Arbitration Strategy for Labor
and Management Advocates

Arbitration Strategy for Labor and Management Advocates

WALT BAER

McFarland & Company, Inc., Publishers
Jefferson, North Carolina, and London

Library of Congress Cataloguing-in-Publication Data

Baer, Walter E.
Arbitration strategy for labor and
management advocates / Walt Baer.
p. cm.
Includes bibliographical references and index.

ISBN-13: 978-0-7864-2796-3
ISBN-10: 0-7864-2796-5
(softcover : 50# alkaline paper) ∞

1. Arbitration, Industrial—United States.
2. Collective labor agreements—United States.
3. Arbitrators, Industrial—United States.
I. Title.
HD5504.A3B24 2007
331.89'1430973—dc22 2006033187

British Library cataloguing data are available

Manufactured in the United States of America

McFarland & Company, Inc., Publishers
Box 611, Jefferson, North Carolina 28640
www.mcfarlandpub.com

For Janet, my wife—
who has made life beautiful for me.
There simply are not words enough.
She is assured her place in heaven.

Table of Contents

Introduction

Each year the number of labor agreements increases. Each year more and more cases are referred to arbitration. And each year thousands of individuals find themselves responsible for preparing, and then presenting, labor arbitration cases as advocate representatives of their companies or unions before an arbitrator.

While hundreds of books have been written for arbitrators, very little information has previously been available for management and union participants—the very people who most need information. These people don't deal with the intricacies of the arbitration process on a day-to-day basis, but when an issue comes to arbitration, it becomes their responsibility to present their organization's position effectively and successfully.

Arbitration is a quasijudicial process. In essence, the purpose of arbitration is the adjudication of disputes by an impartial umpire akin to a judge in a legal action. Unlike a mediator, the arbitrator does not have to suggest formulas and work out agreements. He merely hears the evidence in a dispute and hands down a decision based on the facts. Arbitrators, unlike judges in legal actions, are not bound by legal rules of evidence or by precedent.

The best arbitration is no arbitration. Yet a formal provision for arbitration—preferably, I am convinced, as the "sole and exclusive" means for final, binding decision on contract interpretation or application—is indispensable to sound contract administration. A contract that does not provide for arbitration is the labor relations equivalent of a Manx cat. Something vital is missing, without a sound evolutionary explanation for its absence.

Since World War II, labor arbitration for grievance settlement has grown rapidly. It is now provided for in 95 percent of all labor contracts in the United States. By the time parties to the labor contract resolve to go to arbitration, they are no longer interested in compromise or mutual accommodation. All such efforts have failed in previous meetings and discussions, leaving them with no recourse but to take their chances before a third party, neutral and impartial—the arbiter. Thus, when the heretofore avoidable process becomes unavoidable, each party begins to worry about the "black magic" of the process and what can be done to prevail, to win. And although most parties to labor agreements today enjoy a higher level of sophistication than at any time in the past 35 years, preparation and presentation of cases to arbiters is still too often inadequate and inept.

There is no substitute for thorough, comprehensive, detailed preparation. There is no excuse for its lack. The conscientious, dedicated, and determined advocate has learned the importance—in fact, the absolute necessity—of thorough pretrial preparation. Such an advocate probably already knows what some trial lawyers never learn, that cases are seldom if ever won in court or a hearing room. They are won by the side that has slaved to find all the facts in the case and all its corporal parts, and is fully prepared before any trial begins.

Preparation means giving painstaking attention to every argument, every witness, every exhibit, every precedent, every detail. It means giving equal attention to a systematic, methodical, organized, chronologically purposeful presentation—one that tells a story so logically and persuasively that the arbiter can come to only one conclusion.

The first chapters in this book present important concepts that the advocate needs to understand for assessing and preparing a case. Next, I provide important tips for presenting a case before the arbitrator and discuss the important principles and practices that every advocate should keep in mind. Appendices and extensive references to statutes and case law flesh out the principles. Throughout the text the reader will find the words "arbitrator" and "arbiter." These terms are used interchangeably and have meanings which are synonymous.

In this book I analyze the arbitration process from the most important side—that of the participants. Whether one is a layperson or lawyer, with management or labor, this volume will help avoid the problems and pitfalls of the arbitration process and help chart a course that will achieve the primary goal—being sustained in labor arbitration, the goal of every labor arbitration advocate.

1

The Total Agreement

Before entering a discussion about the advocate's role in arbitrations, it is first necessary to briefly review and familiarize oneself with certain fundamental labor relations concepts and principles. The advocate must first possess an understanding of *all* of the elements that comprise an operating labor agreement, and not just part of them. And the point which must be made at the outset is that when the term *"Labor Agreement"* or *"Contract"* is used here, it does *not* merely have reference to the contract booklet. Although management might like to contend that document comprises the total understanding and agreement between the parties—and therefore is the sole instrument which influences the relationship between the parties—this unfortunately simply is *not* the *whole* reality. The fact of the matter is, there are other persuasive and compelling factors which can have an influence on this relationship. Actually, the labor agreement, or perhaps more properly stated *"The Total Agreement,"* is a pie-shaped affair containing three segments. (see Fig. 1).

Labor Agreement

Of course, the labor agreement itself is the most important segment of this pie-shaped affair. It constitutes the understanding worked out between the parties, which presumably contains all of the terms and conditions under which both will operate for its term. And, this is particularly true of an initial agreement in a newly organized plant where the contract is the first one negotiated between the parties following union organization. But, beginning with the day in which that contract is first placed into effect, and during each succeeding workday thereafter, other

Fig. 1. The Total Agreement.

factors and circumstances come into existence which can have an influence on the future relationship between the parties.

Most managements view the labor agreement as a document which embodies *all* of the terms and conditions which affect the employment relationship of the employee—and that it constitutes the sole and complete scope of the agreement between the company and the union. It presumably represents the compromise and the end result of the bargain that has been reached by the company and the union. Through the process of give and take collective bargaining the parties respectively have attempted to satisfy some of the needs and the wishes of the company and its stockholders on the one hand, and some of the needs and wishes of the employees and the union on the other hand. From the first day of its existence, the contract is intended to govern, regulate or control the behavior of the respective parties. Presumably it contains all of the commitment each party has made to the other and constitutes the total obligation of each party to the other during its term.

However, although the company usually, and the union sometimes, would like to view the contract as a static agreement, and one which provides both parties with the answers to all of their problems which arise during its term, the fact is that it often fails to provide the parties with solutions to all of their problems. Contract provisions which were apparently clear to both parties at the time of their negotiation may suddenly prove to be uncertain and ambiguous when they are applied to a situation which had not been contemplated by the parties. Another factor contributing to the problems of the parties in this connection is that the industrial workplace is not a static situation. It is instead a dynamic one with ever-changing conditions which give rise to new and different problems. When the parties attempt to apply their negotiated agreement to these new and different problems, they often suddenly learn that their instrument is deficient. Either party may claim that the contract provides no coverage whatsoever and that the item in issue falls beyond its purview. Or, they may concur that some contract provisions are appropriate for application to the new and different problem—but are unable to agree as to how or to what extent then should be applied. They may even disagree as to which existing contract provision has relevancy and applicability.

Still another contributing factor to the ever-changing face of the labor agreement is the fact that the union cannot afford to be a static organization. Therefore, although they have negotiated a contract which presumably embraces all the policies which govern wages, hours and working conditions for the contract term, the fact is they view such a contract as the beginning point, and not an end in itself. Throughout the term of the agreement, the union, by its very nature, is compelled to be constantly seeking and attempting to obtain new or expanded benefits and conditions for its members. To the extent that they are successful in their striving, the labor agreement is amended or modified or altered from its original form.

Familiarity with the contract is an essential requirement for all arbitration advocates. If advocates are to function effectively they must be completely informed about the meaning and the intent of all contract provisions. Whenever a question arises about whether language changes have occurred or whether prior discussions have taken place where a change of intent was agreed upon, the advocate must turn to the negotiation records or to participating individuals to fill in this void. Such research will usually concern itself with one or more of the following considerations: (a) Is there a new or changed contract provision on the disputed matter? (b) If a new provision exists, which party proposed the language and what were the reasons for seeking the change, and which party's language was eventually adopted? (c) If the contractual provision has been changed from what appeared in the prior contract, who proposed the change and what were the reasons? In this regard, which party's proposal was finally adopted? (d) Were minutes of the negotiation meetings kept, and what do those minutes reveal regarding the discussions between the parties on the provision in dispute, irrespective of whether it is a new, a changed, or an unchanged clause? (e) Who represented management in these negotiations and was present during discussions on the relevant provisions? Is that individual available and able to supply credible accounts of what the parties intended? (f) Did the union attempt to insert language into the contract to cover an uncovered subject—but fail to accomplish it?

The answers to relevant questions such as these may provide greater insight into the intended application of clauses, the reasons for their presence or absence, and the purpose and meaning of other provisions.

As a preliminary to leaving the confines of the contract booklet, let it be said this early that such resulting agreement is essentially an instrument of government, not merely an instrument of exchange.

Professor Archibald Cox has said that the labor agreement should be looked upon in this fashion:

> A collective agreement also covers a wide range of conduct and an enormous variety of problems. No state or federal statute, except possibly the tax laws, covers as wide a variety of subjects or impinges upon as many aspects of the ordinary company's business or a workers' life—wages, hours of employment, working conditions, health and accident insurance, retirement, pensions, promotions, layoffs, discipline, subcontracting, technological changes, work loads, and a host of minor items. Yet, a collective bargaining agreement must also be kept short and simple enough for the ordinary worker to read and understand. Verbal incompleteness is inevitable; the meticulous detail of a corporate mortgage is unsuited to administration by ordinary workers. The details must be filled in outside of the words.[1]

In other words, because the union did not cover everything it might have, and because simplicity is a desirable goal, the employer may find itself bound to things to which it does not always realize it has become bound or agreed to.

The point is that when the "total agreement" is envisioned, it must be recognized first of all that the labor agreement itself represents an essential and consequential segment of this pie-shaped affair which forms and comprises the "total agreement." *Unfortunately, it is by no means the single portion of this pie.* There are other segments to this picture which have a persuasive and often compelling influence on the labor agreement, on its interpretation and application, and on the relationship between the parties under that agreement.

Past Practice

It will be noted that a second significant portion of the segments comprising "The Total Agreement" is that of the practices and customs of the parties. This is often the contract's silent partner. Labor agreements often do not provide language which gives coverage to all of the situations and circumstances which may be faced by the parties during its term. Sometimes these voids are the result of negligence or inadvertence on the part of the negotiators for the company and the union. Often, the contract remains silent in areas where the parties have been unable to reach agreement on a specific provision. Other times, the contract may be found to contain provisions which appear to treat and give coverage to a particular subject—but careful examination sometimes reveals that the language which has been provided is unclear, uncertain or full of ambiguities. Therefore, in administering the contract, when he is faced with a problem where the contract is either silent or ambiguous—or a little of both, the supervisor is compelled to make independent judgments and take action based upon this. In such an instance, and they are many and varied during the term of an agreement, actions such as these produce a body of practices and customs which can have an influencing affect or a precedent value in some future dispute between the parties. This may prove to be the case despite the presence of certain contract clauses, usually placed there by company negotiators which presumably have a dissolving effect on past practices. Such provisions include so-called "zipper clauses" and "exclusive agreement clauses," which are detailed later herein.

The contract may be entirely silent on the matter in dispute bringing to the forefront management's position on residual rights. However, a silent contract does not *necessarily* dictate that such matters are automatically resolved in the company's favor. Contract language may cover a matter generally, but fail to cover all of its aspects—that is, "gaps" sometimes exist. Or the matter may actually not be covered in any fashion by any contract clause. In such an instance, custom and past practice *may* constitute a significant factor in the dispute. It has been recognized that fixed and established practices act to fill in contractual voids, or to provide clearer meaning for ambiguous provisions.

In the presence of unclear and ambiguous contract provisions, or in the face of a silent agreement not giving coverage to the matter, the advocate's investigation should concern itself with determining the extent and the nature of any existing past practices. In determining if a practice exists, he must determine if it is *fixed* and *established.* In other words:

- Has the practice been known to both parties?
- Has the practice been relied upon before in similar instances?
- How long has the practice existed?
- Does it extend over the term of more than one labor agreement?

- Are there any inconsistencies, contradictions or deviations from the practice?
- Was the practice instituted unilaterally or bilaterally?

Practices are not established by the employees, nor are they established by the union. Practices come into existence and continue from one application of the practice to another *by the action or inaction of management.* Practice develops as a result of the foreman, as a member of the management team, making decisions and taking actions. Or, they develop as the result of a supervisor's acquiescence to union and employee conduct and behavior. Any such practices discovered by the manager, whether during grievance administration or by other means, which are harmful to the company's interests, should be immediately reported and discussed with management's labor relations representatives.

A grievance which claim is based on the alleged existence of a past practice should be thoroughly reviewed. Under no circumstances should the grievance be sustained *prior* to such a review. This is *not* to say that the ultimate result of that discussion may not lead to management's sustaining the grievance claim. But, grievances sustained through the acknowledgement and binding effect of an existing practice can have far-reaching implications and precedent establishing effect. Caution and careful consideration are the wisest guidelines to follow in handling problems of this kind.

It is quite common to find that the parties have inserted a provision into the labor agreement which pertains to matters of this kind, and which limits their relationship to the terms of the contract. Typical of such "exclusive agreement" clauses is a type which reads:

> This agreement supersedes all previous oral and written agreements between the company and the union. The parties herein agree that the relations between them shall be governed by the terms of the agreement only; no prior agreements, amendments, modifications, alterations, additions or changes, oral or written, shall be controlling or in any way affect the relations between the parties, or the wages and working conditions, unless and until such agreement shall be reduced to writing and duly executed by both parties subsequent to the date of this agreement.

If such a provision is contained within the contract, it represents a defense which the supervisor may take *some* shelter behind when disclaiming the validity of some practice. Another contract clause which, in certain cases, may have some relevancy to disputes of this type is one which commonly appears near the back of the labor agreement (the zipper clause) and usually reads as follows:

> During the negotiations leading to the execution of this agreement both parties have had full opportunity to submit all items appropriate to collective

> bargaining. Except as may be expressly provided in written supplement to this agreement, both parties waive the right to submit any additional item for negotiations during the term of this agreement irrespective of whether the item was or was not discussed during the course of negotiations preceding this agreement.

This is still another clause which may be joined in concert with the provision outlined earlier, to provide a defensive shield which *may* under *some* circumstances protect the company from some undesirable practice proclaimed by the union.

However, several words of caution are necessary in this connection. In any such dispute over the weight to be accorded any practice, the case will turn on the particular fact situation, on the clarity or ambiguity of the pertinent contract language, on the bargaining history of the subject matter, and on the nature and extent of the past practice.

Presumably the contract contains what represents the sole and complete embodiment of the commitments each party has made to the other for the duration of its term. But, no contract, no matter how comprehensive, can explicitly and fully cover all situations.

Of course, managements commonly adopt and practice a *residual rights* theory of managing. This concept will be more thoroughly explored in an upcoming chapter. But, in principle, what this concept consists of as far as a management is concerned, is that the employer has all rights it possessed prior to the coming of the union and prior to the existence of any labor agreement. In other words, only to the extent that the labor agreement limits, restricts or prohibits by some expressed provision management's prerogatives, is it so restricted. Therefore, it continues to possess all of the powers and functions that management would otherwise be free to exercise if no union was on the premises. Generally speaking, the ritual of collective bargaining provides the union with an opportunity, legally and statutorily provided, to convince the company to accept limitations upon the exercise of certain of its previously unrestricted managerial freedoms and authorities. Where the union fails to attempt or fails to obtain such limitations on management's rights, the employer continues to possess all such remaining rights undiminished. The residual rights theory holds that the employer retains the residue of all rights it has not bargained away. All rights not bargained away continue to reside in management.

This concept is often argued by managements, before arbitrators, on issues where the union claims support for its position based on some alleged practice. Where the union is seeking to obtain a benefit and it cannot discover supporting language to its case from the agreement, it typically resorts to a claim of past practice. Often such a claim is soundly based. Where the contract is entirely silent on the matter in dispute, it often brings to the forefront managements' argument on residual rights. The company will often assume the position that it is incumbent upon the union to establish that a contract violation has occurred by insisting it point to a specific contract phrasing on the subject. Such contention by the employer is based on the premise that absent contractual provision which prohibits, restricts, limits, or somehow regulates, management has preserved such freedom and right ungoverned.

Also, it is true that the preponderance of arbitral opinion holds to the following view on an employer's residual rights: "it is now a well-established generalization that every employer continues to have all powers, previously had or exercised by employers unless such powers have been curtailed or eliminated by statute or by contract with a union."[2]

While this is *generally* true and fairly typical of the concept endorsed by a majority of arbitrators, it is nonetheless a generalization and there are exceptions.

A silent contract, that is, one which does not provide coverage to a given subject, *does not necessarily dictate* that any or all uncovered subjects are automatically left to management's sole discretion. Therefore it does not mean that any disputes which arise over matters not covered by pertinent contract language will always be resolved in the company's favor. Where this occurs, the customs and practices of the parties during the term of that agreement, and perhaps prevailing under prior agreements as well, may constitute a significant *or even controlling* factor in an arbitrator's final decision over the dispute.

There is no question that the presence of a written agreement imposes certain limitations on an employer's previously unfettered prerogatives. It should be recognized equally as readily that the existence of certain practices and customs under the written instrument may also provide additional limitations on management's rights not expressly indicated by the contract's wording.

Previously mentioned were the so-called "zipper" and "exclusive agreement" clauses. Obviously, at the same time, it is contended here, but not contradictorily, that "past practices" may nevertheless become a forceful and living part of the contract, a segment of the "total agreement" pie. The following case, one of many similar to it, will elucidate this insistence even more clearly. In other words, it will put meat on the bones of an apparently naked contention.

Arbitrator Edgar A. Jones disposed of a dispute between the Fruehauf Trailer Company and the United Automobile Workers, where the contract contained *both* a past practice and a zipper clause. The former provision stated: "This agreement supersedes and cancels all previous agreements, both written and oral and constitutes the entire agreement between the parties." The latter provision stated: "No agreement, understanding, alteration, variation, waiver or modification of this agreement, terms provisions, covenants, or conditions contained herein shall bind the parties hereto unless made and executed in writing by the parties."

The dispute involved a union claim that the employer had violated the job bidding provisions of the agreement and that a prevailing practice should be considered compelling. The employer sought refuge from the past practice behind the above-cited contract provisions. In the substance of his opinion and award, the arbitrator commented:

> The repeated execution of collective bargaining agreements which contain exclusive agreement provisions canceling 'all previous agreements' *has no magical dissolving effect* upon practices or customs which are continued in fact unabated and *which span successive contract periods*. Although *not verbalized* in the current agreement, *such practices may nonetheless comprise a part of it as any of its written provisions* [emphasis added].[3]

Thus ruling, he concluded that the company had committed a contract violation in its job bidding actions.

One of the more eloquent spokesmen in the arbitration process and an arbiter who has sometimes found past practice and custom to be more purposeful than the wording of the agreement, which presumably expressed desires and intentions, is Peter Seitz. Several of his arbitral opinions have so expressed that a possibility exists for such a holding under the right set of circumstances. A typical example is found in the eloquence of his remarks while resolving a dispute between the *Cleveland Press and Plain Dealer* and the Cleveland Newspaper Guild. He is quoted:

> The art of contract interpretation (as subtle and as mysterious an art as exists!) involves a search for what each party has a reasonable basis to expect of the other in consequence of the consummation of a metaphysical thing we call "Agreement." There is general consensus that the best evidence of their "agreement" (their mutual undertakings, their joint will, their bargain), by far, is the word in writing they solemnly signed. Labor-management *arbitrators have not been imprisoned by the word expressed in the printed booklet constituting a copy of the "contract," and in appropriate cases, have put aside the evidence rule to admit and consider side agreements, statements made at negotiations and other alleged proofs of the true substance of the "agreement."* Probably the most frequently urged basis for a departure from the safe and secure harborage of the writing is the existence of an established and accepted practice, custom or usage. *The arbitration reports are replete with instances wherein arbitrators have been persuaded, by either employers or unions, to cast off the mooring lines of the written document and to beat into the hazardous waters of "practice."* This is as it should be, because it is well within the traditions of our legal system, in the course of contract construction, for adjudicators (courts and arbitrators) to conclude that the actions, conduct, behavior, et cetera, of the parties, overtime, have more eloquently manifested and demonstrated what the true bargain of the parties had been than the too general or ambiguous language which they had placed in the document [emphasis added].[4]

These are the words of no less a personage than the man selected to determine whether Wilt Chamberlain could both coach and play in San Diego in the American Basketball Association in his dispute with the Los Angeles Lakers of the National Basketball Association. He also decided the dispute between Jim "Catfish" Hunter, former pitcher with the Oakland Athletics, and team owner Charles O. Finley.

Further thought *must* be noted. These words attach to practices and their weight and affect accorded even where the contract has existing language, either clear or ambiguous, but nonetheless *has* covering provisions, and is *not* totally silent. There can be no doubt. Past practices, prior conduct, and behavior, previous customs and events often are as much a controlling part of a contract as many of its written terms. There can be no question that these are conditions which go into the makeup of what has been called, for lack of a more definitive description, the "total agreement." To remain ignorant of these considerations is to place management's already eroded and eroding rights into danger of greater jeopardy.

Grievance Settlements, Arbitration Awards, and Oral Agreements

Last but not least as a segment of the total pie are grievance settlements, arbitration awards, and any oral or written agreements which have been established by the parties. Each time a grievance is settled or an arbitration award is rendered, a body of common law is being constructed. Therefore, any grievance settlement or arbitration award which is in strict accordance with the written labor agreement, and which is strictly in tune with the intent of the negotiators, merely reinforces that provision of the agreement, and does not detract from it or reduce its power. On the other hand, each time a company resolves a grievance in a manner which is *not* in purest accord with the negotiated document, it either provides the union and the employees with a condition or a benefit they did not achieve at the bargaining table, or—just as bad—it disallows some condition or benefit which the company has acknowledged through its negotiators that it would honor and grant. Either condition is one over which the company should be alarmed: In the one case the company is granting *more* than has been negotiated, in the other case it is violating the agreement and denying the employees something they justifiably deserve. In any case, the result of grievance settlements and arbitration awards is that a body of common law is developed which can play a very influencing and often decisive role in future disputes between the parties. This can be particularly true when such evidence is documented and persuasively introduced before a professional arbitrator.

When dealing with an issue which is *un*familiar or working with a contract clause that is vague and ambiguous, or dealing with a problem in the face of a silent contract, it is always advisable to examine prior grievance settlements to determine the theory and nature of the former settlement that went into resolving these matters. When searching these records the advocate should be alert for the following factors:

- Has the identical issue been raised in a prior grievance and resolved by some mutual agreement of the parties? If so, the resolution of the instant dispute should be in accord with that prior settlement. However, where the grievance has not been mutually settled, but simply has been denied by management at some step of the grievance procedure, and was not appealed further by the union, the desirable recourse is to similarly deny the instant case.
- Has a *similar* or *related* issue been raised in a prior grievance and resolved between the company and the union? If so, and if investigation reveals that the principles and theories utilized by the parties in handling the matter can be associated with the instant dispute, the advocate may discover a guiding principle.
- Have repeated grievances on the same issue been filed and processed by the union? Occasionally, not satisfied with management's denial of a grievance but unwilling to process it into arbitration, a union may persist in raising and presenting the same issue, over and over, on a repeated basis, in hopes the management's position may weaken or change. Faced with this situation, the company has no alternative but to once again deny the claim. This, of course, presumes that the issues are identical and the circumstances and fact situations are alike.
- Has the *same issue* on a prior occasion been processed into arbitration and denied by a subsequent award? Presuming the issue and fact situation were the same, and the new grievance does not embrace factors and changed conditions which would clearly distinguish it from the former, the company should deny the grievance on the basis that this has been settled by the final and binding award of an arbitrator.

Significant to all of these factors is the consideration as to whether the contract language involved in the latter disputes is *the same* as that in dispute in the instant case; and also, whether the contract language has been repeated from one agreement into a subsequent agreement and left unchanged. This "bridge" effect can also be an influencing factor in further reinforcing the finality and conclusiveness of a prior settlement which involves the exact same language. And, when time limitations appear in the agreement for filing and processing of disputes, still another area is present which may influence future claims. When a specified contractual time limit for processing a grievance, from step to step or to arbitration, has expired, and the contract provides that failure by the aggrieved party to file or process a grievance within the time limit shall constitute a settlement, most arbitrators will rule that they, the arbitrators, are not vested with any discretion. The majority of arbiters will declare that particular dispute is deemed settled.

By the same token, if time limits under a contract are to have any meaning, then it follows logically that any ingenious attempts by the union to revive grievances which have already expired by the simple and expedient route of filing a new grievance should be denied on the basis of being previously finally settled. It must be clearly obvious that if a matter is settled it remains settled unless or until some change in the factual situation furnishes cause for a possible re-examination of the subject matter.

Most members of management would like to make a distinction between "collective bargaining" and "the settlement and adjustment of grievances." Presumably the former is the negotiation and establishment of the terms and conditions which govern the relationship between the parties; the latter is merely the settlement of disputes, within the confines of those terms, which arise during the fixed period of the contract. Unfortunately, but understandably, that is rarely the case. In the vast majority of instances, the contract is somewhat widened and broadened during its life by the day-to-day negotiations which take place in the name of grievance adjudication. As each party resorts to whatever power it can apply to compel a particular settlement, the contract takes on new shape and form from that which constituted it at its inception. The end result of all this is usually determined by where the balance of power rested in the majority of settlements—thus resulting in a contract which is more rewarding to the one party and less desirable to the other than was the contract when initially entered. As mentioned earlier, the objective typical of most unions is to expand the original agreement through grievance settlements, during its term, by obtaining that which they failed to attempt, or failed to obtain, during formal negotiations. The objective typical of most managements is to *not* surrender *anything more* during the contract term than it had found necessary to give during the negotiations. And, some cavalier managements even attempt to recover and recapture during a contract term, some of those things which they had presumably surrendered to the union during collective bargaining.

However, in the context intended here, it is assumed that the company (1)has engaged in good-faith bargaining in the development of the agreement, (2) considers the agreement as fully embodying all of the agreements and understandings and terms which are to govern the parties during its fixed period, (3) views the union and the employees as entitled to the full measure of those things provided by that agreement, and (4) wants to resolve grievances in good faith and in full accord with the terms and conditions of the contract—but without making settlements which add to or subtract from its terms, and which do not further limit, restrict, prohibit, curtail or compromise management's future ability to initiate action.

But, irrespective of the particular philosophy followed, one thing is certain—each time a grievance is settled between the parties it has some influence on that labor agreement. Either the grievance is resolved in absolute accord with that agreement under language which is clear and unequivocal; or it provides clearer meaning to otherwise vague or ambiguous contract terms, but is still in accord with the true intent of both parties; or the settlement in some manner and to some degree either adds to or subtracts from the agreement as it was originally intended by the parties. *In any case, each grievance settlement builds a body of common law which surrounds the agreement and the relationship between the parties.* And as each grievance is resolved in a like manner to other grievance settlements, the body of law surrounding that settled issue becomes firmer and stronger, and the precedent value of the parties' positions on that issue becomes more persuasive over other similar or same issues. Such settled issues can supply a great reservoir of tested experience which may prove invaluable in choosing a direction to take on an instant case. What will be the quantum of force given the prior grievance settlements, in the event of an arbitration hearing, will probably turn on the degree of similarity of the issues, and the uniformity of adoption of the settlement principles in such prior cases.

It should be a generally recognized principle that the interpretation of contract language embodied in grievance settlements becomes a part of contract language. As a matter of industrial reality, settled issues should be viewed as having "precedent" value until the parties change their effect in the labor agreement. A central purpose of the grievance machinery is to terminate controversies so that the parties may know where they stand. The only way to achieve this end is to award some weight and influence to settled disputes. Where a prior grievance decision involves the interpretation of the identical contract provision, on a similar or closely related fact circumstance, between the same company and the same union, every principle of common sense, policy and labor relations demands that it should stand until the parties alter or annul it by a newly worded contractual provision.

The reasons are obvious, the benefits are numerous. Considerations such as this contribute to a stabilization in the parties' relationship. They provide the parties with guidelines and general rules they may rely upon if followed. They further remove guesswork from the decision-making process for supervisors, and also further reduce the contractual gray areas which are responsible for the promulgation of so many of the union's grievances. They enable a consistent and uniform contractual administration from department to department, shift to shift, foreman to foreman. They enhance the objective of equality of contractual treatment of all employees.

After a labor agreement has been entered, it presumably embraces all of the terms and conditions which will prevail during its term and thus enables the parties to operate without the need for continuing collective bargaining during that period. This is one of the several reasons why the employer often seeks some form of contract language which will, in effect, provide him with some type of "exclusive agreement" or "zipper clause" insurance. Clauses covering such a contingency have been cited earlier herein.

Despite the presence or the absence of such clauses, situations sometimes arise during the term of the agreement which produce extra-contractual discussions between the parties. And more often than not, even in the presence of such contract language, a supervisor or other member of management will make an oral or written agreement with the union's representative(s), which adds to, subtracts from, or somehow acts as an amendment to the contract. This is usually done in complete innocence and with total unawareness of the implications and possible far-reaching consequences of their act. Normally it is justified on the premise that the necessities of the moment left no recourse—and on some infrequent occasions this may be the case. In the overwhelming majority of instances, however, decision to enter such arrangements can be contemplated and fully considered before the action is taken. During the advance considerations of the subject, it is always advisable to discuss it with the company's labor relations expert before a final conclusion is reached with the union.

The maintenance of records of all types and in a variety of forms is one of the essential requirements leading to successful plant labor relations for management. The company can be assured that a knowledgeable and sophisticated labor organization will be maintaining a wide variety of records to enable it to police the agreement, to ensure that management's actions are consistent and in accord with the contract, and to support and defend its position in any dispute it may face with the employer. It will maintain such records as seniority lists, overtime rosters, wage rate changes of employees, layoff and recall rosters, employee transfers, changes in employees' job classifications, grievance settlements, arbitration awards, and a host of others. It is of no less importance—and perhaps because the union does so, of greater importance—that management maintain its records also. For unless it does, it is clear that it will be at the mercy of the union and any claim made by it, if the union is the sole record-keeper. Naturally the types of records maintained by the company will be very much like those kept by the union. Among this category are a number of records which each supervisor should maintain which have a relevance and bearing on his own particular operating department. Numbered among these are the obvious ones of overtime lists, seniority rosters, absenteeism records and the like. But of equal importance are others which he may have reference to on only an intermittent basis, but which may be of great significance when finally referred to or utilized. Among this type we can list copies of any disciplinary letters he may have issued, copies of any written grievances he may have handled and answered, copious notes he may have made pertinent to some dispute or significant labor relations incident, etc. Although the significance and relevance of maintaining such records may not be instantly apparent—and although the passage of time may further seem to diminish their importance and consequence—the absence of them when they are suddenly or unexpectedly needed will immediately make their essential nature obvious.

Representative of a case where management's use of prior records was of substantial benefit to it was a dispute decided by arbitrator Meyer S. Ryder. This arbiter, a distinguished and extremely knowledgeable statesman in the national labor relations scene, was called upon to determine if a current grievance was arbitrable which dealt with a seniority-layoff issue. An earlier grievance had been filed by another employee but had been based on the same situation and was under the same contract provisions as those involved in the present grievance. The union had failed to appeal the prior grievance, after receiving management's denial, to the next step of the grievance procedure within the contractual time limits. The present grievance was then filed only when it became clear to the union that further processing of the prior grievance was contractually barred. In ruling on the matter, arbitrator Ryder said this:

> It would then seem only fair to hold, if that important means of labor agreement administration—the grievance procedure—is to be respected and honored, the R_____ grievance falls because the earlier H_____ grievance fell. It appears that the parties here had some difficulty in the past in observing the strict time limits in their grievance procedure. In conferences between them it was accepted that such mutually agreed limitations would be observed. Time limits then are of essence in the faithful execution of the labor agreement. Resultantly, the H_____ grievance was disposed of with finality. The union does not seek to resurrect that grievance. But, realistically, the R_____ grievance does; because, as stated hereinbefore, the R_____ grievance only has merit if it is first determined that the Trades Helpers were unjustly removed from their jobs. The R_____ grievance would have to litigate that which the H_____ grievance sought to litigate. To allow this is to really allow by substitution of grievant a relitigation of a matter already dis-

posed of by operation of the contract. [The parties should not construe this reasoning as applicable to a circumstance where no other grievance was filed, or if filed was filed collaterally with the filing of the instant separate grievance.][5]

Now, if this above case is considered in the light of the probable, it is entirely possible, in any plant situation, for that earlier grievance (which was referred to above) to have been denied at the foreman's step and not processed by the union beyond that step—either through neglect, inadvertence or deliberate decision. In any event, the sole company copy of that prior grievance could conceivably have resided with the foreman, provided he retained a copy and also did not forward a copy to any other management member. From there, it is apparent that the later case would have turned almost entirely on his records, notes and relevant testimony of the prior case—or been lost through the absence of the same.

Typical of issues where the employee's past record was a decisive factor was a case where an arbitrator found the employer had just cause for imposing a disciplinary suspension on a crane operator who fell asleep in his cab while his crane was holding a heavy load of steel beams suspended above the plant floor. Influencing on his upholding management's action was the record presented by the company which demonstrated a prior disciplinary history of written and oral warnings.

The admission of an employee's past work record into arbitration proceedings is often objected to by the union on the premise that the arbitrator should only consider the employee's instant, most recent behavior, and not consider any prior instances of misconduct. Or, they may object to the introduction of such records on the basis that the record contained prior employee misconduct which does not relate to the instant case of employee misconduct. Such was the case at Norwich Pharnacal Co., and the ICWU. This grievance dealt with the discharge of an employee for gross carelessness. At the hearing, the company introduced evidence and records relating to written and oral warnings for tardiness and loitering, which had been issued to the employee on prior instances. The union argued that these prior offenses were not related to the offense of gross carelessness and therefore were not admissible in the arbitration hearing. In this point, the arbitrator held:

> In determining whether discharge is too severe a penalty, it is proper to consider Mr. C_____'s past record (prior warnings) as well as the circumstances of the incident leading directly to the discharge. The company contends that its customary practice is to review an employee's complete past record for reasons of discipline, merit and promotion. The union contends that only the past records relating to "poor work," and distinct from minor offenses (tardiness, loitering, etc.) should be reviewed. The October 13, 1958, incident (failure to close the glycerine valve) was in the nature of

"poor work." No contract language or past practice would prohibit the introduction into evidence of the prior warnings given to Mr. C_____ because they were for tardiness or unauthorized absences from his duties rather than for poor or careless work. There is no more reason to exclude part of an employee's good past record for purposes of promotion or merit than there is to exclude part of a bad past record for purposes of discipline or discharge.[6]

The common thread which weaves itself throughout each of these above-cited cases is that in every instance the outcome of the case turned on the introduction of records maintained by the company, based on a practice of doing the same. Had these records not been maintained and not been available for presentation, the outcome in each of the above cases would have been substantially altered—and in every instance would have resulted in the company's position not being upheld. Whether these records are maintained by individual supervisors or in some master location within some other management department is not usually of great consequence; the essential point is that they be maintained somewhere and by someone in management. However, it is evident that certain records are unique and peculiar to a foreman's own departmental operations, and therefore should be maintained and preserved in that location irrespective of their existence in any other management department of the company.

In summary, the first principle being established by this chapter is that the "*total agreement*" is the sum of three essential part: (1) the negotiated labor agreement; (2) the practices and customs of the parties; and (3) any grievance settlements, arbitration awards and oral or written agreements between the parties.

Each of these parts contributes toward the making of the whole. Each of the parts determines in some way—sometimes small, sometimes large—the shape and form, the size and contents, of the total agreement governing the relationship between the company and the union and employees it represents.

It is not uncommon for the union's representatives to attempt to dissolve a foreman's defense by pleading that a grievance should be sustained because not to do so would be unfair. This usually occurs after the union has utilized all relevant contractual provisions and found them lacking, has searched but cannot find a past practice to support its contention, has looked high and low but can point to no other precedent establishing settlements or agreements, and therefore is on the verge of receiving a denial of the grievance by the foreman. At this point, it is not uncommon for the union representative to claim that it is only "fair" for the grievant to receive the relief he is seeking. This approach can be emotionally very appealing and difficult to deal with when made in the presence of employees who are unsophisticated in labor-management relations and the rules encompassing it. Although the temptation may be great, the foreman is best advised neither to sustain *nor* deny grievances on the basis of what is fair or unfair. The total labor agreement stands as the final judge of what is fair or unfair, of what is owed, entitled, intended and deserved. The benefits sought and received by the grievant must be a bona fide product of the contractual settlement negotiated between the parties. It is this bargain alone that determines what is fair and what is unfair.

There is one last point to be covered here before moving on to other relevant, guiding labor relations concepts and principles.

That point is, the well-established rule of law, frequently invoked by industrial arbitrators, that *a collective bargaining agreement, like any other written instrument, must be construed as a whole. Single words, sentences, or sections cannot be isolated from the context in which they appear and interpreted independently of the apparent purpose and understanding of the parties as evidenced by the entire instrument.* Of course, practice should avoid conclusions that adopt an inequitable construction of the agreement and result in an unwarranted general restriction upon the company's managerial discretions. Such conclusions may run counter to the principles of reasonableness and equity—two fundamental prerequisites to constructive labor relations. If the contract is silent on an issue it will commonly bring forward management's position on residual rights. However, a silent contract does not necessarily dictate that such matters are automatically resolved in the company's favor. As mentioned, contract language may cover a matter generally but fail to cover it in all respects—that is, gaps sometimes exist. Or the matter may not be covered in any fashion by any contract clause. In such instances custom and past practice may constitute a significant factor in the dispute. There is no longer any doubt in today's labor-management arenas that fixed and established practice may give meaning to vague and ambiguous contract clauses, fill in contractual gaps and give substance to silent areas by putting meat on the bones of the contract skeleton.

In the great majority of plants, the supervisor's duties are manifold. The supervisor carries a responsibility for meeting high standards of production, quality, and efficiency, while maintaining tight controls on costs and operating budgets. But the job he must accomplish must also be done by and through people—and, in the cases dealt with here, with people organized by a labor union and working under a contractual employment relationship. How well or how poorly he may ultimately perform these vital assigned functions will depend in large measure on how much he understands those forces and regulations which govern that employment relationship, and which guide, determine or dictate his decisions made. In this regard, it is no longer a viable condition for him to be *merely acquainted* with such matters. It is essential, for the continuing industrial well-being of his organization, for the preservation of its rights and powers, for his effective performance of supervisory and managerial function, that he be *intimately familiar* with these compelling concepts and principles of labor contract administration and interpretation.

The labor arbitration advocate's task will be largely enhanced if the cases he handles have been previously handled by other properly trained management representatives.

2

Understanding the Four Sides of the Labor Agreement

Now we move on to a concept which is a little more difficult to comprehend. Principally, it involves the question of what the company gets from its labor agreement.

It gets but one thing. And, it gets that one thing *only* if it is successful in obtaining it during collective bargaining. Unfortunately, there are some employers who fail to obtain even this one thing. Those employers get *nothing* out of their contract with the union.

The one thing referred to here is the no-strike clause.

Prior to the negotiation of the labor agreement—meaning, prior to the advent of the union into the employer-employee relationship—management possessed all rights unabridged, and could establish, change and/or re-establish any wages, hours or working conditions it desired, so long as they conformed with any applicable state or federal laws or statutes. As long as management operated within the law, employers could move wages upward, or downward, unilaterally, without conferring with employees or their representatives. They could change the number of holidays—if any—adding to or taking away as they saw fit in their sole judgment. They could provide vacations, paid sick leave, insurance, funeral leave, cost-of-living improvements, rest periods, wash-up time, and a host of others—or they could discontinue any or all of these, or add to or subtract from any at their sole discretion. Hours of work could be changed, benefits suspended or withdrawn, disciplinary suspensions or even discharges issued without a requirement of meeting a standard of just cause. Employees might be laid off or recalled, transferred, promoted or demoted, without regard for length of service or other seniority consideration. All of these and more could be done, unilaterally and freely, for no regulatory constraints impinged upon the employers' unfettered authority. Now, this is not to say that, therefore, all employers consequently decided and acted capriciously and without regard for employees' needs and desires. It is to say, they could. Management, therefore, gets nothing out of a labor agreement, since it possessed all rights prior to the existence of the agreement—*with but one exception*. That one exception is the no-strike clause of the contract—that is, if such a clause is obtained by the company in the give-and-take of collective bargaining.

This is the one thing management gets—because, prior to the existence of the union contract, the employer's unorganized workers could, under law, engage in lawful work stoppages and other concerted action taking the form of economic force, in labor disputes with the employer.

Therefore, prior to the coming of the union contract containing a no-strike article, the employer had no pledge or assurance from his workers of continuity of operations being maintained. The no-strike clause gives him that *one thing* he formerly did *not* have.

All other provisions of the contract operate as a prohibition, a restriction, a limitation or a regulation on those rights the subjects cover, which were previously the employer's without prohibition, restriction, limitation or regulation. In many cases, they solidify or give rigidity to the wages, benefits and working conditions which will be enjoyed by the workers during the term of the contract.

No longer can the employer add to or subtract from, unilaterally, the number of holidays to be granted. Neither can it add to or subtract from the many other benefits, the vacations, insurance, funeral pay, rest periods, paid sick leave, and the like.

It probably now must (post-contract) follow some detailed procedure when it lays off, recalls, transfers, promotes or demotes—and more than likely, must consider employees' length of service in its treatment of employees in these connections.

And, most consequential, it can no longer decide and act unilaterally, except in those few areas where it has managed to preserve to itself the authority to do so—but even then, management's decisions and actions are subject to the challenge or the question of a work force now organized to speak concertedly. And, even there, where management can still function without prior bilateral intercourse, it is obliged to answer and justify its unilateral decision.

Nevertheless, it must be realized that giving management its desired no-strike article is a substantial compromise for the union.

The union's most effective weapon is the use of, or the threat to use, economic force. They realize that without it their ability to persuade the employer on any given issue that may arise during the contract's term may be markedly impaired. The industrial plant is a dynamic community in which changes frequently occur. Job and work situations may be altered from time to time, decisions made, and actions taken which do not have the unanimous accord of all employees. When differences of opinion occur between management representatives, employees, and union officials, there must be some means by which those employees and union representatives can protest the company's decisions and actions. Without a prohibition on employees' right to strike, their protests against management's decisions can manifest themselves in several various forms. Production output may be controlled and reduced; quality standards may be lowered or disregarded; or employees may totally withhold their productive labor and effort by walking out, sitting down, and so on. Needless to say, these are effective means by which the union and the employees can capture and hold management's attention to the subject of their distress. They fully realize this. To give up these means is a significant compromise from their point of view.

Nevertheless, the basic promise a union can give to an employer in return for the many promises it receives in a labor agreement, is that there will be no strikes. The right to strike is what the union has as a bargaining tool and is the only thing it has to give up as consideration for the agreement. Unless this single promise flows from the bargaining agent to the employer, the labor contract cannot be considered a true bilateral exchange of promises.

The no-strike commitment enables the employer to make plans. Commitments can be made and deliveries scheduled on the assumption of uninterrupted production for the period of the contract. A strike in breach of this basic commitment denies to the employer the sole consideration bargained for and frustrates the economic purpose of the agreement from the employer's point of view.[1]

Consequently, *the no-strike article is one of the four major interacting contractual provisions which hold the rest together* and make it all work. The three remaining provisions are the grievance Procedure, the arbitration article, and the management rights article. These then are the factors which bring into interaction the four sides which surround the remainder of the labor agreement. How these controlling clauses operate and work in concert to complement each other is what will now be reviewed. Their respective locations in Fig. 2 are for a specific purpose, essentially to show that one is the quid-pro-quo for the other, in other words, this one for that one: the grievance procedure for the management rights clause, and the arbitration article for the no-strike provision.

The interaction of the opposing sides is what makes the total contract work. The first side is the management rights or management prerogatives provision which the company typically insists upon, and usually

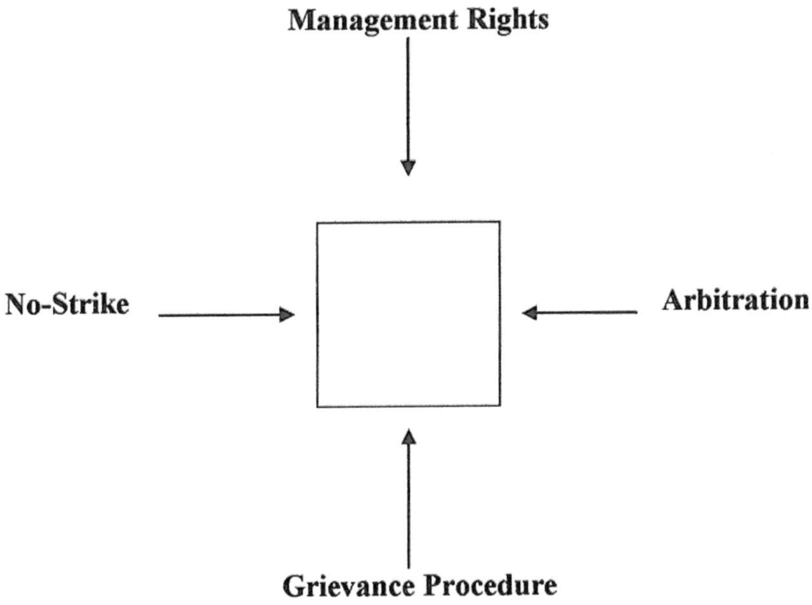

Fig. 2. The Four Sides of the Labor Agreement.

they endeavor to obtain as full and comprehensive an article as is possible. Of course the purpose of this is to ensure that all of the foregoing conclusions made earlier herein are fulfilled by spelling out that management does in fact continue to possess and retain all of these rights not bargained away. Once having acquired such an authority, the company is then obliged to give the union and the employees a means by which they can contest and complain against any actions taken by the management, in the exercise of its management rights, which the union or employees allege are in violation of the agreement. This produces the second, interacting side of this total square, the grievance procedure. This procedure is the machinery provided by the company to the union and the employees, for them to raise, file, discuss, and have handled promptly and fairly any differences between the parties.

As mentioned earlier, from the company's point of view, the most essential ingredient in the entire labor agreement is the no-strike article. This article gives us the third side of the square. The no-strike article forecloses against any work stoppages or interruptions of productive activities during the term of the agreement. So, although the company has provided the union with a mechanism for raising complaints in the grievance procedure, it has pulled the union's teeth by preventing them from the use of economic force to resolve these disputes when it introduces the no-strike article.

This brings us then to the fourth side of the square—the arbitration clause. This is often called the quid-pro-quo for the no-strike article. (the one-for-one exchange between the parties) In exchange for the union giving the company the no-strike clause and its guarantee of continuity of operations, the company provides the union with a fair means by which it can *peacefully* resolve its differences with the company in a prompt and equitable manner, the arbitration article.

Management Rights

The basic principle of the residual rights concept is to the effect that except as management has agreed to restrict the exercise of its usual functions, it retains the same rights which it possessed before engaging in collective bargaining.

The basic philosophy which the company should hold to is that the job of management is to manage. The operation of the enterprise at its maximum efficiency is management's responsibility and obligation. If a management believes in discharging these obligations, it must retain in full measure the so-called prerogative of management. It has the right to refuse to agree in collective bargaining to restrict these rights. If management agrees to limit or restrict certain of its rights through collective bargaining, the agreement should clearly define how far it has agreed to go in this direction.

The question might well be asked as to why it is necessary to have any management's rights clause in the labor agreement if the principle of residual rights is established. If there were no other reason, the fact that unions have either directly opposed or sought to evade this concept would alone provide sufficient justification for inclusion of a statement of management rights in the contract. The reason for the inclusion of a management's rights clause fall into three general categories:

- *Decisions of the courts.* Of particular importance is the Warrior Gulf Navigation Company case decided by the U.S. Supreme Court, to the effect that unless an item or subject is specifically excluded from the area of arbitration in a labor agreement, it is arbitrable per se. Whether the company agrees or not with this decision, it must constantly re-examine its labor agreements in the light of this Supreme Court doctrine. Assuming that in the future under this doctrine, it may be required to arbitrate matters which have either never been discussed in negotiations or have been brought up by the union in negotiations and subsequently dropped, management's case will be materially strengthened if there is a sound management's rights clause in the agreement.

- *Training.* The principle that management retains all rights except those specifically covered by other provisions of the agreement needs expression to assist both union and management representatives in training subordinate stewards or supervisors in the nature of the collective bargaining agreement and in the proper performance of their duties.
- *Practicality.* As a practical matter, it is a significant advantage to an arbitrator to be able to cite or quote explicit language in a labor agreement in making and award, rather than to rely on an unexpressed principle.

The underlying approach of organized labor has probably best been expressed by Mr. Arthur Goldberg, then Chief Counsel for the United Steel Workers, who made the following statement when speaking to the National Academy of Arbitrators on this subject on January 27, 1956. Mr. Goldberg said:

> To the extent that present conditions and methods for change are not revised, they are accepted. Therefore, each party has a right to assume that changes in wages, hours, or working conditions, not provided for by the contract can be made only by mutual agreement or by following practices for making changes which have existed during the collective bargaining relationship, or by virtue of management's exercise of an exclusive right (such as introduction of a new product, new machine, new material, new method of manufacture, etc.).[2]

In further support of this thesis, Mr. Goldberg, who later became a Supreme Court Justice and U.S. Ambassador to the United Nations, commented on the nature of labor-management relationship as follows:

> The real question that arises is, What is the Deal? Is it the contract or something more? I cannot agree that the deal includes the acceptance of the pre-union past as a guide for the future. But the practices which grow up during decades of collective bargaining relationship cannot be swept aside. They have weight which must be measured in a specific case in the light of many factors. These practices, grievance settlements, understanding, etc., inevitably represent the set of circumstances which form the backdrop of the negotiation of the current agreement.

Precisely because this viewpoint is prevalent among representatives of organized labor, it is important that management negotiate the inclusion of not only a sound management's rights clause, but a security clause with respect to past practice comparable to that which has already been presented in Chapter 1. It is imperative that the company clearly understand that it is the implicit right of management to take action as it deems necessary and desirable, and that the only proper action of the union is to protest the action through the grievance procedure rather than to raise the question as to whether or not management has the right to act at all. As Mr. Goldberg himself says:

> The union has a duty, and as a union man the employee has the duty as well as the right, to challenge the company's acts when they violate the workers' rights. *That challenge is made through the grievance procedure, not through rebellion.*

Fortunately, arbitrators have tended to lean more toward the management viewpoint of management rights (the residual or reserved rights concept) as expressed earlier, than toward the union viewpoint as enunciated by Mr. Goldberg. However, it must be recognized that they have not embraced this position as being binding in all respects and under all circumstances.

Almost universally, arbitrators will scrutinize with care and will frequently set aside an action by management, if they are convinced that management's action either (1) is not made in good faith and with sound purpose and/or (2) serves by intent or effect to nullify other provisions of the agreement.

To most employers, "the right to manage" has a basic and concrete significance. It means the right and the ability of management to take such action as the needs of the business demand; and to take such action without extensive and time-consuming haggling with the union over the managerial decision itself, and without having an arbiter decide after the fact (and without regard to what is or what isn't in the contract) that management had no right to make that business decision and to take that essential action.

If it could be summed up in a single word what management is concerned about—what it must have if it is to run the business at a profit, which, after all, like it or not, is the name of the game in our society—what management must have is *flexibility* to meet the competitive needs of the enterprise. For without that there would soon be no enterprise, no jobs, and, for that matter, no management, no employees, no unions—not even any arbitrators.

If it could be summed up in a single word, or perhaps two words, what the union's concern is, it would be "*job security*." Unions are concerned, and it's their business and their right to be concerned, over the job security of their members. That, when it's all said and done, is the name of their game. For without job security, high wages and good fringe benefits are meaningless; and it's up to management to recognize that concern, just as it's up to unions to recognize management's concern over flexibility. So, we're not talking here about some sterile, abstract principle, but a fundamental need of those charged with doing the management job. It is also merely realistic to state that it is incumbent on both sides to recognize that these two concerns, of management over flexibility, and the union over job security, are in fundamental conflict. To whatever extent one prevails in a given situation, the other must yield. This is a fact of our industrial way of life; a necessary friction in the marriage between free enterprise and collective bargaining; and it should be recognized for what it is; a legitimate conflict of interest built into our system.

It isn't the result of the union's deliberately setting out to oust management from its job or to run the business. Unions aren't out (consciously at least) to take over the business or grab a partnership in the running of it—at least most of them are not; and management should recognize this. Unions, for their part, should recognize that not every management effort to obtain more flexibility, or to retain what flexibility it has, is an attempt to undermine or destroy the union. It only clouds the issue and make a sound working relationship impossible when each side misunderstands the reason for the conflict, and attributes only the basest of motives to its opposite number.

While the differences between the viewpoints of management and labor as expressed above are obviously widely divergent, there are at least on the margins certain areas in which of some agreement it may be possible. From purely practical considerations, there are many occasions when it is to the advantage of management to give union officers advance notice of certain management actions which are going to affect significantly a number of employees. The line between timely information and discussion on the one hand, and the area of negotiation on the other, is often times a fine one, and it requires a rather sophisticated viewpoint on the part of management and union representatives to clearly understand under all circumstances the distinction between the two. There are nonetheless frequent occasions when it is highly desirable for management to give timely advance information to union representatives, and under certain circumstances to give them an opportunity to express their viewpoints while preserving carefully the prerogative of management to act. In fact, there are some areas, such as in the matter of plant removal, where the National Labor Relations Board requires, as a point of doctrine, that management give advance information to a union.

With respect to those matters where the viewpoint of organized labor approaches, at least in part, that of management, in the same paper where he made the above quoted statement, Mr. Arthur Goldberg had this to say:

> When a contract says that management has the exclusive right to manage the business, it obviously refers to the countless questions which arise and are not covered by wages, hours, and working conditions, such as determina-

> tion of products, equipments, materials prices, etc. Not only does management have the general right to manage a business, but many agreements provide that management has the exclusive right to direct working forces, and usually to lay off, recall, discharge, hire, etc.
>
> The right to direct where it involves wages, hours, or working conditions is a procedural right.... [I]t is a recognition of the fact that somebody must be boss; somebody has to run the plant. People can't be wandering around at loose ends each deciding what to do next.... [T]o assure order, there is a clear procedural line drawn: *the company directs and the union grieves when it objects.*

Here at least we see by implication a recognition of the fact that it is management who must always act, or take the initiative, and that it is the right of the union to grieve or protest the act, *not to prevent the act from taking place.* This would appear to be obvious to all; but we all too frequently see situations where a foreman's decision to take a certain course of action is challenged by a union steward, demanding to know where in the contract management obtains the right to take such action. All too often at this point, supervisors are prone to engage in a discussion, which is in effect a negotiation, and then to come to their superiors or to the personnel department and complain that they cannot get union agreement to carry out the act. An illustration may be the best method to make the point attempted here. Typically, when a union representative believes that management has violated the labor agreement, he approaches the supervisor and asks him to point out where in the labor agreement there is a provision or a clause which gives the company the right to take the action it took. Also typically, *unfortunately, in many situations, the supervisor attempts to do just that,* leafing the agreement in search of his rights to support the action taken. What each party to this conversation may not understand, and probably does not, is that the company retains and reserves to itself all rights and powers and authorities it possessed prior to the negotiation of the labor agreement—except to the extent that it has restricted, limited or prohibited such rights by a provision of the contract. As has been stated, this is commonly referred to as the *"residual"* rights theory of management—that is, all rights which resided in management *prior* to the contract, *continue* to reside in management *after* the contract except to the extent they have been compromised by the company.

The above ritual puts the shoe on the wrong foot. The fact of the matter is, it is incumbent upon the union to identify some contractual provision that prohibits, restricts, or limits management's right to take the action in the fashion in which it intends. Regarding this approach, it is desirable to distinguish the substantive burden of proof from the procedural burden of going forth with evidence. The substantive burden of proof—whether in a court of law, or in an arbitration hearing, or in a grievance proceeding—rests with the complaining party. The substantive burden of proof never shifts from one party to the other. It may be defined as the burden on the complaining party to prove, by a preponderance of the evidence, his contentions. When the supervisor's defense is to admit all of the essential allegations of the union and to assert affirmatively that his action is justified for some other reason, then the supervisor has used an affirmative defense, and must therefore assume the substantive burden of proving the facts to sustain the defense.[3]

The word "right" is defined by *Webster's New International Dictionary* to mean "any power, privilege, or immunity, vested in one by authority, social custom ... or ... by law." The same reference defines the word "prerogative" to mean the "right to exercise a power or privilege in priority to, or to the exclusion of, other ... for the exercise of which in theory there is no responsibility or accountability as to the fact and the manner of its exercise."

In recent decades there has been progressive invasion of once unchallenged areas of exclusive managerial decision. Many things which once were regarded as the "right" or "prerogatives" of management have ceased to be so characterized. Inroads into management areas have been made by legislation, collective bargaining, and arbitration.

In principle, the supervisor is best advised to function on the premise that the parties have written a contract as an instrument containing specific and limited restrictions on the functions that management would otherwise be free to exercise if there were no labor contract. And, to whatever extent it has not been restricted, management continues to have all those rights that it customarily possesses and did not surrender in the collective bargaining process. Therefore, supervisors are best advised to subscribe to the principle that their management continues to possess the residue of all rights not bargained away. However, they must also be urged to recognize that the union is also a party to the labor agreement; to the extent that the company has agreed to compromise or restrict its managerial discretions, supervisors must realize that such matters are no longer within the province of their authority or control. They are urged to accept the premise that the union also has the right to enjoy the contract benefits and privileges obtained in negotiations with the employer and that matters falling within this area are beyond their authority to alter, modify, or reduce in any respect.

The Grievance Machinery

The grievance procedure is the problem-solving, dispute-settling machinery of the labor agreement. It is the orderly means by which the union or the employee raises and processes a claim alleging a violation by the company of the labor agreement. Importantly, the fact that a collective agreement includes provisions for a grievance procedure and an arbitration clause implies an obligation on the part of the union not to strike during the term of the agreement.[4] And the right of the union to strike during the term of the contract will be determined by the breadth and the scope of the arbitration clause.[5] Arbitrators and courts have called management's agreement to arbitrate grievance disputes the "quid-pro-quo" (one-for-one) exchange for the union's agreement not to strike.[6]

The grievance machinery is the formal process, preliminary to any arbitration, which enables the parties to peacefully and in an orderly, expeditious manner attempt to resolve their differences. It permits the company and the union to investigate and discuss their problems without interruption to the continued, orderly operation of the business. Working effectively, it can bring about the satisfactory resolution of the overwhelming majority of disputes between the parties. Even after an agreement has been negotiated and entered, collective bargaining does not completely end. Union officials are always alert to the possibility of obtaining additional benefits for their membership after the contract has been signed. If, for example, the union can induce a management representative to make an exception and grant some concession not required by contract to one worker, the concession may be used as the basis for a claim of precedent in future cases, or as the basis of a demand for liberalization in the next contract negotiations. In a real sense, it is the unions' view of the labor agreement that it is only the beginning point, and temporary resting place, in their quest for more and better benefits.

In essence, the grievance procedure is a safety valve. It provides a means by which the union and the employees can let off steam. It provides a procedure that allows the employees to give vent to their feelings and attitudes and opinions regarding certain management actions, but in a manner which is constructive, rather than destructive. By so doing, they highlight to management those problem areas which should have management's attention—whether it be a complaint against an unsafe condition or practice, a dispute regarding an allegedly unfair disciplinary action taken by the company, a complaint against an improperly behaving supervisor, or merely an allegation by an employee in which he honestly contends that management has unwittingly erred in its application and administration of the labor agreement.

Grievance procedures take many forms and are designed by different parties with a variety of ingredients. In some labor agreements, the procedure may be lengthy, containing five or six steps where meetings between the parties are held. In another contract, the procedure may be brief consisting of no more than two or three steps. In some agreements, time limits may be rather tight and narrow, while in other contracts they may be fairly liberal in their time limitations for raising, filing, processing and appealing the case. But in any and every agreement—irrespective of the particular ingredients selected by the parties—the primary *purpose to be served by the procedure* is always basically the same from one contract to another. That is, it is intended to provide a peaceful means by which the parties can meet and discuss their legitimate differences without interference or interruption to normal plant operations. The specific purpose of the procedure is to allow the union and the employees to complain against the management's actions. If the company intends to preserve and protect its managerial discretions and its generally unfettered right to make decisions and operate its business based on its own best judgments, it must make the grievance procedure a meaningful instrument which meets the objectives for which it was designed by the parties.

There are some who even refer to the grievance procedure as the quid-pro-quo for the management rights clause. The latter clause enables management to act; the former provision enables the union and the employees to react. With the no-strike clause inserted, employees cannot resort to any forms of self-help or use of any means of economic force. So, some substitute must be provided which will allow them to protest and contest management's decisions and actions. This is the purpose served by the grievance machinery. And, in a well-functioning procedure of this kind, the great majority of disputes will be resolved at the initial step between the foreman, the employee, and/or the union's steward.

When the parties fail to resolve the issue in the grievance procedure, the labor arbitration advocate steps in.

No-Strike, No-Lockout

The basic promise the union gives to the company is the promise that there will be no strikes. This is what it gives to the employer in exchange for the several promises it receives from the company in the labor agreement. Without this commitment, the company really has no guarantee that it will enjoy, for the term of the agreement, a continuity of operations. A revealing examination of the union's political motivations in this connection came from George Brooks, former Director of Research and Education of the Pulp, Sulphite and Paper Mill Workers Union, in his paper "What Our Collective Bargaining Looks Like in 20 Years"–(MIT, 1957).

> It is not the strikes that occur which are important; the important thing is that the idea of strike is present at every negotiation. What gives a settlement its final sanction in the minds of the employees is not that it was "fair" or "generous" or "correct"—but rather that it was "all we could get without striking."

This says it nicely in a very few words. It is the right to strike that the union has as its bargaining tool and it is the only thing it can give up as a consideration for the agreement. Unless it gives this single promise to the company, the labor agreement cannot be construed as a true bilateral exchange of promises.

As mentioned earlier herein, the grievance and arbitration provisions through which the union may seek and obtain relief if it considers management's action improper is the "quid-pro-quo" for the union's pledge of no strike. When work stoppages occur in breach of such no-strike agreements, the union is again resorting to the use of the exact economic forces that presumably had been harnessed for the term of the agreement. When this happens, the bargain has been broken and management is not in fact receiving the guarantee of uninterrupted operations which it thought the union had made.

The following represents a typical no-strike, no-lockout provision which could be found in an industrial labor agreement:

> Neither the union nor any of its agents nor any of its members will, in any manner whatsoever engage in, incite, participate in, aid or condone any strike, sit-down, stay-away, work stoppage, withholding of production or other in reference with production or work, or resort for relief to any form of self-help or other direct or indirect action during the term of this agreement; and the company agrees that during the term of this agreement it will not lock out any of the employees covered by this agreement.
>
> The company retains the right to discharge or otherwise discipline employees in the bargaining unit who have committed acts prohibited by the provisions of this article. The company shall have the right to discipline employees and to administer different penalties or to refrain from taking such disciplinary action for violations of the provisions of this article. The union shall have the right to protest and appeal any action constituting discipline administered to any employee by the company under this paragraph; however, the only issue which can be subject of a grievance and which can be reviewed by the arbitrator is limited to whether the employee has committed acts prohibited by the provisions of this article.
>
> If any controversy or dispute of any nature arises between the management of the corporation or its other divisions, subsidiaries or associated companies, their employees and unions representing these employees or attempting to represent such employees, and further that if any controversy or dispute of any nature arises between the management of any company performing work on company premises, or for the company under other conditions, their employees other than the employees covered by this agreement and the unions representing those employees or attempting to represent such employees, or any company which supplies raw, semi-finished or finished material manufactured by the corporation, their employees and the unions representing those employees or attempting to represent such employees, such controversy or dispute shall not affect in any way the rights and obligations of the parties herein established by this agreement; and if

> any such controversy or dispute results in or threatens to result in any strike, stoppage of work, or other interference with production, the parties hereto agree to abide by all the provisions of this article of this agreement, and to fulfill their obligations in accordance with the terms of this agreement.
>
> Neither the violation of any provision of this agreement nor the commission of any act constituting an unfair labor practice or otherwise made unlawful by any federal, state or local law shall excuse employees, the union or the company from their obligations under the provisions of the article.

Such a no-strike pledge enables the company to make plans. Commitments can be made and its deliveries scheduled on the assumption of uninterrupted production for the period of the contract. A strike in breach of this basic commitment denies to the company the sole consideration for which it bargained. Despite the presence of such a clause and in the face of differences of opinion between the company, the employees and the union officials, it is not uncommon for the employees or the union to resort to self-help and violate this pledge. However, sophisticated and informed union officials of today recognize that management must run its plant and give orders to employees, which it can expect will be obeyed.

This is especially true where the parties have set up a grievance and arbitration provision to handle management's mistakes. Under the usual contract today, the normal recourse of the affronted employee is to follow orders and file a grievance if he believes his contractual rights have been offended. It is an established principle in the administration of labor agreements that the proper procedure for protesting alleged violations of the contract is to use the established grievance procedure. To view this matter otherwise would invite the type of chaotic conditions which the presence of the no-strike article in the contract is designed to prevent.

Arbitration

A collective bargaining agreement is an effort by the parties to erect a system of industrial self-government. The grievance machinery under the agreement is at the very heart of the system of industrial self-government. Arbitration is the means of solving the unforeseeable by molding a system of private law for all of the problems which may arise, and to provide for their solution in a way which will generally accord with the variant needs of the parties.

When the union agrees to arbitration, it usually gives up its right to strike over the issue submitted. When the company agrees to arbitration, it thereby gives up its right to take unilateral action *unopposed* on the matter which is under dispute. Arbitration constitutes the terminal point for solving differences between the parties with the award of the arbitrator being final and binding upon them.

Grievance arbitration, which provides an alternative to strikes and lockouts, has been referred to as a judicial process because it requires the arbitrator to interpret that private source of law which regulates the parties, the labor agreement. As a dispute settling process, it is almost as old as the recorded history of man; history relates how Solomon acted as the wise and respected neutral.

Approximately 94 percent of all labor-management agreements in this country provide for grievance arbitration for the peaceful resolution of disputes, and the use of such arbitration is growing.

Management's quest for stability and efficiency, ensured by the guarantee of continuity of operations, which took the form of a no-strike agreement from the employees and the union, left the union without its strongest weapon, the strike, to resolve its grievance disputes with management.

To achieve its objective of untroubled and uninterrupted operations, management was obliged to provide some equitable system for dispute resolution if it expected the union to sacrifice its primary power, the use of economic force. The grievance and arbitration clauses were intended to provide just such a fair, equitable, and just solution to the parties' problems during the term of the contract.

The labor arbitrator is usually chosen because of the parties' confidence in his knowledge of the common law of the shop and their trust in his personal judgment to bring to bear considerations which are expressed in the contract as criteria for his judgment. His essential qualifications are assumed to be high integrity, understanding, and strict impartiality, coupled with an adequate knowledge of labor law and economics. The parties' objective in using the arbitration process is primarily to further their common goal of uninterrupted production under the agreement and thereby make the agreement serve their specialized needs.

The process of arbitration differs from two other common methods of promoting a settlement of labor disputes. It differs from mediation and conciliation which are processes usually initiated from the outside and which the parties are at liberty to refuse. Such mediators and conciliators do not necessarily propose agreements but aim at persuading the parties to reach their own agreement by enabling them to see the other party's viewpoint and by offering recommendations to narrow such differences.

Arbitration also differs from so-called fact-finding procedures. These also, as a rule, originate from the outside. Except for the emergency dispute provisions of the Taft-Hartley Act, fact-finding boards usually formulate proposed agreements, but the parties again are under no obligation to accept them.

However, under most labor agreements which contain arbitration provisions, the award of the arbitrator is final and binding upon the parties. Such arbitration clauses customarily contain provisions which limit, regulate and circumscribe the authority of the arbitrator and require him to arrive at his decision from his interpretation and application of the labor agreement. Most parties do not think that the agreements they draft are inept or incomplete. On the contrary, the average collective bargaining agreement, particularly in those industries and companies which have a long history of union relations, is rather a carefully and laboriously prepared document. Having gone to the trouble of so carefully constructing a document which is usually quite lengthy and fairly comprehensive, the parties prefer to prevent an arbitrator from adding to, or overturning their applecart. The parties are generally determined not to share their decision-making function with the arbitrator. So far as most parties to labor agreements are concerned, their conception of the role of the arbitrator is that he is essentially a judge. His task is to do justice in accordance with the rules imposed by the parties' contract. He decides the controversy entirely on the basis of the arguments and the proof presented to him while the parties are confronting one another face to face. He does not attempt to mediate or conciliate and to do so would be to compromise his role as adjudicator. He strictly avoids any private communication with the parties after the hearing. To them the arbitrator is a person of principle, a person who respects the institutional limits of his task; a person who conscientiously refuses to exploit his powers for ulterior purposes, however benign.

The arbitral process may not always produce decisions rendered from the Olympian heights of objectivity, but is the best procedure yet devised for industrial self-government that meets the twin objectives of getting disputes settled peacefully and avoiding interference or interruption of production.

In summary, what this chapter has intended to demonstrate is how these four critical contract provisions operate, interacting and complementing one another, and how these are the four contract clauses which surround the other benefit and operational provisions of the contract, making it possible for everything to hang together and work in harmony.

Management has agreed in the labor agreement that when carrying out its responsibilities, it will follow certain procedures or take into account specified factors involving the equities of employees. In such situations, management's failures to perform the particular responsibility in the manner agreed upon are subject to challenge in the grievance procedure which may be subject to appeal to arbitration.

Moreover, even with regard to managerial rights not in any way regulated or limited by a labor agreement, management should act wisely and justly. The arbitrary and inconsiderate use of power is a sure invitation to ultimate limitation of that power. In union-management relations, management's injudicious use of its rights and responsibilities affords the union ammunition for demanding further contractual limitations on management in future negotiations.

3

Implied Limitations in the Contract

Many arbitrators are confronted today with arguments that they must supply by implication a significant term which has been omitted from what may otherwise appear to be an obviously thorough and complete and carefully prepared collective bargaining agreement. Obviously, if arbitrators are faced with this problem, supervisors must first encounter the issue before it reaches the arbitrator. More and more today, whenever the union has difficulty finding a provision of the labor agreement which specifically supports their grievance contention, and they cannot find or are not content with an existing past practice, they are insisting that there are *implied* restrictions to be found in the contract which limit or restrict management rights. The ultimate question here is one of *intent;* and if there is a single presumption *not* warranted in the labor-management context today, it is that management, when it staggers bloodily away from the bargaining table, really *intended* to give up *more* of its management prerogatives than it left there. As a matter of fact, quite often there is ample evidence that the true intent of the company in the negotiations was precisely the opposite of what the union or an arbitrator might impute to it by "implication." That is, that management was *not* to concede the limitations sought by the union and perhaps even specifically rejected a language proposal made by the union for that purpose.

More often than not a reading of all of the terms and conditions of the agreement leaves one with the definite impression that its authors fully intended to state clearly every point of importance in their minds.

It is often difficult to conceive of parties to a contract, who are usually diligent in their contact's preparation, purposely omit a vital condition. When the union *implies* the existence of such a vital condition, the only possible conclusion that can be drawn is that such condition did not in fact exist. Despite this, the union persists. For example, alleging violation of the "recognition clause" is a favorite tactic.

Dealing with the recognition clause as a source of implied limitations on management action, we are in the area of implications, *not* express terms. The average recognition clause contains *no* express agreement to continue the unit or the operation without change—*no* express grant to the union or its members of jurisdiction over the work.

If a manager is faced with a claim that the recognition clause has been violated in any type of grievance, he should firmly, flatly and quickly reject this claim. Recognition clauses create no labor agreement rights as such. Their only meaning is to include in a formal fashion, in the contract, the company's already existing legal obligation to bargain with the union.

A typical approach of the shop steward is to demand that the manager show him where in the agreement it specifically states that he had the right to take a contested action. This is a shrewd tactic which may catch the unsophisticated supervisor unaware; and having fruitlessly searched the contract, such a supervisor may be led to admit that he cannot locate a specific source for that right. Clearly this puts the cart before the horse. The supervisor's answer to the steward on such an approach should be:

> You show me where it specifically limits or prohibits my right to take the action you contest—for only to that extent may my action be viewed as improper.

The answer that should be given to any claimed violation of the recognition clause should be as follows:

> The recognition clause, as such, creates no right. All it does is include in the labor agreement the company's legal obligation to recognize the union as the bargaining agent of the company's employees. We have recognized, and will continue to recognize, the union as such agents.

The union seizes upon this clause after painstakingly combing the agreement for a thread from which it can spin an interpretative argument that supports their claim that such a clause contains a right or a limitation. However, ordinary interpretation, common sense and sometimes even the history of negotiation clearly demonstrate that such limitations are *not* there and were never in the minds of the parties who wrote the clause.

There are still other reasons why the recognition article does not and cannot have the scope which some unions would attribute to it. To hold, as some arbitrators and most unions do, that the ordinary recognition clause prevents any change in the composition of the bargaining unit, or the work assignments of its members, is to attribute to it all of the force and effect which is elsewhere called a *scope* clause or a *work jurisdiction* clause. Anyone familiar with these clauses, which typically appear in building trades agreements and in the entertainment industry, is well aware of how substantially such clauses *differ* from the ordinary recognition clause. Such clauses are extremely detailed in describing the work they cover. To assert that the broad language of the recognition clause has the same effect—lacking, as it does, the essential elements of detail of the *scope* and *work jurisdiction* clauses mentioned—is to call an alphabet a dictionary. Under the recognition article the company recognizes the union as the representative of its employees. Such a clause does not operate to require the company to use *only* its regular employees, or to hire new employees, or to perform work in its facilities. As a matter of fact, such clauses operate *only after* an employee has been hired and the employer-employee relationship has been created, and the average clause of this type also merely indicates to which of the employees so hired the provisions of the contract apply. Such a clause describes the unit of the employees for whom the union treats, and thus delineates the operative scope of the agreement itself. But, it serves *no substantive function*. That is, it does *not* deal with, and has *no bearing upon*, the terms and conditions covering the employment itself. To read substantive provisions into the recognition article through arbitration or grievance settlements, is to use these processes as a means for expanding the agreement which the parties have made, rather than just interpreting and applying its substantive provisions in specific situations.

The recognition article is not the only clause seized upon by the union to claim that implied limitations emanate therefrom. Others typically used, either singly or in combination, are the seniority clause, the list of job classifications the hourly wage schedules which reflect employees' rates of pay for given tasks, and other such clauses. These will be treated later.

But the recognition clause is, plainly and simply, a creature of the National Labor Relations Act. That act requires of the employer what he says, in the recognition clause, that he *is* doing, namely, recognizing the union as the exclusive representative of all of the employees in the bargaining unit.

The presence of recognition clauses in collective bargaining contracts is historical. Their significance dates back to a time in the 1930s when many a union would gladly have settled for a statement in writing, signed by the employer, doing no more than extending recognition to the union. Bitter battles were waged over that simple issue. Nowadays, the contract itself—extensive and complex as it so often is—testifies to recognition of the union's status in a far more impressive manner than any recognition clause, and the need for such a clause in terms, therefore, is negligible.

Nothing in the act expressly requires such a clause, although the fact of recognition is itself compulsory under the act. But the very element of compulsion, which takes the recognition clause *out of the area* of items to which the employer is entitled to agree or not to agree, points up the utter fallacy of attempting to base any "implied agreement" on the recognition clause. In a very real sense, the recognition clause is unique in the labor agreement, in that it is the only term whose inclusion is completely nonvolitional insofar as the employer is concerned. The National Labor Relations Act, as the Supreme Court has said, does not compel the making of agreements.[1] All other terms of the collective agreement are terms to which the employer could refuse to agree, subject to the economic consequences of his failure to agree. But the recognition clause is different. He *cannot* withhold recognition, he cannot refuse to "agree" to recognize. Nor, having "agreed," can he refuse to put the fact of that agreement in writing and sign.[2] It follows, therefore, that, whatever may be properly "implied" from other, volitional clauses in the agreement, no element of volition or implied agreement can be ascribed to or derived from the recognition clause.

There is another reason why the recognition clause cannot be said to have any continuing effect as a promise or undertaking. It is a verbal act, completed as soon as it is said, and the union is "recognized" as required by the statute. The very remainder of the contract is evidence that the union has, in fact, been "recognized." In other words, the function of the recognition clause (if it can truly be said to have one apart from the statute) antedates the negotiation of the contract and is complete when the negotiations culminating in the contract have taken place.

Finally, there is the fact that the typical recognition clause is wholly inappropriate to the crucial uses to which some arbitrators would put it. It completely lacks the necessary ingredients. Thus, if the recognition clause were to have the force and effect which the union seeks to give to it, it would be because it constitutes an exclusive assignment of work jurisdiction to the union. But the recognition clause is hopelessly vague for that purpose. The "jurisdiction" it spells out is simply "production employees" and "maintenance employees." Where are the boundaries and limits? How could work jurisdiction be administratively applied and enforced, if it did exist? These are only a few of the many questions this issue obviously raises, but cannot answer.

Subcontracting is a principal act by management that commonly generates heat. But first, what is subcontracting? Many people become emotionally involved when discussing it, since in industrial parlance, subcontracting has become a glandular word—the mere utterance of it causing the pulse to throb, the thyroid gland to secrete and the temperature to rise dangerously. The ironic point is that this same reaction is typical of both union and management representatives.

When rational, how do these same people define it? In its broadest sense, subcontracting means arranging with another firm to make goods or perform services which could perhaps be performed by bargaining unit employees within the company's facilities.

Since such a simple definition is possible, why is so much heat generated by its utterance?

First of all, there is no question that an entire book could be devoted to the views of the National Labor Relations Board on management's action in contracting out. After concluding that document, a second book could then be written on the rulings of the courts and their impact upon subcontracting. But, although the parties to labor agreements much too often find themselves in these arenas, the tribunal they frequent more often is that of arbitration. Since this is the area that plagues them most, and should concern advocates most, this is one I shall explore.

For the sake of brevity, I intended to dismiss contracts expressly defining the company's authority to contract out. Contracts with such express provisions generally either limit management's contracting-out prerogatives, in whole or in part, or they expressly provide management with an unhindered right.[3] Therefore, I am limiting my attention to the more elusive subject of implied limitations,[4] and how arbitrators wrestle with this issue.

Where the contract is silent and contains no explicit language to bar work from going to subcontractors, arbitrators who imply limitations usually turn to one clause, or a combination of several clauses, to find some implied intention to limit contracting out.

The provisions most frequently referred to, singly or in combination, are (1) the recognition clause; (2) the seniority clause; and (3) the list of job classifications. I will deal briefly with each of these.

The Recognition Clause

As stated before, the recognition clause is merely the statement in the labor agreement that the employer recognizes a particular union as the exclusive bargaining agent of employees in the appropriate unit. However, some arbitrators, and many unions, have said that this clause implies an agreement that the employer may not, by managerial decisions, remove work from employees in the unit by subcontracting it to others.[5] This theory was articulated by arbitrator C.R. Schedler in a United States Potash case, where he said:

> There is no express language either prohibiting or authorizing contracting out. What is more important is that the contract contains a clause recognizing the union.... The infraction here is in the unavoidable effect on these rights. To me it is clear that the work belonged to the unit which contained employees fully capable of executing it. The contracting out had the inevitable impact of derogating the union's status as recognized exclusive representative.[6]

The essence of the error into which arbitrators fall when they employ this clause as a source of work jurisdiction is the failure to recognize that the required recognition of the union under the National Labor Relations Act is a recognition of the union as the representative of *"people," not* of *"work."*

Perhaps the most complete answer to those who seek erroneously to find an implied agreement or limitation in the recognition clause was given by Professor Herman Gray of N.Y.U. who met this issue head on in a case with Hearst Consolidated Publications, wherein he stated:

> In my view, the purpose of the recognition clause is no more than to enunciate the legal status of the bargaining union. It describes the unit of the employees for whom the union speaks and thus delineates the operative scope of the agreement itself. It serves no substantive function. That is, it does not deal with and has no bearing upon the terms and conditions governing the employment itself. To read substantive provisions into the recognition clause through arbitration decisions is, in my judgment, to use arbitration as a means for expanding the agreement which the parties have made, rather than just interpreting and applying its provisions in a specific situation.[7]

Perhaps I have dwelt too long on this point; but it is the recognition clause which most frequently captures the fancy of those arbitrators who search for implied reasons to limit management's contracting-out actions.

The Seniority Clause

Presumably, the seniority clause merely establishes a preference for longer service employees over shorter service employees, for work when made available by the employer. Since such a clause provides that the latter (shorter service employees) will be laid off before the former, it obviously recognizes that the volume of work can diminish.[8]

However, arbitrator Saul Wallen rejected the management rights clause and turned to the seniority provisions of the labor agreement in his decision at New Britain Machine, when he said:

Job security is an inherent element of the labor contract, a part of its very being. If wages is the heart of the labor agreement, job security may be considered its soul. Those eligible to share in the degree of job security the contract affords are those to whom the contract applies....

> The transfer of work customarily performed by employees in the bargaining unit must therefore be regarded as an attack on the job security of the employees whom the agreement covers and therefore on one of the contract's basic purposes.[9]

Naturally, arbitrators, being only human, reserve the right to reconsider, then sometimes change their minds, and it appears that this occurred ten years later with Arbitrator Wallen. In a Hershey Chocolate Corp. decision, he had this to say:

> In the same way the seniority provisions guarantee, not a constant employment opportunity for each category of employee covered by the contract, but a set of rules for the parceling out of employment opportunities, the availability of work can be affected by diminished work volumes due to changes in the market, due to changes in technology, or due to changes in the realm of good faith managerial decision-making.[10]

The consolation is that it appears, in subsequent years and in subsequent cases, we have here at last one arbitrator who eventually amended his views on this whole implied limitation controversy. Far too many others continue to seize upon this provision to read a limitation into a contract where none is expressly provided.[11]

The List of Job Classifications

Typically, the listing of job classifications is attached to the contract as an appendix, and it is *nothing more or less* than a list of job titles and their representative wage rates to be paid *when* those jobs are manned.

Arbitrator John Sembower's award at Continental Can is a good example of how the job classification list has been used as a basis for implying a limitation on contracting out work. In his opinion he said:

> The agreement is not silent on the matter of subcontracting. If it does not speak out on it, *it at least whispers* when it spells out, in Appendix "A" that janitors are included in the bargaining unit. When the company specified job classifications in the recognition of the bargaining unit, it, in effect, gives up its right to subcontract in that field, unless something is added in the way of a contract provision giving the right to subcontract [emphasis added].[12]

Once again, we are dealing with another contractual provision over which there is not unanimity of arbitrator opinion. It is also *not difficult* to find arbitration rulings which deal with precisely this same issue, and *do not* bestow ownership of work upon employees, *nor bar* subcontracting despite the discovery of a listing of job classifications and their wage rates.[13]

What about arbitrators who refuse to imply restriction? What do they use as a basis for their awards? Basically, they apply a simple, straightforward view to the effect that management has reserved the right to contract out, unless, by specific contract language, this right has been limited.

But most arbitrators of this type impose a certain standard to evaluate the propriety of the subcontract action.[14]

The standards listed below are not intended to be all-conclusive, but are merely factors which singly, or in combination, have been decisive in certain cases:

- *The effect on the union.* Was the subcontracting done to injure or discriminate against the union and did it substantially prejudice the status of the unit?[15]
- *The availability of qualified employees.* Was the skill possessed by available members of the unit adequate to perform the required work and are such employees readily available in the numbers needed?[16]
- *The availability of facilities and equipment.* Were equipment and facilities currently available and, if not, could they have been readily and economically acquired?[17]
- *The duration and regularity.* Was the contracting out for a temporary or permanent period and was it done frequently or spasmodically?[18]
- *Negotiation history.* Has the subject been discussed in negotiations—has the union made demands to limit the right to subcontract?[19]
- *Past practice.* Has work been contracted out in the past, and to what extent?
- *Type of work.* Was the work contracted out customarily done by unit employees; was it done for economy or security; was it an emergency or special job, or done to augment the regular work force?
- *The effect on the unit.* Did the contracting-out action displace or lay off employees, or cost them regular or overtime earnings?

Managements usually don't quarrel too bitterly with arbitrators who expect the company to meet such tests of reasonableness and good faith. What they quarrel with is the kind of muddled reasoning which makes a clause mean one thing if the arbitrator thinks the employer is in good faith, and quite another thing if he thinks the employer is in bad faith.

It is conceded that an employer should not be motivated by hostility toward the union, or a desire to injure or destroy the union. Criteria such as those herein enumerated are essentially criteria used by arbitrators for determining whether such hostility or improper motivation exists.

Why is management faced with this implied limitation type of threat to its right to manage, and most important, what can be done about it?

Sophisticated employers say unions aren't taking away management prerogatives. They say the prerogatives are being given away, day to day, in the way the plants are run. And there is a good deal of truth in that. But that's not the biggest source of danger today. For a change, management is not its own worst enemy. The right to manage is literally in the center of a great pincer movement.

One claw of that pincer is the NLRB. It's no great secret that, in the past several years, that claw has pinched into areas heretofore considered unquestionably the exclusive province of management.

But, it's the second pincer claw we are dealing with here. Two factors have combined in recent years to drive many companies to the wall. One is the drive of unions toward a concept of "property right" in a job, and the other has been a kind of "peace at any price" philosophy, which many managements have been pursuing.

Some have now awakened to find that "peace at any price" is no more workable as a philosophy in labor relations than it is in foreign relations.

In the unions' quest for greater job security, managements' assignment of work must be a principal target. Unfortunately, some managements have been frightfully lax in fighting these unions' quests for property rights in jobs. And that's where the second pincer claw, arbitration, is used as the instrument to endanger management's properly unilateral decision.

The Supreme Court has also dealt a body blow to the reserved rights theory by its holding "everything management does is subject to the agreement when it contains arbitration."

The court also said that, once arbitration exists in a contract, "only the most forceful evidence of a purpose to exclude" a given type of claim will keep it out of arbitration.

In the face of these conditions, management must devise contractual language to shore up its rights to expressly exclude the arbitrator from those areas in which it does not intend for him to operate. There is no question that getting such language changes will not be easy. Unions have come to expect little pressure for language changes in defense of management right. Employers are on the short end of the propaganda battle between job security and management rights, with the latter becoming almost as nasty a word as profits.

But, it is easier to reinforce possession of rights which the union knows perfectly well haven't been given up, than it is to recapture those same rights later. Management must soon advocate an attitude of rights preservation, while it still has something to preserve. Only through such action will management raise its rights out of the twilight zone in which some of them reside today. Managers can assist in this endeavor by not ceding them away by ignorance or inadvertence in their handling of implied limitation contentions.

4

Discipline or Discharge of Union Officials

The most delicate type of discharge or discipline case is one that finds a union official the target of management's action.

The dual role of local union officer, as an employee and also as official of a labor organization, gives an added dimension to his conduct which is not shared by ordinary employees. In the role of employee, he has the right and privileges of other rank-and-file employees within his bargaining unit, and he is governed by the rules and regulations which apply to his co-workers. While in his job as an employee of the company, the requirements of attendance, punctuality, quality, production output, and the like, are the same for him as they would be for any other employee of the company. But while operating in his capacity of union representative, he enjoys a certain latitude and freedom in his day-to-day application, administration, and implementation of the union contract. As a union representative, he becomes co-equal with the company's supervisors, thus enabling him to represent and advocate the positions and interests of his constituents.

Management's discipline or discharge of a union official frequently raises the questions: Is the motivation for its action union animus or discrimination? Was the union representative's act performed during a time when he was operating in his role as an employee, or was he acting as a union official and, therefore, by reason of this representational cloak, entitled to some special consideration or immunity?

This chapter will describe some representative informative cases dealing with the punishment of union officials for on-the-job rules violations while acting in their dual role of employee and union official. To enable the company to better see the several principles involved, various arbitrators' decisions are reviewed for supporting authority, and to show how the issues raised by such cases are commonly dealt with.

Insubordination

In cases involving alleged insubordination by individuals who hold the office of union steward, the penalties are generally the same as for rank-and-file employees if the steward was insubordinate *as an employee.*

In one such case, at the Dominion Electric Co. where a union official refused a job assignment related to his particular tasks as an employee, the arbitrator concluded that the company did not discharge him with intent to discriminate but rather for his refusal as an employee to carry out a proper order.[1]

At the American Can Co., the employer was found justified in discharging for "gross and defiant insubordination" a union president who repeatedly left his bargaining unit job without proper supervisory leave to investigate grievances.[2]

At Chrysler Corp., under a contract which obligated the chief steward to report to his foreman the number and nature of grievances he wished to investigate, the employer was found justified in discharging the steward after his refusal to perform unit overtime work. The steward claimed he was investigating grievances (and so could not work overtime), but refused to identify them as required by contractual provision. In upholding the dismissal, the arbitrator ruled that the steward had been instructed by his foreman to report for the assignment and he had been warned to identify the specific grievances under investigation, or return to his job, or be discharged.[3]

In a case with a different twist, the arbitrator sustained the discharge of a union steward who functioned continually in the capacity of a union official outside of a fixed, agreed upon hourly period established for stewards to handle grievances and to otherwise discharge their duties. Although he was acting as a union official, his refusal to stop was in total disregard of specific contractual regulations which limited that union activity.[4]

The labor agreement's provisions are the controlling factor here. The regulations and practices under the contract determine when an employee-union representative can function as a union official, and to what extent. Absent some contract arrangement to the contrary, the general rule holds that such workers have two obligations—*first* to their job as an employee, and *second* to their capacity as a union official—and, in that particular order of priority.

But where the steward is on union business, the usual requirement of "obey first, grieve later" is most often not applied by arbiters, *if* the orders given are *in conflict* with the union's rights under the labor agreement.

In one such situation, upon dismissing the compliant, an arbiter held that:

> There is a clear distinction between the case of a supervisor telling an employee to go back to his job and supervisor telling the union to stop investigating a grievance. The company and union have met equal terms and adopted a contract recognizing each other's right.... If he (steward) could rightly be penalized, it would put the entire grievance machinery, set up by agreement of the parties at the highest levels, at the mercy of supervisors with the possibility of great harm to the relations of the parties, even to a complete breakdown of the grievance machinery.[5]

A new and different type of remedy was rendered by another arbitrator. Where a union committeeman was discharged for refusing to perform assigned work which he believed was not covered by his classification, the arbitrator concluded that the committeeman's trouble was due to overzealousness in his union office. He reinstated the committeeman without back pay upon the condition he resign from office as union committeeman and pledge to remain out of such office.[6]

Gambling, Dishonesty and Drinking

Insubordination is not the only offense for which union representatives may find themselves subjected to discipline. All plant rules and other regulatory conditions which govern employee behavior are also applicable to local union representatives in equal measure while in their capacity of employee. Union officials have found themselves in serious trouble with management for their transgressions in a number of areas. For example, the discharge of a union steward was found to be a warranted exercise of managerial discretion when the company established that the steward (as an employee) was guilty of submitting false piecework tickets, thus claiming additional compensation for work which he was unable to prove he had performed.[7]

When a union president was discharged for excessive absenteeism, the question was asked: Where is the proper balance between the latitude provided him in his capacity as union president and his obligations as an employee? In examining this situation, the arbitrator said:

> The grievant was out an inordinate number of days for a variety of reasons: outside union business, illness, personal reasons. He was warned repeatedly about this, even to the extent of being given a disciplinary layoff.... Knowing that the company took a serious view of his absences and his leaving the job without first securing permission, he made little effort after the disciplinary layoff, to comply with the reasonable requirements

> expected of him, but continued to absent himself on union business, aware on the basis of his previous record, that the chances were good that he might also be out for illness. Under these circumstances I consider the company has justified its charge of excessive absenteeism. The grievance is denied.[8]

In the case above, there was a mixture of absences for illness and personal reasons, and others for purposes of engaging in union business.

By no means is there unanimity of arbitral opinion on this point. A representative case of their disagreement is one in which the arbitrator ruled that the employer was not justified in discharging a union president for chronic absenteeism and tardiness, in accordance with the plant rules, even though the president had received prior warnings regarding the excessive number of his unreported absences. The arbitral premise here was that the majority of absences and occasions of tardiness apparently were necessitated by *legitimate* union business, and the remaining number of absences were *not* sufficient to constitute chronic absenteeism.[9]

Here again we see that distinction drawn between duties and functions as an employee, as contrasted with the second part of the dual role, the activities and responsibilities as a union representative.

Union officials have also been disciplined for gambling on company time and on company premises. Under a plant rule providing for immediate discharge of "any employee drinking or gambling on the company property," an employer was found justified in discharging a local union officer who had been operating baseball and number pools at work. In upholding the discharge, the arbitrator said:

> Patently the issue here is whether the grievant was discharged for just cause or if, as the union charges, the dismissal was capricious and discriminatory. The company avers the discipline meted out was just and proper because: (1) all four types of gambling games conducted by the grievant violated the criminal code and had they adopted a laissez-faire policy and closed their eyes to such violations they could have been ejected from their premises by the very terms of the lease agreement; (2) rule 6 of the company rules and regulations provides immediate dismissal for gambling; and (3) the gambling activities conducted by the grievant adversely affected plant productivity as is evidenced by substantial productivity improvement after the grievant's discharge and the gambling ceased.[10]

Here again, the employee-union official violated a plant rule while acting in the capacity of employee. His union office did not cloak him in immunity.

Falsification of the employment application of a newly elected union officer was reason for yet another discharge. While the officer was militant and aggressive, and his discharge followed by one day the union's strike vote over grievances he had been processing, the arbitrator found that the employer's action was *not* discriminatory or premised on the employee's union activities. In his decision he commented:

> Whether or not he had been a union official his falsification would have supported discharge. That he was a union official would not mitigate against the impropriety of what he had done.... The grievance dismissed.[11]

Again, consequential to the arbitral findings was the absence of any discrimination or union animus on the part of the employer.

The discharge of two union officials who drank on the job on company premises on Christmas Eve was sustained by an arbitrator who ruled that drinking on the job was dangerous to the employee and to his fellow workers. In this case, it was also a direct violation of the contract. Despite a union argument that both men were officers of the local and that the company had failed to *detect* other employees guilty of the same offense, he ruled that these considerations were immaterial and sustained the company's discharge action.[12]

In still another interesting, insightful case involving violation of plant rules and regulations, a union president was discharged for (1) preparing an order which directed the removal of exterior plant floodlights, (2) forging a plant superintendent's signature on the order, and (3) filing the form as a legitimate order. It proved of no consequence when the union president-employee alleged that he merely wanted to play a joke on a night watchman, since in the arbitrator's view the faked order might have resulted in loss of company property by fire or theft, thus making this a serious offense. In commenting about the effect of a union president's discharge on the relationship between the parties, the arbitrator said:

> It was contended on the part of the union that L_____ had been a longtime faithful and competent employee of the company and that he had been a union member from the time that the union had first been recognized by the company and was, in effect, president of the union at the time of his discharge, and was also chairman of the negotiating committee dealing directly with the company for the renewal of the contract at the time of his discharge.
>
> If laxity to the extent of permitting the subscription of that of a superintendent's name to an order affecting the company's property is to be permitted to the president of a union, the example set for the general workers in the plant is not conducive to sound labor-management relationship and mutual respect in their varied dealings.[13]

Here we have a case containing an additional complicating ingredient—the company's action was taken during the time that bargaining was in progress for a renewed labor agreement, with the union president a key participant. But that fact notwithstanding, (1) the company's action showed *no* union animus, (2) there was *no* other aspect of discrimination, (3) the company *met* a test of bearing the burden of proof, and (4) it *met* a standard of just cause. This was then sufficient to overcome the problem of the event occurring during the period of collective bargaining, and those suspicions attendant therefore.

Ignorance of the Law

It is common for arbitrators to weigh the length of time a union official has been in office and thereby consider his degree of sophistication and familiarity with the scope and responsibilities of his union authority when reviewing any punishment of the official. Arbitral opinion often holds that a new or inexperienced steward's improprieties in office may be excused, or partially justified by the fact that he is not completely informed. Such was the story in a case when a union committeeman was disciplined for violating a company rule forbidding distribution of handbills on company property. The committeeman had acted in the honest belief he was within his rights because of a recent NLRB decision involving a different company, which found illegal the company order prohibiting distribution of union leaflets on company parking lots.[14]

Another arbitrator went a large step further in resolving a dispute over a discharged steward who, on his first day in office, told his foreman he was entitled to go where he pleased and proceeded to "roam" up and down, in disregard of his foreman's repeated orders. Although the arbitrator fully censured the behavior of this steward, he reasoned that:

> ... (the steward) would nevertheless have taken immediate proper directions from his own chief within the union, the divisional steward. However, this opportunity to give the inexperienced steward timely correction was ignored by the foreman. The green steward was given a further opportunity to repeat his mistake and to sink further into the consequences of his blunder.... Modern personnel relations require from both sides and their representatives at least a reasonable degree of sympathetic tolerance. On the night of the dispute, S_____ was an inexperienced, newly appointed steward. Management appears to have been guilty almost of entrapment of the steward into a harsh consequence of an ignorant mistake, instead of cooperating in a charitable and tolerant effort to correct his erroneous assumptions.[15]

Although most arbiters will not go quite so far as this, generally speaking, *the majority give ample consideration to the factor of inexperience, in union officials*. An arbitrator who joined this majority reinstated discharged union officers even though evidence established that they had instigated and participated in a strike in violation of the contract. This arbitrator also considered the inexperience of the union officials, the newness of the employer's operations, the local union and the labor contract, as well as the accumulation of grievances which had led to employees' unrest, all to be mitigating factors in this case.[16]

The best course of action for a manager therefore is to (1) give the erring new union official a thorough counseling on all the breadth and limits of his union freedom and responsibility before any disciplinary action is deemed applicable, (2) give him a warning and a second chance to correct his improper conduct before action is taken, and (3) advise higher union officials of the complications experienced and solicit their cooperation and higher authority to get the right message across to their inexperienced brethren.

Countermanding Management's Orders

For the most part, there does appear to be unanimity of opinion among arbitrators about the impropriety of the union countermanding management's orders, so long as the order deals with matters generally falling within management's domain. Harry Shulman, respected spokesman and statesman in the arbitration process and former umpire with the Ford Motor Co. and the United Auto Workers, articulated this philosophy in one of his many cases when he said:

> No committeeman or other union officer is entitled to instruct employees to disobey supervision's orders *no matter how strongly* he may believe that the orders are in violation of the agreement. If he believes that an improper order has been issued, his course is to take the matter up with supervision and to seek to effect an adjustment. Failing to effect an adjustment, he may file a grievance. But he may *not* tell the employee to disregard the order [emphasis added].[17]

The overwhelming weight of majority opinion in arbitral circles reflects the view that an industrial plant is not a debating society. When controversies arise, as they inevitably will, the operation of the enterprise must go on while the dispute is being discussed and resolved. The authority for directing that it go on is vested *solely* in supervision. The grievance procedure is designed to adequately recompense employees for any abuse of authority by supervision. But the remedy under the labor agreement for violations of rights lies in the grievance and arbitration provisions.

For the union representative, or the individual employee, to disregard or countermand supervision's orders is to replace the grievance with the extra-contractual method of individual determination and action. And such must be the advice of union representative to his constituents. The only exception to this are orders which would require the employee to perform a criminal or unlawful or immoral act. Also in this category are supervisor's directives which, if carried out, would jeopardize the health, safety or welfare of the employees. But if the management order falls within its proper boundaries, the union representative's posture should be that the employee is obliged to obey the supervisor's instructions and to seek redress and correction through the grievance procedures. The efficient and orderly operation of a plant requires that employees and union representatives alike respect the authority of their supervisors. Union representatives who advise employees to circumvent or disobey reasonable instructions issued by the company open themselves to possible disciplinary action.

Union Officials' Responsibility

Generally, arbitrators hold that local union officials not only have similar responsibility as other employees with regard to performance of their regular jobs, but also carry an additional burden, as union officials, of enforcing the contract and influencing other employees to comply with its terms. For example, where a union official participated in an unauthorized work stoppage, his offense is graver than that of the other participating employees.[18]

This principle was voiced in a situation where the employer imposed a suspension against a shop steward for engaging in a strike in violation of the labor agreement. In his award, the arbiter said:

> The proposition that affirmative obligations of leadership in upholding the grievance procedure and opposing work stoppages devolved upon an employee, who by reason of seniority and status as a union officer must be held to have achieved a position of influence, has hitherto found acceptance under this and other agreements. Implicit in it is the thought that if those prominent and influential in the affairs of the union fail to so support these vital provisions of the agreement, the parties' expectations that they will be complied with during the life of the agreement become altogether illusory.[19]

Some arbitrators have even viewed a union official's passive behavior in the face of known employee violations of the contract as a type of "negative leadership." *This general principle of "negative vs. affirmative leadership" is one shared by many arbiters.* One such opinion was expressed in a case where the local union president, union committeeman, and shop steward were disciplined for failing to prevent an unauthorized work stoppage.

> ...Local union officials are the spokesmen for the workers. They are their leaders. They, therefore, have responsibilities *over and beyond* those of the rank and file. Local union officials are *obligated aggressively to oppose actions* that violate commitments undertaken in good faith. Local union officials are bound by virtue of their office to set personal examples of opposition to contract violation. *They cannot be passive; they must vigorously seek to prevent contract violations by their constituents* [emphasis added].[20]

Although this view is shared by the great majority of arbitrators, a few dissenting voices are occasionally still heard. Supervisors should also be aware of these minority opinions as well, and not be deluded by a belief there is total unanimity. Typical of such minority opinions was a decision where the employer was ruled to not be justified in discharging a union committeeman who had participated in a wildcat strike, since the committeeman had neither incited nor led the strike, and no other employee who participated in the strike was penalized. The arbitrator held that the fact the discharged employee was a union officer did not warrant a greater penalty than that imposed on other employees. The arbitral position here was that the responsibility of committeemen as union officers was not to the employer but to other employees and the union.[21] No further comment will be made on this type of holding. Suffice it to say that this does represent the *minority* view of the principle of negative vs. affirmative leadership.

Union officials also have been held answerable for their personal behavior in carrying out union duties. Despite the relaxed and loose usage of shop vernacular, arbiters have upheld discharge of stewards for verbally insulting and intimidating members of management.[22] Whether the remarks exceed the typical and normal shop vernacular of the particular institution, and are threatening, insulting and intimidating, are factors in what the ultimate arbitral determination may be. Also it may be relevant if the behavior is such as to threaten the dignity of the supervisor and his office in the eyes of other employees, and bring this into disrepute, impinging upon his image as an authority figure.

On the other hand, an employer was not sustained in his attempt to discharge a union official who personally instigated filing of a large number of grievances.[23]

Employees may go only so far in demonstrating their dislike of a supervisor. But when that employee is also a union representative, his conduct and behavior should be somewhat different from that of the other employees. This was the view of one arbitrator who upheld the discharge of a union steward. Following his demotion from a job in the plant, the steward filed several grievances contending the demotion was punitive; he later filed a grievance alleging that his supervisor cursed the men, was discriminatory, and was unfit to be a boss, which action finally resulted in his discharge. The arbitrator, in examining all the facts of the case, decided that here was more than a mere overzealous steward. Here was an individual whose combination of behavior patterns exceeded the reasonable limitations on a steward's conduct in a plant. In rendering this award he stated that mere zealousness or militancy could not justify management discipline. But repeated and unfounded written accusations of a criminal or semi-criminal nature against management personnel, threats of physical violence in retaliation, and public bullying tactics could not be condoned by upholding his grievance. Doing so would place some degree of approval on a pattern of behavior which would place the plant's collective bargaining relationship at the level of the jungle.[24] In a somewhat similar affair, the company was found to be justified in discharging a union chief steward for filing a grievance in which he falsely charged a supervisor with manhandling another employee, a story fabricated out of whole cloth.[25]

The discharge of a union steward, who had received many prior warnings for violating a contract ban on unauthorized union activities during working hours, was sustained when he again took working time on union matters which should have been handled by the union's financial secretary in accordance with an established and satisfactory procedure. In discussing the steward's misconduct, the arbitrator said the steward.

> was guilty of a serious disservice to his fellow workers, in that he needlessly gave rise to irritation and friction which especially, if repeated, must inevitably result in injury to the morale and productive efficiency of the plant, as well as to good labor-management relations.
>
> It cannot be pointed out too often that the position of a steward is an important and honorable one, and that the individual filling the office should be a person who, while fully carrying out the important responsibilities of his office, and protecting the rights of his fellow workers, is nevertheless able to retain the respect and goodwill of management by the exercise not merely of zeal alone, but also of good common sense.[26]

By virtue of his office, a union representative has a special obligation to observe and respect the collective bargaining agreement. He is duty bound to protect employees in the grievance procedure against violations of the agreement by management. The agreement gives him special rights and privileges in order that he may perform that function. He cannot with impunity turn his back on the very agreement which it is his duty to defend.

A union steward is also a leader; indeed, it is reasonable to assume that it is also because he is a leader that he acquires his union office. It follows then that when a steward participated in a work stoppage, making no effort to police *that* contract violation as he does others, or bring it to a close, he sets an example for the other employees and indicates by his action that the stoppage has his tacit approval and sanction. *This is a graver offense than participation by an ordinary employee and may justify a more serious penalty.*[27]

Arbitral Standards

Although parties to labor agreements have achieved, and enjoy today, a higher level of sophistication than at any time in the past fifty years, cases involving discharge and discipline for union activities are still a too frequent issue in arbitration. An analysis of the many hundreds of published cases on these subjects may lead one to various conclusions. The parties have still a long way to go before they have achieved a desirable level of understanding of the rights and responsibilities incumbent on each, and also those possessed by the other. Perhaps, at least in part, this reflects the failure of both parties to assume their proper responsibility to develop, train, and instruct their respective representatives as to the proper role of each. Perhaps it also reflects a failure of the parties to realize that each is here to stay, that each is entitled to its respective needs, positions, principles and philosophies, and that the only road to a peaceful and constructive relationship lies down the path of mutual acceptance, respect and understanding.

But laying this aside and examining only the manner in which most arbitrators view such disputes generally speaking, arbitrators concur in their views regarding the bounds of union authority and the degree of behavioral freedom of the union representative. They impose the same criterion of just cause where disciplinary action is taken against the steward for alleged misconduct as an employee. When a union claim is made of anti-union discrimination in the absence of conclusive evidence of this, the burden of proof to support this claim falls in the union. But in judging such cases certain arbitral standards are used.

- What has been the relationship between the parties? What is generally the atmosphere between the company organization and union as an institution? And, what has been the acting management representative's relationship with the particular union representative being disciplined?
- Is there any evidence of discrimination or union animus? Has the disciplined steward been a troublesome, aggressive, militant individual—perhaps one who has filed many grievances or abused paid union time provisions of the agreement? If there is any evidence of union animus, the burden of disproving it will fall on the employer.
- Was there in fact a proven violation; did the steward commit the offense of which he is accused; and can the company meet fully its burden of proof?
- What has been the company's disciplinary treatment of other employees who are not union representatives, for similar offenses where the circumstances were similar and related to this case?
- Was the union representative's conduct provoked, and did the management's representative also engage in similar conduct—threats, name calling, intimidation, and so forth?
- Did the incident, if provocative and inflammatory, occur in the presence of other employees, or did it happen in the privacy of a meeting between the principals only? And were the remarks and the behavior well beyond the customary shop vernacular and mode of conduct—customary in this context, meaning that which is typical, accepted and routine in this particular plant's day-to-day climate and atmosphere?
- And, was the union representative being disciplined new to his office, recently elected or appointed, with a small amount of expe-

rience and understanding of his proper role and responsibilities? Or was he a knowledgeable and informed individual, with considerable experience and understanding of his duties, his rights, and his obligations?

A management sensitive to the above criteria, a management that give full consideration and weight to each of these factors that may be applicable in any particular case, should find itself better equipped to defend its action and have it sustained or supported by the arbitrator—the only person who, in the final analysis, sits in a position to overturn a management decision.

The final answer to diminishing such problems rests in a realization by each party of the rights of the other. If the number of such cases is to be reduced to a realistic level, indicative of mutual respect and understanding, each must assume its educational and informational responsibilities and create an industrial climate wherein there is, in fact, joint respect, understanding and cooperation.

This section will aid the labor arbitration advocate in making a reasoned, calculated judgment about the viability of his case.

5

Grievance Procedure Time Limits

The labor arbitration advocate needs a full appreciation of the arbitral attitudes toward the time limits written into the contract's grievance procedure.

Many labor advocates contend that the company's attitude toward grievances under a union contract governs the peacefulness of the contract period to a large degree. Many in management will contend that the union's attitudes in this matter are even more influential in determining the relationship between the parties. There is generally little argument from either side that the ingredient of good faith by both parties is vital to truly compatible understandings. Despite this mutual agreement, bottlenecks still occur in settlement of grievances.

Without good faith on both sides of the labor-management bargaining table, grievance settlements would be worthless. Why then the incorporation of time limits in contract grievance clauses? There are many good reasons.

Neglect in giving attention to employee complaints has proved to be a *major cause* for labor-management discord. In an effort to take some corrective action, many labor agreements are written with specific time limits incorporated in grievance clauses. Such clauses typically apply time restrictions for filing of grievances after incidents have occurred; specify the time restrictions upon management's review of, and answer to, the grievance; and denote the time restriction for union appeal from one step to another. This often includes a time period within which arbitration must be moved into.

Typical grievance procedure clauses provide that grievances are to be filed and time limits are to commence from the date of "the occurrence" or "its discovery" and, naturally, not all grievances are discovered at the time they occur. Such questionable issues often cause consternation among arbitrators, but most frequently, they decide that a grievant cannot be expected to file a grievance until he is, *or should have been*, aware of the event upon which he claims a violation.[1]

Some contracts contain no specific time limits for instituting grievances, but instead, impose the general requirement that "grievances must be filed with reasonable promptness." In such cases, arbitrators have generally still held that grievances must be filed promptly, unless *justifiably* delayed; but the interpretation of what is "prompt filing" by one arbitrator may be quite different from that of another arbitrator.[2]

Arbitrator P. Kelliher in a Creamery Package Mfg. case ruled that filing of a layoff grievance *three weeks after* the employee was laid off was *not* "prompt" within the meaning of the contract.[3]

On the other hand, arbitrator R. Seward in a National Tube Company Case ruled that a *ten month* delay in filing a grievance did not bar consideration of its merits where management had *deliberately withheld pertinent information* from the union.[4]

Although grievances must be initiated within a stated period of time in 81 percent of labor contracts (88 percent of manufacturing, 60 percent of non-manufacturing), time limits applicable to later steps of the grievance procedure are written into only 53 percent of the contracts (61 percent of manufacturing, 29 percent of non-manufacturing).

Discharge appeals are subject to special time limitations generally shorter than those applying to other types of grievances.[5]

Such time limits are placed in labor agreements to be observed and respected by the parties. Employees have the right to expect prompt and expeditious treatment of their problems. Management has an interest in preventing grievances from festering, wasting and souring. Whether or not the particular labor agreement contains expressed penalties for time limit defaults, the foreman should treat each case as though the time limits are binding and mandatory. This is not to say where additional time is essential, that an extension of time cannot be mutually agreed upon between the parties. But such cases should be infrequent and unique. Secondly, even if the particular labor agreement contains no expressed time limits of any kind, the foreman should still require that the union and employees raise and process their claim within reasonable periods of time after the date of the alleged violation. Repeated failures by the company to require the union to accord with procedural time limitations on the filing and processing of grievances may lead to the result that such time limits are rendered meaningless. The manager should approach his administration of this matter with the presumption that the parties placed such procedural conditions in the contract to be faithfully observed. Typical of such grievance clauses are ones which read:

> Any employee who claims a grievance shall present such claims to his foreman within (X) working days after the occurrence upon which the grievance is based.
>
> If the grievance is not settled as a result of the above discussion, it shall within (X) working days following the conclusion of the discussion, be set forth in writing on grievance forms, signed by the employee involved and the department steward, and given to his immediate supervisor.

With or without specific penalties for defaults on such time limits, it is certainly clear in the above example that the parties intended for grievances to be filed within specified periods. It is the foreman who first faces the employee's complaint. To a large extent, whether or not the union and the employees comply with such time limits will be determined by the foreman's enforcement of them. It is true that management can raise such objections to time limit defaults in the higher steps of the grievance procedure, if the foreman has failed to do so earlier—*but,* some arbitrators have been known to *overlook the company's objections* because of the company's failure to raise the issue at the very outset.

Although the majority of arbitrators appear to recognize valid claims of procedural defectiveness raised anytime during the grievance processing, some have ruled that the company has waived its right to contest the procedural correctness of grievances *by processing it without raising any question of its procedural defects until the arbitration hearing.* For example, arbitrator Harry H. Platt, in a case between the Republic Steel Corporation and the United Steelworkers, had this to say on this point:

> Quite apart from the merits of the dispute, the company maintains that the grievance is defective because it was signed by the grievance committeeman and not by any of the affected bloom mill employees.... Notwithstanding this fact, however, the company processed the grievance as presented and not once thereafter raised an objection. No mention of this procedural defect was made in any of the company's answers to the grievance. Not until the arbitration hearing did it maintain that the grievance was defective. Moreover, it was acknowledged by supervision that the subject of this grievance had been discussed in some detail before it was received and that it was known, when the grievance was filed, that it concerned "all people in the rolling units ... (who were) affected...." Under all these circumstances, I find that the grievance is properly before me for a decision of the merits.[6]

Still another ruling which is typical of the thinking of those arbitrators who embrace the philosophy that management must raise its procedural objections early in the procedure is that of arbitrator Stanton W. B. Wood. In a case involving a time limit objection by the company he remarked:

> We further believe that the grievance is arbitrable because of the company's action in agreeing to the appointment of an arbitrator to hear and decide the matter in dispute. Even had there been merit in the company's position that the grievance was untimely such a contention was waived when the company voluntarily consented to go to arbitration.[7]

The point made by all of this is an obvious one. Not only should the supervisor insist upon employee and union compliance with any contractual time limits; it is further advisable for him to express an objection to any default of such time limitation, *as soon as he discovers the breach*. Obviously by failing to do so, he may be exposing management to an unnecessary risk—particularly if the matter is ultimately reviewed by certain arbitrators who view the management failure to do so as constituting a waiver of the procedural issue.[8]

The observance of contractual time limits in the handling of labor grievances is a two-way street. The foreman cannot insist upon strict compliance by the employees and the union and be negligent in his own expeditious treatment of worker disputes. Investigation should occur while the facts are still fresh and a full and prompt answer supplied *within* any prescribed contract time limits. This should be assumed as an obligation by the foreman *irrespective of whether* the labor agreement imposes time limitations upon him for handling such matter.

Penalties for Default

Frequently labor agreements provide that if the company does not answer within the prescribed time, the union may appeal the grievance to the next step of the procedure. The failure of management to answer in the time allowed is generally not interpreted as an admission of default in the grievance, since the burden of moving the complaint to the next step rests with the union and the grievant, the moving parties—not with management.

Less frequently encountered are grievance clauses which consider complaints settled in accord with the demand of the grievance when management defaults in observing the prescribed time limits.[9]

On the other hand, if *both* parties have been guilty of contract violations within the grievance procedure, the time limitations will usually *not* be enforced by arbitrators.[10]

But even in the absence of a "settlement penalty" against the company for its untimely handling of a complaint, every effort should be expended to deal with the matter in a prompt manner without delays or hesitation. Unions usually go after such clauses against the company during negotiations because management's representatives have been inattentive or neglectful to their obligation to *meet* promptly, *discuss* promptly and *answer* promptly, the employees' grievances.

Where an early and opportunely timed objection to some time limit defect has been raised by the company, arbitrators have generally held that clear, unequivocal time limits must be met by the union, or by the employee, if the grievance is to be deemed arbitrable.[11] This view was expressed by arbitrator James A. Doyle in a case where a worker objected to his rehire as a new employee because he thought he should have been recalled from layoff, with all seniority rights intact, but lost his case because the grievance was untimely. The contract required that a grievance be filed within three days after the occasion giving rise to the grievance, and the company argued that this required filing within three days after rehire. Arbitrator Doyle agreed, and, in fact, suggested the employee should have known that the company had changed his status even before the rehire.[12]

Time limits are primarily provided to safeguard against stalling and avoidable delays, thus preventing the accumulation of stale, unresolved cases. They are not to be avoided or aborted by some clever or technical manipulation. For example, i00f the foreman is absent from his department during the period of time when certain time limits are running, and no other management member is available or qualified to handle the matter, he should not toll the time against the grievant. If the time limit is figured in terms of "working days," as opposed to "calendar days," he should not count weekends, or holidays, or vacation shutdown periods, unless the grievant has scheduled work days during such time. He should not stall in giving an oral answer to an oral grievance until the time limit for filing a written grievance under the contract has expired—and then claim the employee filed the written claim beyond the time limitation. These are merely a few of the types of practices which *must be avoided* if the integrity of the grievance system is to be preserved and the confidence of employees earned and maintained.

Labor relations is not a game to be played between a foreman and his stewards and employees whereby shrewd and clever trickery by one party causes the other to default on its contractual obligations. Extremely short-lived will be the success derived from this type of chicanery. The foreman who causes the union or employees to fail to comply with time limits through his own action or inaction should voluntarily declare a waiver of the time limitations for that case and for that reason. However, in such instance, he should make it clear to all concerned as to why he is pardoning their filing of the claim beyond the time limits, and make it clear that it is for that case only. In the absence of similar mitigating factors, in the future, he will require their full compliance with all procedural requirements. And, such waivers of compliance with time limitations should be the infrequent exception, not the rule.

It is a generally accepted principle of contract law that if the parties grow lax in the application of a provision imposing a time element, the party which first seeks to return to the strict observance to which both parties are entitled must issue a warning to that effect. In 17 American Jurisprudence 2d 773, Contracts Par 344, it is stated as follows:

> ... the rule is especially applicable where there has been a waiver of the time stipulation in a contract. Time cannot again be made of the essence without notice to the party in default requiring performance within a reasonable time to be specified in the notice and stating that if there is not performance within this time the contract will be abrogated, or without conduct equivalent to notice....

Virtually every jurisdiction has its decisions supporting this view, but in *Crocker Chair Co. v. Edward Hines Hardwood & Hemlock Co.* (201 Wis. 415, 230 NW61, 75ALR 603), the Wisconsin Supreme Court gave typical expression to it by holding that before one party may impose a default upon the other because it has failed to meet a deadline which theretofore had been largely ignored by the parties, it is *necessary to give warning* that such course of conduct no longer would be tolerated and that the terms of the contract henceforth would be enforced.[13]

So, if the company allows the administration of time limitations to be laxly observed, over a period of time it may reduce the effectiveness of such time requirements. In such event, the management generally may have to serve effective notice upon the union that in the future it will insist upon strict observance of such limitations, in accord with its right under the contract.

Handling Untimely Claims

If the union or the employee has filed or is processing the grievance beyond the contractual time limits, and if this fact is known to the company's advocate prior to discussions on the merits, the advocate should present his arguments on the timeliness issue *first,* giving all of the reasons for considering it untimely. *He should make it very clear to the grievant and particularly to the union representative that the company is denying the grievance first on the basis of its timeliness.* Now, this is *not* to suggest that the advocate should *not* proceed into a discussion of the grievance on its merits if the grievance is untimely. But first he should make it clear that the company is denying the grievance on the basis of its timeliness and irrespective of its merit. Having made this point clear, the company should *then proceed* into the discussion of the grievance *on its merits* and carry on with the subsequent orderly processing of the dispute. When faced with this type of problem, it is recommended that the company give two reasons for denying the grievance in its written answer:

1. *Grievance denied*—it does not accord with the mandatory procedural requirements of the agreement.
2. *Grievance denied on its merit*—no contract violation occurred.

Naturally, these same answers may be used if the grievance is otherwise procedurally faulty, assuming the contract provides that such other procedural requirements are also mandatory with any faults rendering the grievance defective.

In any case, it is strongly recommended that the manager not take the position that he will not accept, nor process, nor discuss the case on its merits because he so strongly believes it is untimely—henceforth a nullity. That may very well be the ultimate arbitral conclusion, but it is not one that a manager should set himself up as judge and jury to decide, finally and indisputably.

The reasons for this recommendation are several.

First, a manager's refusal to accept the case denies the union and the employees access to the rest of the contractual procedure. In that procedure, each succeeding step brings representatives of higher authority together for the respective parties, who may view this particular issue differently based on their greater labor relations knowledge and expertise.

Second, if no discussion is held relative to the merits, the company will not be informed about the important details of the problem. If an arbiter does not support the manager's singular contention on the time limit question, the company will not be equipped to put forth any viable case on the merits. And, they may even be contractually precluded from doing so if the agreement prohibits the introduction of evidence into the arbitration hearing which was not previously presented during the steps of the grievance procedure.

Third, the manager who takes such a singular stand on time limits is actually supplanting the arbitrator, who is the only final judge of contractual rights and wrongs.

This whole approach would put too many eggs in one basket—an unwise and reckless course when compared against available alternatives which have been previously recommended.

Continuing Violations

However, when handling grievances which appear to be procedurally irregular in the time limit area, remember that some violations may be of a "*continuing*" nature. In the second BNA edition of *How Arbitration Works* (1960), the authors (Elkouri and Elkouri) state that (pp. 107–108):

> Numerous arbitrators have held that 'continuing' violations of the agreement (as opposed to a single isolated and completed transaction) give rise to 'continuing' grievances in the sense that the act complained of may be said to be repeated from day to day—each day there is a new 'occurrence,' these arbitrators have permitted the filing of such grievances at any time, this is not being deemed a violation of the specific time limits stated in the agreement (although any back pay ordinarily runs only from the date of filing).

An example of a "continuing violation" would be as in a case where the company erroneously was paying an individual employee less than the prescribed contractual wage. Every day this shortage occurred would constitute a new violation which would start a new time period tolling within which the matter could be timely grieved.

Clearly, one of the purposes of time limit provisions in a grievance procedure is to prevent the filing of stale grievances, where the incident giving rise to the grievance occurs only once, at a specific time and place. An example of this would be a warning given to an employee for leaving his work area without permission. It is generally clear that the parties do not want grievances of this kind presented two or three weeks (or later) after this incident occurred.

It is also equally clear that parties do not want one party to the contract to be able to engage in a *"continuing"* violation of its terms, and get off scot-free if the other party fails for one reason or another to present a grievance within the time limit following the very first occurrence. If such an interpretation as this was permitted, it could encourage violations of the contract where this might be to the advantage of one side or the other—since the rule would then be, if one doesn't get caught the first X-number of days, one may continue the violation with impunity.[14] This is obviously not the good faith intent of either party. Therefore, anytime the supervisor is inclined to take the position that a grievance is *fatally* defective procedurally so as to bar an arbitrator from considering it on its merits, he should be as certain as he possibly can be that his position is valid. This is not a suggestion that procedural defects should be excused. It is merely a caution *not* to raise this issue for reasons of trickery and as a technical roadblock to frustrate the proper resolution of procedurally correct disputes.

But again the point that must be repeated is that management's failure to contest the procedural propriety of any grievance may be viewed as a waiver of any such objection.

Arbitrators' rulings reveal that such is the result, and another view typical of this was that expressed by arbitrator Samuel H. Jaffee who decided a dispute between Celanese Corporation and the United Mine Workers, in which he remarked:

Discussion and Conclusions

Waiver of Procedural Defect.

> 1. Under Article V a discharge grievance begins with Step 2. Instead, the union took it up direct with Mr. Black, superintendent of personnel, in Step 3 and he received the formal grievance on March 21. Despite some testimony to the contrary, *the weight of the evidence is that no objection was made either to the delay or the skipping of the second step procedure*. Rather, the evidence is that the company indicated that the only way the matter could be disposed of on the merits would be through arbitration. Mr. Black, at the union's request, wrote to the American Arbitration Association for the necessary forms and the AAA rules. *Under all the circumstances I am satisfied that the company waived any procedural defects* and that the dispute is presently arbitrable [emphasis in original].[15]

Taking this same premise and associating it with the supervisor, it is clear that he too, at his grievance step, may often encounter a similar situation. The same theory will apply to observance by the union, and generally by employees, of any procedural steps or time limitations imposed by the contract at the foreman's level. For example, skipping a contractually mandatory oral step and filing a written grievance first—a common occurrence at the foreman's step—may constitute a procedural defect under the right set of circumstances. This is merely an example of the many different types of contractual defects which the foreman may discover if he is alert—and if he carefully and thoroughly examines each case before engaging in an examination of the issue of its merits.

One final example of this proposition is illustrated in a published decision by arbitrator Hubert C. Callahan wherein is stated:

> Article VII provides that grievances must be referred to the departmental steward who shall take them up with the departmental foreman within three days of the time they arise. If the grievance cannot be adjusted in the department, the steward shall take the matter up with the shop chairman who shall reduce the grievance to writing and take the same up with the duly authorized representative of the company. The shop committee, a representative of the union and a representative of the company shall then seek to adjust the matter....
>
> The grievance was formally discussed at a grievance session on December 12 and filed in writing at a similar session on December 28. Obviously, the procedure used in the processing of this grievance was not in strict accord with the provisions of Article VII of the contract. However, *there is no evidence that the company raised any objections to such a procedure. Therefore, the grievance cannot be invalidated because of procedural deficiencies* [emphasis in original].[16]

Because of this waiver of procedural complaint, the arbitrator was privileged here to review the case on its merits—and in so doing, sustained the union's grievance, imposing a healthy back-pay liability upon the company. *Had timely and appropriate objections been raised* by the company—and in view of the grievance's procedural deficiencies—it is probable that the arbitrator *would have found it not arbitrable on its merits* and thereby refrained from ruling on that issue.

Unions sometimes claim that an improper layoff commences a "continuing" grievance, contending thus on the basis that each day the employee remains improperly laid off constitutes a new opportunity to grieve, and still have it be timely. This is *not* the case. A layoff does not constitute a "continuing" violation type grievance. A layoff occurs only once, at the time the employee leaves employment and last performs work for the employer. For a grievance to be filed correctly under the contract, it must be filed within the expressed numbers of days specified in the grievance procedure, immediately following the layoff action of the employer.

Retroactive Adjustments

Most labor agreements contain some provision for regulating the amount of liability and retroactive adjustment for which the company may become obligated in any grievance case. Such a provision is connected to, and interrelated with, the time limit conditions found in the grievance procedure. A time limit is customarily provided within which the grievance must be initiated. Usually the time limit governing retroactivity is a like or comparable time period beyond which no company liability is incurred.

Typical of such clauses is that which read:

The settlement of a grievance shall not be made retroactive for a period exceeding ten (10) working days prior to the date the grievance was first presented in writing.

In this case, the contract from which this was extracted required a *commensurate period* of ten days from the date of the occurrence of the alleged violation for the grievance to be reduced to writing. However, also common to many agreements is language which provides for a more flexible and liberal retroactive time element. Typical of such clauses as that would be one which reads:

> The settlement of a grievance shall not be made retroactive for a period exceeding ten (10) working days prior to the date the grievance was first presented in writing, provided that in the case where the employee and steward had no way of knowing of the occurrence of the event upon which the claimed violation is based, and the grievance is presented within five (5) working days from the date either the employee or steward by the exercise of reasonable diligence should have known of the occurrence of such event, then the settlement of such a grievance may be made retroactive for a period

not to exceed thirty (30) calendar days prior to the date the grievance is first presented in writing.

In the contract from which the above language was extracted, the time element within which grievances had to be initiated in writing was corresponding ten days—but, it further provided that if the employee or the union had *no* knowledge of the event upon which their claim was based within that time period, they could file the claim timely within five days of the time they would have known of the claimed violation by their exercising reasonable diligence.

However, a review of certain contract language such as the above examples is hardly sufficient to provide adequate coverage to this subject. More important is an examination of how such clauses have been administered and how arbitrators have ruled when passing judgment on that administration.

An employee whose seniority rights have been violated fell victim to contract language comparable to the above in a case at International Harvester Company involving the UAW. In his award arbitrator Whitley P. McCoy found it necessary to withhold assessing any money damages despite the violation due to the presence of such a retroactivity clause. He said:

> The difficult question of how to measure his damages is unnecessary to determine, because it is quite clear that his delay in filing a grievance bars any claim prior to May 26, the date of the grievance, and the only damages claimed by the grievance are his losses prior to May 25. Article VI, Section 2, reads:
>
> "Retroactivity of grievance settlements effected under Article VII, 'Arbitration,' shall be limited to the date the grievance is presented in writing in the grievance procedure, except where the circumstances made it impossible for the employees, or for the union as the case may be, to know that he, or the union had grounds for such claim prior to that date...."
>
> Since I have found that [the employee] had knowledge of the facts on April 5, it cannot be said that it was "impossible" for him to have knowledge before "that date" i.e., the date of filing the grievance, May 26.
>
> Where there has been a violation of right, it is no pleasure to me to deny a remedy on the ground that delay in asserting the claim bars back pay, and the express words of the contract bar back pay because of the delay. The grievance must therefore be dismissed.[17]

In the above-cited matter, there was no question or argument that the employee had knowledge of his grievance, for some period, prior to his filing the claim. But often the employee does not have such prior information, or at least he alleges he did not. Where this occurs, the burden of proving that the employee did have some knowledge, or should have reasonably concluded that he did by related associations, this proof rests with the company when the parties sit before the arbitrator. *To argue its case of either un-timeliness of grievance filing, or to defend its position that retroactive should be limited or eliminated, the company must be prepared to present persuasive evidence to show that the union or employee somehow were in possession of information regarding their present claim which they failed to promptly act upon.*

A case containing these elements was decided by arbitrator David A. Wolff. The contract applicable here contained provisions barring back pay as discussed earlier herein and the case involved a seniority grievance raised by a group of laid-off female employees. Their grievance was filed more than ten days (the contractual limitation) after junior men had been given work. Although seniority lists had been posted by the company subsequent to such action, the lists failed to include the women's names. Arbitrator Wolff's pertinent remarks on the question of back pay indicate that the matter of "proof of employee or union knowledge" rests with the company on issues of this type.

> On the proof submitted, the chairman concludes: that the company failed to post the names of the considered employees during the period as alleged by the union; that the failure to post was contrary to the agreement; that it is reasonable to believe, and no convincing proof to the contrary has been shown, that the considered employees did not know of the facts which entitled them to recall before the ten day period prior to the filing of the grievance; that it is reasonable to believe, and no convincing proof of the contrary has been shown, that the union did not know, or could not have been expected to know of the rights to recall of these particular employees, or any particular one of them, prior to ten days before filing the grievance. Article II, Section 16 specifically provides for a written notice of claim to be filed within ten days from the time the company first failed to give an employee work to which his seniority entitled him. The Section, contrary to some others in the agreement, such as Article II, Section 14, indicates no possibility of contemplated exception. However, contractual limitation of right in this type of situation can only fairly be based on a knowledge of the occurrence of the event on which the right is founded, or a reasonable opportunity or way to know of the event. Any other interpretation would mean that a claimant could be barred from a proper claim by failure of the party against whom the claim was made to comply with their mutual agreement. The chairman cannot believe that such a situation was here contemplated. Knowledge was not shown to have been present here. An opportunity or way to obtain knowledge, as provided by the contract was not made available. The chairman finds, therefore, that in this case the union is not barred by the limitation.[18]

The issue of retroactive adjustment sometimes turns on the effect of the union's own behavior as it related to their grievance. In other words, after learning of a company action or a company decision did they react as though such exercise of management discretion was acceptable to them? or was perhaps acquiesced to by them. Or, if it is a grievance answer they have received from the company, did they conduct themselves as though it were acceptable or acquiesced to—or did they appeal it in a prompt and expeditious fashion? Similar to this were the circumstances surrounding a case decided by Joseph Brandschain, the arbitrator of a reclassification dispute between the Kewstone Reamer and Tool Co. and the UFW. This arbitrator ruled that questions of whether the union committee had actually agreed to waive its first reclassification review provided it by the agreement, and whether it had authority to waive such reviews, were irrelevant to the back-pay issue since they failed to use the remedial processes of the grievance machinery without delay.

> The demand first presented on August 5, 1946 was not pressed again by the union from the time its representatives met with management shortly after August 5, until the revised list was presented on February 5, 1947. Whether the union committee actually agreed to waive its demand, or had authority to do so, the failure to press the demand and follow it up amounts to a waiver. The contract provides grievance procedures under which any difference between the company and union can be settled, in the manner that the present difference is being settled. Such matters should be handled expeditiously and without delay. The union had the opportunity to appeal the matter through the subsequent steps of the grievance procedure, if it was dissatisfied with the company's action following discussion with the shop committee. Its failure to do so until after the next semi-annual reclassification period occurred, must be taken as an indication that the union did not intend to contest the decision of management, or that it waived its right to appeal from it.[19]

In summary, a review of these cases, and the many others which are available on the subject, offer a common thread of arbitral opinion. Where the contract contains a *clearly expressed limitation* on the amount of retroactive liability the arbitrators are careful not to abuse the authorities afforded them by the contract. Where the contract provides a more *flexible retroactivity provision*, one which permits later filing and processing of claims due to the absence of knowledge of basis for a claim by the employee or the union, the arbitrators will allow accrual of a larger retroactive liability where the employee or the union can provide reasonable justification of their delay. However, where the employer is asking the arbitrator to disallow completely, or curtail liability in part, the *burden of proving* the employee or union knew, or must have known, of the events upon which their claim is based, rests *solely* with the company. If the employee or union say they knew nothing of their alleged claim until the date they initiated it, the employer must persuasively show otherwise if he hopes to limit his liabilities. Of course, if the case involves a deliberate act of the employer to conceal or withhold information, thus causing employee or union delays in the grievance handling, the arbitrator has little choice but to make the employee whole—at least from the point that the employer's conduct is shown to have been deliberately improper. Familiarity with these contract provisions, as well as all time limit conditions, is a must for the supervisor, if he is to avoid making commitments on retroactive adjustments which exceed the contractual requirements. It should go without saying that such supervisory knowledge is necessary also to insure that adjustments, when made, are not less than that amount to which the employee is contractually entitled.[20]

Time Limits and Demands for Arbitration

A review of arbitration awards shows that arbitrators expect the parties to observe the procedural time limit requirements as a "condition precedent" to their assumption of jurisdiction over the case. Time limits bind the parties as they do the arbitrator.

It is not unusual for a complaint to be timely filed, processed through the grievance procedure in timely fashion and then be deemed *not* arbitrable by an arbitrator *due to one of the parties faulting in observance of a time requirement for demanding arbitration.*

In a case where time limits had not been followed and the issue of arbitrability based on jurisdiction had been raised, arbitrator Edwin R. Teple stated:

> Although the arbitrator has a natural reluctance to dispose of these grievances solely on procedural grounds, the issue of procedural arbitrability is clearly and properly presented. Where the parties themselves, in their agreement, have specifically set forth the steps to be taken in the course of the grievance procedure, to and including the arbitration step, and have clearly stated time limits within which these various steps musts be taken by each party, the arbitrator actually is left with no choice in the matter.[21]

The grievance in the case above was denied because of the procedural defect.

Arbitrator Walter G. Sinsheimer in the Aluminum Industries, Inc., case expressed the problem succinctly when he stated the following in denying the grievance due to a procedural defect:

> It is this arbitrator's preference to rule on the merits of a case, as not to do so invariably means that nothing is actually settled. Ruling whether a grievance is arbitrable or not, no doubt gives one party a victory, but it is this arbitrator's feeling from long experience in labor-management relations, that when the union-management relationship develops into a contest and the parties become opponents with one side or the other's main purpose being to win a contest, that nothing but trouble can result. The grievance procedure, including arbitration, should not be an arena with the parties drawn up as if for battle, but should be for the purpose of getting along with each other, as well as for interpreting and giving meaning to the contract. This of

course, is somewhat idealistic. However, even under ideal situations *rules cannot be ignored* [emphasis added], and the rules in this case are those set forth in the agreement. Obviously, whether the relationship between the parties is one of contest or cooperation, such rules are necessary. The contract is the constitution; the by-laws governing the relationship between the parties and the time provision are a sort of 'statute of limitations.' The situation might be likened to the rules and ground rules for a baseball game. The basic rules are often the same or similar from one area to another, but the ground rules vary from one ballpark to another, just as the agreements in contracts vary from one company to another. No matter what the variations are, however, they are the rules for a 'ballpark' in which the umpire must make his decisions.

Arbitration case books indicate numerous cases (some cited by the company) where grievances have been ruled inarbitrable due to timeliness, where the time late involved was only two or three days. In such cases there can always possibly be such things as the responsible union representative being out of town, sick, etc., which could create perhaps extenuating circumstances—yet invariably, arbitrators have stuck with the contract and ruled the case inarbitrable.[22]

Arbitrators have long held that time limit provisions set forth rules which must be punctually adhered to in the strictest sense. Arbitrator Clyde Emery in the Deep Rock Oil Corp. Case held that time limits in the grievance and arbitration provision were "mandatory" and that the time limits imposed for submitting the case to arbitration were "peremptory."[23]

A careful analysis and critique of a similar situation was made by arbitrator Whitley P. McCoy in the case of Management Service, Inc., where he stated in denying the grievance on procedural grounds:

The arbitrator, unlike the courts, derives no authority from the common law, the constitution, or statute. He is in no sense an official of any government or governmental agency. He is a private person, employed by other private persons, in the same way that a doctor or a lawyer may be employed. He has only such power as the employers who employ him see fit to bestow upon him, just as a surgeon has power to perform an operation only if the patient gives him that authority.

The authority or power of the arbitrator is to be found in the agreement of the parties, either a specific submission agreement applying to only one case, or a general arbitration agreement embodied in a collective bargaining contract. In the case now before me, the power of the arbitrator is confined by the general collective bargaining contract. Since the parties themselves confer the power, they are at liberty to confer as much or as little power as they see fit, with such limitations as they see fit.

In the contract between the parties before me, the parties have expressly specified that they agree to arbitration, that is to an arbitrator assuming jurisdiction over a case, only if the union gives the company written notice of intention to appeal to arbitration within ten calendar days after receipt of

> the company's decision at Step 3 of the grievance committee. That limitation is contained in Article V, Section 1. In other words, the company has agreed to arbitration of only certain disputed, namely those as to which notice of appeal is given within ten calendar days. It has not agreed to arbitration of any other disputes.
>
> Now, when these fundamentals are borne in mind, namely that I have no power to arbitrate any disputes except such disputes as the parties have agreed that I may arbitrate, this case becomes very simple. Written notice of the union's intention to appeal this case to an arbitrator was not given within ten calendar days after receipt of the company's decision at Step 3. This is therefore a dispute that the parties have never agreed could be appealed to an arbitrator.
>
> I think the union recognized the truth of the fundamentals stated above, but seeks to avoid their force by certain arguments bearing on questions of fairness and hardship. My power is derived from the parties. I cannot confer any power upon myself, whether on the ground of hardship, fairness or any other ground.[24]

The point made by arbitrator McCoy is clear: time limitations *must* be scrupulously followed at *all* steps. The factor of why the union was dilatory is unimportant. The salient point is that they totally ignored the time limits and thusly precluded themselves, by a procedural reason, from looking into the merits of the situation since no grievance can then exist.

In some instances, a procedural elimination of the grievance is not valid. As explained by arbitrator McCoy in *Management Services, Inc.*, supra:

> There are only two circumstances under which an arbitrator might proceed with a case even though it had not been appealed to him within the time limits, namely, first where the company has waived the default, and second where the company is estopped from setting up the expiration of the time limit.
>
> Neither is there anything upon which to base an estoppel. An estoppel arises when one mistakes the facts, so that it would be unfair for them afterwards to take advantage of the other party's having been misled.
>
> I see an unfortunate series of circumstances which resulted in the appeal not being taken in time, but I do not see any greater or different hardship in this case than exists in any other case where time limits have been inadvertently allowed to expire. Even if there were an unusual and quite a different hardship in this case, I know of no principle which would make that a justification for my conferring power on myself, unless I could apply the well recognized principles of waiver and estoppel. My only power as an arbitrator comes from the parties.

In ruling against the grievant in *Autocar Company*, John R. Abersold succinctly stated:

> Having determined that the union did not file its appeal with the time limit established by the June 25, 1948 contract, the arbitrator does not have

jurisdiction to decide the second issue, namely whether the company violated the contract by assigning the trimming of cabs with embossed fibre board to the Final Cab Assembly.[25]

The reasonableness, and necessity, for time limits in grievance and arbitration procedures is not unwarranted. Economics is, of necessity, a factor involved. "Stock piling," an onerous device that is repugnant to a sound relationship, is eliminated when time limitations are embodied in a contract and enforced by the parties. Arbitrator Paul Dodd in *Bethlehem Steel Co.* expressed this view when he stated:

> Reasonable safeguards must be recognized in the successful administration of the terms of working agreements. If time limits are not set on the filing of submission or closing of grievances, obviously an unscrupulous party might dig out the skeleton of a grievance long since thought buried and forgotten by the other party. It is only good business practice to provide for the expeditious settlement or treatment of grievances which do arise even in the best of industrial families.
>
> It is very unfortunate that grievances must be considered closed because of a technical default of one sort or another, especially when the grievance may otherwise have merit. But these are the rules of the games set down by mutual agreement between the parties, and, when one questions the other on technical grounds, the rules must be applied if they are to give proper guarantees to each party.
>
> In view of the facts surrounding the submission of Grievance No. 254, I must rule that the arbitrator does not have jurisdiction to hear the case on its merits since its submission to arbitration was not made within the time limits set down under the terms of the working agreement.[26]

As can readily be observed, arbitrators do not hesitate to observe the limitations placed upon the parties in processing grievances to arbitration. This is also so in *Republic Oil Refining Co.* where arbitrator Peter Carmichael stated:

> The question is now as follows: Did the failure of the union to take steps for the arbitration within five days after the grievance hearing on January 21 forfeit its right to arbitrate the dismissal? When the five-day period for initiating an arbitration elapsed, the right of the dismissed employee to the arbitration lapsed with it. In view of the pledge of the parties to endeavor to effect a fair and prompt disposition of grievances, this may be unfortunate; but to effect such a disposition of grievances a considerable machinery of procedure has been created in the contract. Unless this procedure is followed, the contract is not followed. But the parties, as well as the arbitrator on the case, are bound by the terms of the contract. If either party departs from these or fails to perform his part, the consequence for him and for others may be unfortunate. But that is a consequence which cannot be helped by arbitration where the only question under arbitration is, as it is here, a question of the proper interpretation of a contract.[27]

As can be ascertained from the above cases, procedural limitations must be followed in order to make a grievance arbitrable on its merits. Conditions precedent, which have been incorporated into a written agreement, become part of the administration of the contract. If this were not so, the contract itself would be obviated as to all of its written provisions. It is a time honored policy among arbitrators, as can be seen above, that the express procedural qualifications in processing grievances and in processing grievances to arbitration must be strictly adhered to by the parties. The courts, too, have substantiated this position.

Procedural Limitations Discussed in Court Cases

In *Brass Workers Union vs. American Brass Co.,* affirmed by the U.S. Court of Appeals, 7th Circuit, the court stated:

> Action by a union against an employer, under Section 301 of the Labor-Management Relations Act, for specific performance of an arbitration clause of a collective bargaining agreement. Action Dismissed.
>
> Procedural compliance is a separate issue, distinct from the question of the discharges. While the company may raise the question of waiver of rights as a defense, this does not go to the merits of the discharge issue. The company has not consented to submitting this additional issue to the arbitrator.
>
> The conditions, in unambiguous language, provide for a specific period of time in which requests for arbitration must be submitted. These terms do not appear unreasonable or harsh on their face.
>
> On the absence of the union's compliance with the specific procedural requirements of the agreement, the company's refusal to arbitrate is not in violation of the agreement, notwithstanding the absence of any forfeiture provisions coupled to the conditions precedent of the arbitration promise. The union has lost its rights to enforcement of the arbitration promise by noncompliance.
>
> It is neither equitable, nor does the court have the power to rewrite the contract entered into by the union and the company.[28]

Without equivocation the court decided above that the need to fulfill procedural obligations was a condition *precedent* to having the grievance become an arbitrable matter on the merits. The obligations to follow the express provisions must be deemed the intent of the parties. In view of this the remarks of Justice Steuer in the Mark Cross Co. case are highly apropos:

> It is not disputed that the sole right to arbitration is founded in the contract. As a consequence, it is limited by the contract and must be had, if at all, in according with it.
>
> It is plain that the provisions of the contract were neither followed nor waived. It has repeatedly been held that where there are specific time limits

for a demand for arbitration that they bar demands thereafter. This agreement to arbitrate is a contract and the one seeking to have the other perform must show that he himself has complied with its terms (Heogelf & Stern vs. Financial Employees Guild, 81 N.Y. 5.2d 532). Here there is no compliance. It is not for the court to say that where the parties have made careful and elaborate provisions that these can be ignored on a plea of substantial justice. No such plea can justify the court in changing the terms that the parties have agreed to.[29]

The above cited case was quoted with approval in another New York case; here the court held that failure of the employees to comply with procedural requirements of the grievance procedure under the terms of the collective bargaining agreement *barred* arbitration of the employer's grievance against the union under the arbitration clause of the contract, since the procedural requirements are not permissive, but adherence thereto is made a condition precedent to arbitration.[30]

Justice Eder, in the Ketchum & Co. case, stated the company's position herein succinctly and concisely:

> The provision is, in effect, a statute of limitations, and the right to demand arbitration is barred by failure to give the required notice within the time prescribed, unless waived. The union terms this a mere technicality. I disagree. It is more than that. It is a matter of contractual right, and is one of substance. If this provision may be glossed over and ignored, why not any other?[31]

Mandatory vs. Permissive

The framework of any contract, labor or other, is built around the use of words in expressing the intent of the parties to formalize their agreement. The use of the words "may" and "shall" designate an intentional distinction which the parties agreed to in the contract. *Webster's New Collegiate Dictionary* defines "may" as indicating: liberty, opportunity, permission, or possibility. It defines "shall" as expressing obligation or compulsion on the speaker's part. The implication here is not meant to be facetious but is simply expressed to aid herein in understanding the intent of contracts. The inherent distinctions have been strongly expressed in law as well as before arbitrators. In the M.H. Rhodes Inc. case, the arbitrator stated:

> Contract providing that grievances "may" be taken up in writing within ten working days permits arbitrator to consider grievance on merits even if it was not, as claimed, taken up in writing within ten working days, in absence of strong evidence that parties meant something other than what they said when they used *permissive* word "may" instead of *compulsory* word "shall."[32]

Today there is a tendency, on the part of many people, to overlook the fundamentals in contract interpretation. We live in a period of "sophisticated" union-management relations where the mechanics of an operation (contract) are bypassed in an overt attempt to secure stabilization. Such an attempt, while entered into with good will, most times results in a contravention of the intent of the parties, creating greater problems than had been anticipated. There is a reason, in the contract, for inserting time limits and mandatory language in the grievance and arbitration procedure. The word "shall" indicates the stringency of the time requirement. Neither the time limits nor the mandatory language should be ignored. To do so would be an error in that the arbitrator could place the company in danger of never knowing what cases were appealed in any step, and further would preclude the orderly process and prompt disposition of cases. This danger is clear and concise if the contractual, procedural time limits are not strictly enforced.

Absent specific time limits for the arbitration demand—arbitrators have sometimes ruled "it is implied"—that such application must be made "within a reasonable time" where strict time limitations are provided to all other steps within the procedure.

Claims that the parties have waived the time limits or conditions, either by expressed consent or by an unequivocal course of conduct showing that the parties have acquiesced in the waiver, may become material facts which the arbitrator may consider in deciding if the dispute is arbitrable.

For centuries, there have existed statutory periods of limitation within which various legal actions must be instituted. The primary purpose of these statutes is to defeat stale and long-neglected claims after evidence, by which they might have been defeated, has been forgotten or destroyed. In Courts of Equity, the doctrine of laches is analogous. Of similar origin are the requirements that, during each step in legal and equitable proceedings, certain definite time limits must be observed to insure reasonable diligence on the part of every person seeking to enforce or defend a right. If such were not the case, there would be no end to delays.

It is for this purpose that grievance time limitations exist. To whatever extent they eliminate festering, wasting and souring employee complaints, they have earned their place in the grievance clause.

The labor arbitrations advocate needs to be fully aware of the arbitral attitudes toward contractual time limits.

6

Arbitrability

The question of the arbitrability of given issues is considered in about one of every ten arbitration clauses in manufacturing agreements and one of every eight in non-manufacturing contracts. Both of these figures represent substantial increases over the corresponding percentages of only a few years ago. Most such provisions state that the question of arbitrability is one for the arbitral umpire himself to decide. A very few require a court proceeding to determine the question of arbitrability.[1]

A contract with the Ladies' Garment Workers, for example, includes a clause of this agreement on the arbitrability (substantive or procedural) of any complaint, dispute or grievance thereunder; the Impartial Chairman shall have exclusive jurisdiction to determine such question, issue or matter and his decision shall be final and binding.[2] This provision would appear to foreclose either party from initially or even subsequently referring the question of arbitrability to the court.

As mentioned previously, a few collective bargaining agreements provide that such questions be referred to court. In the following example, that is the requirement unless the parties agree to do otherwise: "Any dispute as to the arbitrability of a given matter shall be resolved by a court of competent jurisdiction and not by an arbitrator, unless the parties specifically agree otherwise in writing."[3]

In still another arrangement, either party appears to be able to seek a judicial determination, but only after an arbitrator has submitted his decision:

> If the Company believes the stated dispute is not arbitrable, it shall advise the Union within five working days after receipt of the request for arbitration stating its reasons therefore. If the Union decides to proceed with the arbitration, it will advise the Company in writing within five working days after receipt of the Company's notice that the Company believes the

dispute is not arbitrable. The arbitration will proceed in the following manner:

(a) The arbitrator will be required to rule first on arbitrability. If he finds in the affirmative, he shall then rule on the merits of the grievance at issue.

(b) If either party challenges the arbitrator's finding regarding the arbitrability, it may within thirty calendar days after receipt of the award, file suit in a court of competent jurisdiction to seek a judicial determination of the arbitrability of the subject matter. The Court in its determination shall be entitled to treat the matter as though originally submitted to it and neither the record of the arbitration nor the finding of the arbitrator shall be given any consideration by the Court.[4]

The clause appears to give to the party contesting the arbitrability of the grievance "two bites at the apple," one before an arbitrator and, if that is lost, again before a court. Few agreements make such elaborate arrangements beforehand; only about one in ten mentions the method to be employed to obtain final disposition of any question of arbitrability. This does not mean that parties without contract coverage are left without avenues of relief; it merely means that they either have not contemplated the problem or have not formalized an agreed-upon approach for disposing of such an issue.

First, complaints about the contract should not be steered toward the courts if there is no question of substantive or procedural problems not within the arbitrator's jurisdiction and authority. In most instances, the court will merely refer the matter back to the parties and the arbitration process, particularly if the contract and its grievances and arbitration provisions cover the dispute.

The law of the Steelworkers Trilogy is predicated in part upon the proposition that labor arbitrators are better equipped than judges to deal with questions of contract interpretation. Associate Justice Douglas's opinion in *Warrior and Gulf* tells us that arbiters perform functions that are "not normal to the courts,"[5] that the considerations that help arbitrators fashion judgments may be "foreign to the competence of the courts," and that arbitrators have a knowledge of "industrial common law" and the effects of a particular measure on productivity, shop morale, and intraplant tensions, which even the ablest judge cannot be expected to bring to bear upon the determination of contract questions.

These were not the only remarks of the court on the subject of arbitral jurisdiction and authority. The Supreme Court has also stated that grievances are not to be compelled to arbitration when they are "so plainly unreasonable that the subject matter of the dispute must be regarded as nonarbitrable because it can be seen in advance that no award to the union would receive judicial sanction."[6]

A collective bargaining agreement typically has a dual purpose: It fixes the substantive terms of employment to prevail in the enterprise, and it establishes the procedural means for resolving disputes arising from the interpretation or application of those terms.

Despite the Steelworkers Trilogy opinions, in the case of Enterprise Wheel and Car, the court offered a word of caution: "An arbitrator is confined to interpretation and application of the collective bargaining agreement; he does not sit to dispense his own brand of industrial justice. He may of course look for guidance from many sources yet his award is legitimate only so long as it draws its essence from the collective bargaining agreement. When the arbitrator's words manifest an infidelity to this obligation, courts have no choice but to refuse enforcement of the award."[7]

In summary, it can be said that unless the parties expressly exclude a matter from arbitration, the court will conclude that they intended to make it subject to arbitration. Therefore, it appears to be well that the federal courts are limited to determining whether a contract between the parties which contains an arbitration clause is in force, whether there has been a violation of that labor agreement, and whether the violation is within the scope of the contract. Further, in consideration whether to issue an order compelling arbitration, the courts have been instructed by the United States Supreme Court not to inquire into the merits of the grievance, but to determine whether the claim itself is covered by the contract.

In addition to these general principles, in subsequent cases, the courts have established certain specific criteria for determining whether arbitration should be ordered. Taken together, these cases comprise a new body of law covering arbitrability. Briefly stated these cases establish:

- If a contract has an arbitration clause and if the contract covers the subject matter in dispute, the court should order arbitration without considering the merits of the claim.
- An award limited to the "interpretation and application of the collective bargaining agreement" will be enforced without any review by the court of the reasoning leading to that award.
- Issues of damages for violation of a no-strike clause will be treated by the courts in the same manner as any other issue. That is, the court will decide whether the parties agreed in their contract to have such issues decided by the arbitration process. If they have, the issue will be arbitrated. If not, the court will decide it.
- The arbitrator, not the courts, decides issues concerning whether there has been compliance with the contract's procedural requirements, which is a condition for hearing the case on its merits.
- State courts have concurrent jurisdiction with the federal courts in suits for breaches of agreement. But the state courts must apply

federal law in any situation in which the state and federal laws are in conflict.

- An award which is beyond the scope of the collective bargaining agreement may be set aside by the courts. However, the courts may not review the reasoning pursued by the arbitrator in making the award.[8]

A promise to submit grievances arising from the interpretation or application of the agreement to arbitration presents two separate questions of arbitrability. First, resistance to arbitration may be based on the claim that particular subject matters have been excluded from the promise to arbitrate; for example, the grant of a merit increase, the discharge of an employee for cause, the contracting out of work, the methods of performing an operation. The assertion is that a claimed violation of a claimed substantive rule is not within the purview of the arbitration commitment. It presents a question of *substantive arbitrability*. Is the subject within or without the promise to arbitrate?

Second, resistance to arbitration may be based on the claim that the steps preliminary to arbitration have not been followed—that the grievance was not submitted within a time limit, the time prescribed for taking the grievance from step to step was exceeded, or arbitration was not requested in the proper manner or within a certain time period. This would present a question of *procedural arbitrability*. Was there compliance with the conditions precedent to arbitration?[9]

Since the disputes fall under the umbrellas of two general categories, substantive and procedural, the following cases are cited to illustrate how arbitrators have dealt with the questions in the arbitrational forum.

Meeting Precedent Conditions

There are any number of contractual provisions that could impose conditions on one or the other party as the case develops and proceeds toward eventual arbitration. For example, a contract states that a grievance must be filed within ten days of the occurrence of the event on which it is based, and one is filed six months after the event—and also after the union had knowledge of it. The company takes the position that the grievance is untimely. In view of the contention of procedural deftness, is it arbitrable?

The contract states that the employee must be signatory to his grievance. A grievance is signed by a union committeeman on the employee's behalf. Is it arbitrable, or has it failed to meet a mandatory condition, which renders it null?

In a four-step grievance procedure, the union demands arbitration immediately after filing its complaint, skipping all of the contractual steps. Will it ultimately prove to be nonarbitrable because of the procedural irregularity?

In the absence of a specified time limit for invoking arbitration, is a reasonable time to be inferred? What constitutes a reasonable time?

It is plain that questions of procedure deal with the minutiae of the arbitration process. They are the details of a scheme that, in its overall aspect, is taken for granted as the method of dispute settlement. Questions of contract interpretation are subsumed under the uncontested promise to arbitrate unsettled grievances. For example, the question of whether a reasonable time limit to invoke arbitration is to be assumed in the absence of a specifically prescribed time is answered, in major part, by a judgment about the function of grievance handling. A valid judgment may be that a grievance should be handled promptly or be considered dropped; avoidable delay in its prosecution should be discouraged as dilatory handling allows an unhealthy accumulation of stale grievances. If so, it follows that arbitration should be invoked within a reasonable time or not at all. And this is a value subsumed under the arbitral scheme. Similarly, questions of fact are highly particularized. What constitutes a reasonable time, for example, is almost entirely related to the special circumstances of the individual situation.[10]

The ways in which some of these procedural questions have been answered by arbitrators are worth reviewing. Although a grievance may be procedurally defective, the defect may be excused and therefore have no effect on the validity of the claim if it is not challenged in time. At McLouth Steel Corporation, an arbitrator refused to dismiss a grievance for not having been filed according to the contract when the protest against improper filing was not made until the arbitration hearing. It was held that procedural issues of this nature were ordinarily considered to have been waived if not raised in the previous grievance steps.[11] A review of a large number of published decisions shows that a preponderance of arbitrators has concurred with this concept.[12]

With clear contract language delineating the proper grievance process, most arbitrators will rule that the parties themselves have established the procedural requirements to be observed. However, failure to protest an infraction in time can result in the company's forfeiture. On this point, arbitrator Langston T. Hawley ruled as follows:

> The Company is contending that the grievance should be dismissed because it is not signed, in accordance with Article XXIX, Section 1 of the Agreement by aggrieved employee. The arbitrator believes that the grievance should be handled on its merits and not dismissed on technical grounds. This grievance was processed through all steps of the contract prior to its submission to arbitration. The Company had five months prior to the hear-

ing to raise objection on the grounds now being urged and yet its first objection was made known to the Union at the time of the hearing. In the light of these facts, the arbitrator believes that the signature on the grievance of an authorized representative of the aggrieved employee is sufficient.[13]

In addition to this type of procedural difficulty, where the employer had failed to contest the union's technical error, there are a variety of other types, a few of which merit examination. To demonstrate the contrasting rulings in two such cases, reference is made first to a decision by arbitrator Clare B. McDermott in a case between the U.S. Steel Corporation and the United Steelworkers:

> The grievance in Case USS-5145-H was filed by thirteen Grievance Committeemen, attempting to allege a violation of an obligation of "... the Company to the Union as such," under Section 6-E, on behalf of all other unnamed employees who did not receive Labor Day holiday pay and who neither filed individual grievances nor signed one of the seven grievances in USS-5145-H.
>
> From the beginning, Management has insisted that this is an improper subject matter for a union grievance under Section 6-E. When the defect was pointed out in Step 3, the Union said it could name individual employees referred to and their particular circumstances, and the employees so identified. No such identification was given. Holiday pay provisions of the Agreement can be applied only in light of specific fact situations, which are of nearly infinite variety, some of which would qualify an employee for holiday pay and others of which would not. Thus, the grievance in USS-5145-H without stating the particular situations of any named aggrieved employees, really does not present any holiday pay question which this Board can decide, and does not "... allege a violation of; the obligations of the company to the union as such." Accordingly, it will be dismissed.[14]

In contrast with this award, in another case in which the facts were somewhat different, arbitrator Saul Wallen found a grievance did meet the necessary procedural requirements with regard to being filed in sufficient detail:

> Article XXI, Section 7(c) requires that a written grievance "be in such detail as to identify the nature of the complaint, the name of the aggrieved employee or employees, the date and the place of the complaint." The company objects to the grievance on the grounds that it did not specifically list the names of the grievants but instead had a seniority roster of Operators appended to it. We find that the grievance filed is sufficiently definite for the company to identify the persons who actually were discharged and constituted sufficient notice of the union's challenge of that action. The inclusion of the names of those not discharged does not detract from the validity of the protest for those who were. Thus, the grievance meets the requirements of Section 7(c).[15]

A careful examination of the two awards readily reveals the rationale employed by the two competent arbiters. Although the factual differences were not substantial, they were clearly sufficient to produce different findings.

In the next two cases, the question was whether a regulating agreement existed.

A grievance arose after a contract had expired and before the parties had agreed to abide by the old contract pending enactment of a new one. It was ruled arbitrable. The influencing factor was that a supervisor answered the grievance in accordance with contractual procedures after the parties had agreed to be bound by the old contract. This indicated to the arbitrator that the company was bound to arbitrate and that it should have felt itself obligated to follow each procedural step after the supervisor's "answer."[16]

In another situation, a discharge grievance was arbitrable even though the discharge occurred before the employer and the union had executed their contract. The circumstances were as follows: (1) the employer and the union had operated in accordance with the contracts in effect between other contractors and unions at the job site prior to signing their own identical agreement; (2) the union had attempted to settle the discharge dispute through contractual grievance procedures, and the employer had dealt with the union on that basis, thereby implicitly acknowledging that contract procedures were applicable; and finally (3) the employer did not raise the question of arbitrability prior to the arbitration hearing.[17] Even if this last factor had not been in the picture, it is doubtful that the outcome would have been much different, if at all.

Given the types of questions involved in procedural arbitrability, are they more properly resolved by judges or by arbitrators? In *Livingston v. John Wiley and Sons*, the Second Court of Appeals had this to say concerning the issue:

> Indeed, it may well be that the arbitrator can make his most important contribution to industrial peace by a fair, impartial and well-informed decision of these very procedural matters. To hold matters of procedure to be beyond the competence of the arbitrator to decide would, we think, rob the parties of the advantages they have bargained for, that is to say, the determination of the issues between them by an arbitrator and not by a court. A contrary decision would emasculate the arbitration provisions of the contract. It is of the essence of arbitration that it be speedy and that the source of friction between the parties be promptly eliminated.... The numerous cases involving the great variety of procedural niceties ... make it abundantly clear that, were we to decide that procedural questions under an arbitration clause of a collective bargaining agreement are for the court, we would open the door wide to all sorts of technical obstructionism.[18]

In other words, in separating the question of substantive arbitrability from that of procedural arbitrability, the promise to arbitrate the merits of disputes evidences a fundamental commitment to the arbitral process. One may therefore assume that the procedural questions are secondary and have been entrusted to the arbitrator as part of the whole scheme.

Issues Inside or Outside Arbitral Scope

Perhaps the most frequently claimed basis for nonarbitrability is that the issue is not covered by the contract and, therefore, the arbitrator has no jurisdiction to hear the matter. The matters covered above dealt with issues involving questions of nonarbitrability for procedural reasons. Those to be covered now deal with questions of nonarbitrability due to substantive preclusion.

In *Warrior and Gulf*, the company argued that a question of subcontracting was nonarbitrable on the basis that it was purely a management function and not limited by the labor agreement. The union argued that the company violated the contract by its action of contracting out. The arbitration provision at Warrior and Gulf read as follows:

> Issues which conflict with any federal statute in its application as established by Court procedure or matters which are strictly a function of management shall not be subject to arbitration under this section.
>
> Should differences arise between the Company and the Union or its members employed by the Company as to the meaning and application of the provisions of this Agreement, or should any local trouble of any kind arise, there shall be no suspension of work on account of such differences but an earnest effort shall be made to settle such differences immediately in the following manner:
>
> If agreement has not been reached the matter shall be referred to an impartial umpire for decision. The parties shall meet to decide on an umpire acceptable to both. If no agreement on selection of an umpire is reached, the parties shall jointly petition the United States Conciliation Service for suggestion of a list of umpires from which selection shall be made. The decision of the umpire shall be final.

The limitation embodied in this clause is primarily exposed in the particular phrase "or matters which are strictly a function of management shall not be subject to arbitration under this section."

The Supreme Court said that such a limitation excluded only some issues from arbitration. Regrettably, for those seeking explicit and definitive distinctions, the exact boundaries of the exclusion are unclear. The Court stated: "Apart from matters that the parties specifically exclude all of the questions on which the parties disagree must therefore come within the scope of the grievance and arbitration provisions of the collective agreement." What does this mean in effect and practice? Basically, the conclusion was that an arbitrator may determine what constitutes a management function. Where a given activity is "management function" is a question to be decided by the arbitration process because it involves a determination of the "meaning and application" of the contract.

The Court's ruling in no way vitiated the force of the management-rights clause. Rather, it assigned the issue to the proper forum to determine whether it was binding.

The scope of an arbitration clause may determine whether a matter is excluded from arbitration. The scope of management-rights articles and operating clauses may also influence whether the issue raises a substantive question. Essentially, the argument in *Warrior and Gulf* was that subcontracting was a matter outside the contract and, therefore, not within the arbitrator's jurisdiction. The function of the court is a limited one: It may determine only whether a party seeking arbitration is making a claim which on its face is governed by the contract. The arbitrators decide the merits of the question.

Decisions on substantive arbitrability may either uphold the claim or reject it as nonarbitrable on its merits. A sampling of both types is useful in order to discern the rationale behind them.

An employer demanded that the union be required to furnish to employees who were not union members the funeral benefits and free periodicals furnished to members. The company's theory was that the contract in general as well as the contract's union-security provisions implicitly or otherwise obligated the union to do so in consideration of the fact that such employees had to pay the union a sum equal to period dues paid by members. The contract did not in express terms or by "any interpretation to which the language is susceptible" permit the arbitrator to confer on nonmembers the benefit that under the union's constitution were available to members only.[19]

Another employer's refusal to allow an employee to return to work after a two-year absence caused by a non-occupational illness was not an arbitrable issue. Under the agreement, an employee who was not able to work due to non-occupational illness was to remain on the payroll for a period of 90 days and "his status thereafter shall become a subject of negotiations between the company and the union." The contract merely required the employer to negotiate with the union concerning the return to work of the employee. Once that was done, as it had been here, the employer had no further obligation. The arbiter held that the contract did not require that such negotiations result in agreement or provide that failure to reach agreement was a matter for arbitration.[20]

Occasionally, the conduct or alleged misconduct of a management representative will provoke a grievance demanding that he be disciplined or ousted. And sometimes a supervisor's attitude and demeanor may leave much to be desired by both the employees and management. Of course, management should take the necessary and adequate steps within its own organization to censure and correct any instance of supervisory misconduct. However, in the overwhelming majority of such cases put before an arbitrator where the arbitrability was contested by management, the arbitrator has most often ruled against the union unless the parties had agreed by contract or otherwise to give him jurisdiction to decide the grievance on its merits.

Typical of commonsense arbitral rulings in this area was that in a case involving the King Powder Company, where a grievance demanded the discharge of a foreman for using abusive language and improperly docking wages. Arbitrator Dudley Whiting, an experienced and capable member of the National Academy of Arbitrators, commented as follows:

> It is a fundamental principle of American industry that the selection and retention of foremen or other supervisory personnel is the sole prerogative of management, particularly where they are excluded from the benefits of the collective bargaining agreement covering other employees. There is no doubt that the union may not, as a matter of right, demand the dismissal or demotion of a foreman and that such a demand is not a proper subject matter for a grievance.[21]

To provide some balance to this analysis and to emphasize its important points—important because arbitrability issues are often upheld—the following examples are offered in review.

Whether the employer had the right to retire an employee for reasons of age was considered an arbitrable issue under a contract defining "grievance" and "any dispute involving the effect, interpretation, application, claim of breach or violation of the contract and allowing arbitration of any and all grievances so defined." The mere fact that the agreement contained no provision specifically dealing with the retirement question did not itself preclude the matter from arbitration.[22]

A dispute over the employer's failure to grant maternity leaves to three employees was deemed arbitrable, notwithstanding the fact that pregnancy was not listed in the contract as one of the causes justifying a leave of absence. The deciding factor was that the subject of leaves as such was dealt with in the contract and was, therefore, in the view of the arbitrator, a matter over which management did not have unlimited discretion in handling the issue.[23]

In a final example, the issue was whether an employee who had incurred injury in the course of his employment was entitled to the difference between his regular wages and workmen's compensation benefits. Despite the employer's claim that there was no provision in the agreement requiring such pay, the issue was held to be arbitrable because the contract allowed for arbitration of all differences, disputes, or grievances pertaining to the terms of the contract. However, the arbitrator made it clear to both parties that in passing on the question of arbitrability, he was not prejudging the issue itself.[24]

Merits Versus Threshold Issue

When the validity of a grievance is in question for procedural or substantive reasons there are two potential issues to be presented to the arbitrator. The first question is a threshold matter: Is the grievance procedurally or substantively faulty to a degree that renders it nonarbitrable? If it is deemed arbitrable, the next issue is whether the claim has sufficient merit to be sustained. Several results are feasible. If the employer is raising the procedural issue and seeking to have the grievance denied, both on the arbitrability question and on its merits, the company will have "two bites at the apple"—two opportunities to have an award in its favor. In such case, the union has to survive two tests in order to achieve its objective. Of course, the employer may lose on both counts. However, the point should be made that a grievance may raise technical questions about arbitrability and at the same time have intrinsic merits, with both facts recognized by the employer. For example, an employee may be discharged improperly and without sufficient cause—or without any cause at all for that matter; because of contractually improper processing and grievance handling, he may never have his case heard or decided on its merits by reason of it being deemed nonarbitrable. This is an example of one of the inequities of a system for which few mutually acceptable solutions have been found.

In order to have sufficient authority as provided for under the parties' contract, the arbitrator must be appointed in accordance with the terms of the contract. If his appointment does not square with those requirements, his authority may be invalid and his award unenforceable.

It will be remembered that under certain contracts an appointing agency is empowered to make an arbitral selection for the parties. If, in such a case, that agency does not accord with the contractual regulations, the appointment could be, and most likely would be, invalid. Also, if by the contractual arrangement it is merely to proffer names, the agency could not make an appointment in the face of one party's refusal to participate in the selection process. If the agency makes an appointment without the participation of one party, that party must then decide whether it will participate in a hearing or allow it to proceed *ex parte* (in his absence). If its position is that the appointment is procedurally invalid and therefore any award would not be enforceable, the courts would probably set aside an award upon such a showing. However, in view of the Steelworkers Trilogy and subsequent cases, it would appear that, if the appointment is procedurally correct and the arbitrator is satisfied after an ex parte hearing that the issue is arbitrable, the courts will be likely to refuse to review a claim that the subject matter was excluded from arbitration by the contract.

With regard to separating the threshold issue of arbitrability from the question of the merits of the grievance, some parties have provided contractual coverage. In one major labor agreement, the arbitrability of the dispute is to be decided before it is considered on its merits:

> If either party shall claim before the Arbitrator that a particular grievance fails to meet the tests of arbitrability ... the Arbitrator shall proceed to decide such issue before proceeding to hear the case upon the merits.... In any case where the Arbitrator determines that such grievance fails to meet said test of arbitrability he shall refer the case back to the parties without a decision or recommendation on its merits.[25]

The language appears to be clear in restraining the arbitrator from rendering a decision or opinion on the merits of a case that he has found nonarbitrable. However, it may leave certain other questions unanswered.

One may infer from the contract that both issues—arbitrability and merits, as well as the arguments for and against them—are to be presented to the arbitrator at one and the same hearing.

In other words, can the threshold issue of arbitrability be presented in an initial hearing, separate and apart from a hearing on merits? Can an award be rendered on that issue alone before the arbitrator hears anything whatsoever about the parties' respective positions with regard to merits? Granted, such procedure would require two separate hearings. However, such an approach is often in the best interests of the party contesting the arbitrability of the grievance. It must also be acknowledged that more often than not the arbitrator will prefer to consider both issues at one time, thus saving himself time and travel. As a consequence, he may render a decision on the threshold matter without going into the merits. The arbitrator, however, is a servant to the parties; if their mandate is that the issues be heard separately, he must abide by that arrangement.

Dividing the case into two distinct hearings is sometimes viewed as desirable for psychological reasons. The arbitrator would not be influenced by the merits of the case while considering the purely technical arguments about arbitrability. Arbitrators are only human after all. After having heard both cases in full, the arbitrator would have to have a well-disciplined mind and a stable emotional constitution to keep the two issues segregated and to resist the temptation of finding a case with merits arbitrable if his ruling to the contrary would render it null. The closer the decision on arbitrability, surely the more difficult it is for the arbitrator to rule a case nonarbitrable when it appears to have substantive merits.

These are valid considerations when the parties weigh a decision to combine or separate the issues.

The parties may mutually agree to arrange for two hearings. If so, the arbitrator is originally presented with only the parties' respective positions, arguments, and evidence, on the procedural or substantive arbitrability question. Nothing relating to merits is revealed—or only so much as is essential and necessary to deal with the question of threshold. The hearing is closed, and only if the arbitral finding is in favor of arbitrability is another hearing necessary. Also, if it is deemed arbitrable, the parties may then choose to present the dispute on its merits to a different arbitrator.

There is one other adversary approach to handling this question of presentation of threshold issue versus presentation of merits. It involves some willingness to engage in brinksmanship. Again, it has to do with an ex parte hearing. If management is adamant in its desire to deal with the two issues in two separate hearings, it should advise the union of its stand during grievance processing and pre-arbitration discussions. This should be made clear to the agency making the arbitral selection or submitting panels of names. It should be made clear to the selected arbitrator, before and during the hearing on the threshold question. He should be advised that he has not been selected to consider the merits of the dispute or empowered to do so. He should be advised at the outset of the hearing of the party's intention to withdraw at the close of the hearing on that single, initial issue and of the party's refusal to be bound by any decision that may be subsequently rendered in an ex parte proceeding. At the appropriate time, the party should leave—and pray a little, of course. There are risks involved, but attaining most things worthwhile involves taking some risks.

In the majority of instances, the arbitrator will try to persuade the parties to do it all in one sitting. That is understandable. Also, in the majority of cases, it is unlikely that he will proceed with a hearing at which one party is absent, especially if there is any doubt about his having been given jurisdiction over the second issue. However, if he has been given jurisdiction over that issue, the party is foolhardy to attempt this approach, and its chances for a favorable outcome are extremely doubtful. Under those circumstances, being absent at an ex parte hearing is not brinksmanship, but hara-kiri.

The procedural question is of course whether the arbiter should rule on arbitrability before either party presents its case with regard to merits, or whether he should reserve his conclusions on the threshold question until the full case, including merits, has been completely presented.

In summary, it is well to examine the comments of professionals from different schools of thought.

Arbitrator Harry Dworkin believes that the ruling on arbitrability should be made before the presentation of the case on the merits:

> The Chairman is of the opinion that when a party raises the issue of arbitrability, it is better practice to pass upon this issue at the time it is presented, and before hearing the dispute on the merits, for the reason that whenever possible, parties should have the right to an interim decision or ruling until after the conclusion of the hearing.[26]

Arbitrator Douglas B. Maggs is a spokesman for the point of view that the ruling on arbitrability may be reserved until the full case has been heard. In a dispute involving Barbet Mills, Inc., he remarked:

> The arbitrator may properly reserve his ruling upon arbitrability until after he has heard evidence and argument upon its merits. A contrary rule would cause needless delay and expense, necessitating two hearings whenever the arbitrator needed time to consider the question of arbitrability. Furthermore, in many cases, it is only after a hearing on the merits has informed the arbitrator of the nature of the dispute that he is in a position to determine whether it is of the kind covered by the agreement to arbitrate.... This procedure does not, of course, preclude the party who loses from obtaining any judicial review of the arbitrator's decision to which it is entitled by law; to reassure the company about this I explicitly rule that its participation in the hearing upon the merits would not constitute a waiver of its objections to arbitrability.[27]

Dworkin and Maggs have clearly expressed different points of view on this question. As advocate and as arbitrator, the author has held both points of view, depending upon the role he was playing at the time. As advocate, he favored Dworkin's view, almost always urging the arbitrator to rule in favor of a total separation of the issues. However, when looking at the question from the vantage point of the arbitrator, he was most often inclined to believe that one's position on this particular question is somewhat influenced by the chair he is occupying at the arbitral hearing table.

However, there is a commonsense middle ground between these two positions: The choice should be based on consideration of all the circumstances of the particular dispute. This procedure is followed by the Connecticut State Board of Mediation, which states:

> The Board will inform the party protesting arbitrability that it will be permitted to raise that issue at the hearing. The Board will then first hear arguments on arbitrability before it proceeds to the merits of the dispute. The Board makes clear that at the hearing both parties must be prepared to proceed on the merits after the Board has heard them on arbitrability.
>
> After the case on arbitrability has been presented, the Board will assess the circumstances, then obtaining to determine if it will proceed directly to the merits.

> Under its policy, the Board reserves the right either to require the parties to go forward on the merits at the same hearing or to determine that the decision on arbitrability should be made first before proceeding on the merits.

This is certainly a more flexible arrangement. It attempts to ensure that each decision about whether to separate the two aspects, threshold and merits, is based on the peculiar facts of the case. Nevertheless, it too fails to meet the special needs of the party definitely committed to the separation of issues or one determined to see them treated together.

In any case, the overwhelming majority of published conclusions shows that arbitrators customarily separate the two issues in their written opinions, putting the question of arbitrability and its answer before the discussion and conclusion on the merits of the case.

Needless to say the labor arbitration advocate must possess a full familiarity with these court and arbitral attitudes.

7

Some Basic Principles of Discipline

No attempt is going to be made here to cover all of the complex aspects of industrial discipline and discharge, its application and administration. It would take an entire volume to do justice to this subject totally.[1]

Purpose

The purpose of discipline is to correct improper conduct, not merely to punish for it. Therefore, in any given case, only the amount of punishment necessary to get an employee's attention and surely get the corrective message across to him is the amount of penalty applied. The objectives of management in applying discipline are basically as follows: (a) to enforce reasonable rules; (b) to help the employee help himself to be a better worker, to protect his job and thereby his family's security; (c) to save the company's investment, plus its training and replacement costs; (d) to protect the health and safety of all employees; (e) to protect the company's property and equipment; (f) to warn other employees that improper conduct will be punished; and (g) to thereby deter other employees from similar misconduct on their part in the future; (h) to obtain a full day's work; and (i) to teach a concept of self-discipline to all employees. Growing out of this is a means by which order is maintained, and limits are set for individual behavior which preserves the well-being of the entire group. The responsibility for all of this rests with the management, since only it can act—not the union, not the employees.

Ignorance of Law

In society at large, ignorance of the law generally constitutes no excuse. The citizen who alleges ignorance to defend his violation of a given law is seldom excused by law-enforcement people. A somewhat different condition exists in industrial society where it has been customarily held that an employee cannot be expected to comply with rules and regulations he is not aware of.

Rarely has a management attempt to discipline an employee for violating a rule that was not published or adequately promulgated been upheld. The employee's ignorance of it constitutes a sustainable defense if he can establish that he could not have known of the alleged rule. This is why some employers have chosen to enumerate their factory rules and regulations fully and prominently within the covers of the labor document. Still others publish them in an employee handbook, while the majority seems to prefer to use bulletin boards scattered throughout the operating facility. In any case, a management will find it extremely difficult to have a disciplinary action sustained by an arbitrator unless it can be established that it has taken steps to communicate its rules effectively.

Just Cause

Most labor agreements contain a provision in the Management Rights Article which states that the employer may discipline or discharge employees for "cause" or "just cause." Consequently, what is this standard of "cause" or "just cause" which must be met when discipline is meted out?

Very basically it consists of three parts: (1) was an improper act, in fact, committed; (2) consequently, is the offense serious enough to warrant discipline; and (3) if so, is the penalty imposed appropriate to the offense?

The company must justify each of these three parts. The union can protest and appeal any one or more of these parts, and an arbitrator reviews all three parts. The union may contest whether or not an improper act was actually committed and, if it was, whether any discipline should be imposed based on the facts and circumstances, and they can also grieve the penalty on the basis it exceeds the amount of action necessary to correct the employee without being onerous or punitive.

These three parts then are those which shore up the foundation of "just cause."

Arbitrator Carroll R. Daugherty has developed seven criteria that he has set forth and applied in a number of published decisions on discipline cases. The stature of this arbiter makes these particular standards noteworthy. They are embodied in seven questions.

1. Did the employee have foreknowledge that his conduct would be subject to discipline, including discharge? (This, of course, involves the "Ignorance of the Law" principle earlier enunciated.)
2. Was the rule he violated reasonably related to the safe, efficient, and orderly operation of the company's business?
3. Did the company make a reasonable effort before disciplining him to discover whether he in fact did violate this rule?
4. Was its investigation fair and objective?
5. Did it obtain substantial evidence that the employee was guilty of the offense with which he was charged?
6. Was its decision nondiscriminatory?
7. Was the degree of discipline given him reasonably related to the seriousness of his proven offense and/or his record with the company?[2]

For an employer's discipline or discharge to be upheld, all seven questions must be answerable in the affirmative. If any one question evokes a negative response, the company's action will either fall or be amended. It should be noted, all of these seven criteria fall under the fundamental and general umbrella definition of just cause herein previously given.

Burden of Proof

It seems to be a well-established tenet of labor relations that the burden of proof in disputes over *discipline or discharge* must be carried by the party holding the affirmative of the issue—that is, the party who initiated the challenged action. *The employer is therefore called on to establish the facts it asserts as the basis for having taken positive corrective action. The company must bear the burden of proving its action met the standards of just cause.*

The employee is innocent until proven guilty, and is presumed so.

In the grievance procedure the employer should put forth the facts and evidence it holds in support of its action. Nothing of any relevance should be withheld.

If the case goes to arbitration, the company as the moving party here will undoubtedly be required to put on its case, in chief, before the union goes forward. Nothing should be withheld. On the other hand, nothing can be presented there in evidence against the employee, which has not been revealed and given to the union prior to the arbitration hearing. In fact, many contracts preclude the introduction of any matters not presented between the parties during the course of arguing the case within the steps of the grievance procedure.

The employee need not testify during the arbitration hearing. His waiver or refusal to do so will *not* raise any presumption as to his guilt or culpability. He need not prove his innocence—the employer, the moving party on discipline and discharge actions, must prove his guilt.

Was a crime committed? Was this the employee who committed the offense? Was he previously aware it would be deemed improper? Was corrective action merited? Was the amount of discipline imposed no harsher than should have been necessary to correct the problem?

The burden is not on the union to disprove the employer's action. The burden is on management to prove its decision was just and necessary.

Five Types of Industrial Offenses

There are basically only five different types of industrial offenses, and all of the specific violations of rules and regulations can be divided among, and assigned to, one of these five families.

1. A violation of the contract. In this category one will generally find offenses like refusal to work overtime if otherwise mandated by the labor agreement, refusal to accept a work assignment or a transfer to another job, or even engaging in a work stoppage or other action in contravention of the No-Strike clause.
2. A violation of a plant rule. In this family of offenses one will generally find disputes involving violations of safety rules, carrying firearms, being under influence of alcohol or drugs, smoking, sleeping, etc.
3. Engaging in misconduct, *on* plant premises, which *is* illegal in the community. Examples of this type of offense would be stealing, rape, molesting other employees, fighting and assault, and various manifestations of moral turpitude.
4. Engaging in misconduct, *on* plant premises, which is *not* illegal in the community, but which *does* affect the employee's relationship with the company. Numbered among this type of offense would be horseplay, littering, neglect or abuse of tools and equipment, gambling, etc.
5. Engaging in misconduct, *off* plant premises, which may affect the employee's job, his fellow employees,' supervisor's, or the company's good will or reputation. Examples of this are various.

An example of the fifth type might be when an employee confronts and attacks his supervisor, off plant premises, perhaps even many miles away from the workplace. This is nevertheless misconduct which warrants disciplinary action if such actions on his part resulted from him carrying a work-related grievance off-premise—meaning, the problem had its origin or its roots in the workplace.

Another example could be an employee selling or giving formulae or trade secrets of his own employer to one of its competitors.

Or, another instance could be that of a male employee engaging in off-premises conduct of an immoral or obscene nature, public indecency or attempted rape—with the consequence that fellow female employees were fearful or refused to work with the offender any longer on premises. Such instances as those briefly cited above, and a host of others, may constitute off-duty, off-premises conduct which justifies the employer in imposing some form of disciplinary or corrective action.

Reasonableness of Rules

The majority of Management Rights Articles contain a provision which in effect says that the employer may "establish reasonable rules and regulations for employees to observe." The sense in which the term "reasonable" is used is what I will attempt to define here.

Rules which are reasonable are basically those which are (1) reasonable in context; (2) reasonable in their administration and enforcement; and (3) reasonable in the penalties meted out for violations of the rule.

The union may normally be free to grieve any one of these parts: the context of the rule, the matter of enforcement of the rule, and the penalties imposed for violations.

A rule that is reasonable in context is one that has a bearing upon or relatedness to the safe, efficient and orderly operation of the enterprise. Therefore, a rule prohibiting smoking in a potentially explosive or volatile work situation would certainly be deemed reasonable in context—whereas a rule of no smoking in a foundry where there is already molten metal, sparks, fire, heat and smoke, could very probably be viewed as unreasonable in context.

A rule that is reasonable in enforcement and administration is one in which employees are treated relatively equally for infractions. It is unreasonable if misconduct by some is overlooked while others are held to strict compliance. Therefore, a rule may be reasonable in context, but unreasonable in enforcement unless it is applied consistently, uniformly and regularly, between and among all employees.

A rule that is reasonable in the penalty imposed is one where the punishment fits the crime. For example, a rule against littering may be reasonable in its context; it may be uniformly enforced; but it is nevertheless unreasonable in terms of punishment if an employee is instantly fired, for a first offense, of inadvertently dropping a tiny piece of paper on the floor.

These are rather extreme examples, but deliberately so, to illustrate by dramatization the points being made.

Offers of Compromise

The purpose of the grievance procedure is to provide the parties with an orderly, regulated means for peacefully resolving their differences during the term of the agreement. For this process to operate effectively the parties must each feel at liberty to suggest, and to offer, various remedies for such problems. They must feel they have the freedom to search for solutions which are accommodating to their respective interests. Such suggested remedies are put forth, and analyzed, weighed and considered, sometimes to be accepted, other times to be declined or responded to with a counterproposal.

This is as it should be. And, to insure and preserve this grievance-bargaining freedom, many labor agreements contain a provision, usually found in the Grievance or Arbitration Article, which basically states that such offers of compromise are not introducible to an arbitrator as evidence against interest of the compromise-offering party.

However, even though such provision may not appear in the contract, arbitrators will typically disallow the introduction of any information of this type into the arbitral record.

The reasons for this customary holding are obvious. For example, the company discharges an employee and during the grievance procedure offers to reinstate him, less any back pay, with a 30-day suspension remaining on his record. The union declines, demanding full back pay as well, and no suspension whatsoever. The company refuses this union demand and the parties proceed to arbitration on the issue of the discharge.

The union in this case would be precluded from introducing to the arbiter the fact of the company offer to reduce their discharge action to a 30-day suspension. The arbiter would disallow this presentation. He must do so to preserve the parties' bargaining freedom in the grievance procedure. If he were to allow either party to introduce evidence of prior offers of compromise, and allow them to influence his decision, it would act to hinder or throttle the parties in their efforts to resolve problems by compromise and accommodation. Under those circumstances, each party would take stiff-legged, unbending positions throughout all steps of the grievance process, not offering in any way to compromise or otherwise seek solutions, since if they did so, such could be subsequently revealed as evidence against their own interests.

Let us refer back to the discharge case just previously mentioned. After discharging the individual, which action was based upon certain facts, circumstances and evidence, a grievance results and the parties meet to discuss it. Previously it was described that the company here offered to reduce their discharge action to a 30-day suspension from work without pay. Let us presume that such offer of compromise came because the union offered mitigating evidence and circumstances. They feel it is sufficient to warrant removing all disciplinary action. Obviously the company seems to feel it does affect their case, but not sufficiently to merit reinstatement in whole. So, the company offered to reduce its action—the union refused to accept. In the situation cited above, the employer withdrew its compromise offer, let its discharge action stand, and the parties proceeded to arbitration.

It is that rather typical company position that I wish to address. In such a case as the one here mentioned, or any others of a related nature, I would recommend a different company position.

Its discharge action was based upon certain facts, circumstances and evidence. The union comes along and produces mitigating circumstances and evidence, not known and/or considered by the company when it decided to discharge. This information acts to somewhat compromise the viability of the company position. At this point the employer offers to reduce its action to a 30-day sentence without pay. If this offer of compromise is declined by the union, I would urge that the employer unilaterally implement its offer of compromise—that is, advise the employee of its revised action of a 30-day suspension without pay, and inform him when he is due back at work. In other words, the employer should not withhold the compromise, basing its implementation upon union acceptance of it. If the *total* facts and evidence point toward that as a more appropriate disciplinary treatment, the arbitrator will undoubtedly think so too. So why let the employee do *to* the company, what the company can do *for* itself. Additionally, all of the foregoing *is* material and facts which *can be* presented to the arbitrator as evidence of the employer's reasonableness, willingness to compromise, and determination to do what's right, because it's right, and not because it has been ordered.

Double Jeopardy

It is a well established principle in labor-management relations that an employee cannot be punished twice for one offense. This is evidently an outgrowth of our constitutional prohibition against subjecting a person in a criminal proceeding to double jeopardy. The basis for the legal rule is the view that to try and then retry an accused for the same act would be an oppressive exercise of the power of the state against the individual. Our notions of fairness are offended by the thought.

This rule has been considered to have applicability to disciplinary proceedings in an industrial plant, for, as one commentator has said, double penalties "would be contrary to fundamental concepts of justice."[3]

Generally, the concept of double jeopardy is not found applicable in discharge cases involving a series of minor offenses when management has imposed corrective discipline properly.[4] Corrective discipline is progressive. Unless the employee's offense is so grave as to merit immediate discharge, the degree of punishment will be decided by how often he has erred before and how important the rule is that he has broken. A first offender guilty of a minor infraction of a rule is given a minor punishment, perhaps an oral warning or a written reprimand. If he breaches a similar or comparable rule on a second occasion within a reasonable time, a more serious penalty will usually be assessed. Further and harsher penalties may follow up to and including discharge. Each severer penalty is telling the worker that the gravity of his misconduct is increasing, and each affords him another opportunity to improve so that the terminal point of discharge may be avoided.

Each step probably constitutes a grievable situation, and every discipline imposed by the employer must stand the test of just cause. If the union challenges it unsuccessfully or lodges no grievance at all, the incident becomes a part of the employee's work record. Therefore, in an arbitration hearing on a dispute, the worker's prior disciplinary record is a highly relevant consideration. Thus its introduction into the arbitration record does not expose the offending employee to any threat of double jeopardy.

Demotion—Withholding Benefits

Demotion as a form of discipline to correct improper employee behavior is an action to be discouraged. While it is true that a small *majority* of arbitrators disapprove of such action as a type of discipline, admittedly a good number would permit it unless clearly disallowed by the contract. I believe this is fallacious reasoning in the majority of such cases.

The opposite view is urged here. Demotion should only be considered and employed where the contract expressly provides for it. The single exception is one to be mentioned later herein. But, for the most part, demotion as a form of discipline should be shied away from.

Demotion does not correct an employee action of misconduct. It merely transfers it to a lower level, to another location, perhaps even to a different supervisor. It is a cop-out, an evasion, an escape-hatch which, when used by the supervisor, enables him to avoid facing the employee's problem. Of course, what I'm talking about here are cases where the employee has violated some established plant rule or regulation designed to control his behavior—such rules as those covering absenteeism, tardiness, horseplay, smoking, drinking, loitering, littering, drugs, misuse of working time, and the like. Demotion is not an appropriate remedial action for correction of these types of misconduct.

As a matter of fact, it can be persuasively contended that to demote, unless specifically allowed by contract, denies the affected employee a contractual benefit. It probably affects his seniority ranking in some negative way. It probably results in a material reduction in his wage or salary—and such a penalty as that is on-going, payday after payday, with no eventual terminal point. It in affect constitutes a form of withholding of a negotiated contract benefit. There is very little difference between that type of action, and telling him he will get only eight holidays instead of ten as contractually assured or his insurance coverage will be unilaterally reduced below other employees' coverage, or everyone else will get the contractually provided rest periods, but his are to be denied. By demoting an employee, management can be imposing a penalty of indefinite duration. Its action can affect the seniority rights of not only the penalized worker but also others, who then become unintended victims. It can weaken the demoted employee's job security by making him more vulnerable to layoff. It may jeopardize his ability to obtain more meaningful and profitable positions in the future. It is too often a substitute for intestinal fortitude—an easy or at least less troublesome way out of a situation meriting discharge or another form of discipline. Further, it can result in the imposition of unequal penalties: One worker may be demoted three labor grades while another who is guilty of the same offense under similar circumstances may be demoted two or four.

The one exception, alluded to earlier here, is in essence, that any demotion should be related to the employee's competence and qualifications for the job, not to breaches of plant rules, which call for discipline.

Moreover, if an employee *has the ability* to perform a job and *is withholding* it, this constitutes a condition that *also* is subject to correction through progressive discipline. The reason for the behavior is really irrelevant. Whether it arises from a misplaced sense of independence, work group pressures, or circumstances in his private life, there is no justification for it as long as any such conditions are *within* his control.

A case involving the Bethlehem Steel Company embodies this view. The arbiter held that management's demotion of an employee was improper because his record indicated that he had the requisite ability for the job, stating that disciplinary action rather than demotion was proper remedy where substandard performance was found to be temporary.[5] The two significant facts are that the employee possessed ability and that he had demonstrated it. His failure to apply it to his task was merely temporary. The expectation was that he would regain his previous level of performance.

The arbitrator of another dispute held that the Boeing Company could use demotion when the employee was *not capable* of performing the work, but it was *not* entitled to demote where the evidence showed that errors were the result of *negligence* rather than *inability*.[6] Similarly, an arbitrator deciding a case involving the Republic Steel Corporation ruled that it could *not* use demotion as a form of discipline for occasional carelessness or failure to obey instructions on the job.[7]

All these decisions express the concept that as long as an employee is able and qualified to carry out his work, his failure to do so represents a fault that should be corrected by discipline rather than demotion.

Indefinite Suspension

If an employee is suspended from work without pay, as discipline for a work rules infraction, the employer should put a beginning and ending time and date on the suspension action. It should not be left open-ended.

There are several faults with handling it otherwise.

If the duration of the suspension is not clearly defined, the company is leaving its length to the discretion of the offender. Imagine this: An employer orders an insubordinate employee to go home, and not to come back until he is disposed to follow the rules: The employee takes the company at its word, leaves, and six months later, or after any other period for that matter, comes back and says he's now inclined to follow instruction. It sounds like he's more in command than the employer.

Another fault with such an approach is equally or even more consequential: Such actions will not be supported by arbitral ruling.

The purpose of the discipline is to correct a given form of misconduct for the offender. In the occurrence described, a specific period of suspension should be given. The employer's presumption should be that the action taken has served its purpose when the worker returns following a suspension of a stipulated period. If the insubordinate or abusive employee continues his improper conduct upon his return or thereafter, he is subject to further disciplinary action for repeating the offense, up to and including discharge.

Workers should not be left to decide their own punishment. The responsibility for assessing the proper degree of penalty rests solely with the employer. He has failed to meet that responsibility unless he clearly declares the beginning and terminal dates of the discipline.

8

Precedent Value of Arbitration Awards

The matter dealt with here is the problem of the relation of prior arbitration awards to current controversies and their status under the same, a succeeding or a different contract, and before the same or a different arbitrator. Is an arbitrator bound to follow the same doctrines that would ordinarily be applied by a court in considering earlier disputes and decisions of other tribunals? This question has been the source of continuing argument for many years, and the very nature of the arbitration process, as it exists today, conceals from its own disciples a definite, specific answer.

It appears that the great majority of arbitrators are willing to give only "some weight" to prior awards. It then seems to boil down to the question of what do arbitrators consider to be "some weight."[1]

It seems to be generally agreed as an established principle in the arbitration process that arbitration opinions are not precedents—that each case stands upon its own feet. However, it also appears to be a well-established principle that the interpretation of contract language embodied in an award becomes a part of that contract language. This is a doctrine which is not seriously threatened even by those who protest against "citations" and "precedent." As a matter of industrial reality, a decision is "precedent" and continues until the parties change its effect in the labor agreement or another arbitrator changes or confuses it with a contrary ruling.

It can also be safely stated that arbitrators seldom give much notice to the legal differences which dictate the effect which must be accorded various types of precedents. *Res adjudicata* is the familiar judicial doctrine universally recognized which forbids retrial of matters which have been previously definitely settled by a binding decision. The rule rests upon consideration of judicial time and public policy (factors not necessarily present in private arbitration hearings) favoring the establishment of certainty in legal relations. When a court has entered its final judgment on the merits of a cause of action, the parties are thereafter broadly bound not only as to every matter which was offered and received to sustain or defeat the claim or demand but also as to any other admissible matter which might have been offered for that purpose whether or not it was actually considered. The judgment of the court puts a practical end to the dispute so that none of the includable issues can be brought again into litigation between the parties upon any ground whatever in the absence of fraud or some other overwhelming factor which would operate to invalidate the judgment.[2]

This is not so in the arbitration process!

Arbitrator's awards do not have a corresponding authority or force; they are not accorded this weight of "judicial authority" in determining future controversies, even between the same parties or over the same issues. Arbitrators do not consider prior awards conclusive or binding in subsequent cases. In arbitration, all questions of fact and law are deemed to be referred to the arbitrator for decision. Unless restricted by the contract, or submission agreement, or an applicable state statute, arbitrators do not bind themselves by strict rules of law or evidence. As long as he remains with in his jurisdiction, the arbitrator invariably feels free to decide the issues submitted to him, notwithstanding any prior awards between the parties, unless the parties have agreed otherwise.

What, then, is the "some weight" given by arbitrators to prior awards?

An examination of a large number of reported cases reveals that prior awards often do play a part in arbitration. But rather than carrying the weight of "judicial authority," they exert a "persuasive" force which compels consideration. The extent to which this persuasive force is in fact persuasive and compelling in a given case is generally influenced by such factors as the following:

- Is the present fact situation the same as the prior fact situation?
- Are the same two parties involved in the present dispute who were involved in the past dispute?
- Is the language of the labor agreement identical to that of the prior case?
- If the same parties and the same labor agreement are involved, has a contract negotiation occurred during the intervening period between hearings, and if so, were the contractual provisions changed?

- Subsequent to a prior award has a practice come into existence, mutually agreeable to the parties, which has the effect of modifying all or part of the prior award?[3]
- Has another award been rendered which reverses or is contrary to the prior award?
- Is the same evidence and argument involved in the present case or is something new being presented not considered in the prior case?
- Did the prior award enunciate just and reasonable principles of conduct and contract interpretation?

It appears that one of the problems frequently encountered by arbitrators is where a party to an arbitration hearing puts forth citations of other published cases, presumably identical or very nearly on all fours with their case, which upon close examination by the arbitrator prove to be dissimilar or unrelated.[4] Naturally, the parties do not enhance the value of their cited cases, a value already dubious and questionable, when they do not exercise extreme care in their research and selection practices.

Reference to such elusive precedent reminds one of the story told by Erick Heller in which a clown appears on a stage completely darkened except for a small circle of light cast by a street lamp in one corner. The clown, his face deeply worried and long-drawn, walks round and round this circle of light, obviously desperately looking for something.

"What have you lost?" asks a policeman passing by.

"The key to my house!"

Whereupon the policeman joins him in his search. Finding nothing after a while, the policeman inquires, "Are you certain you lost it here?"

"No," replies the clown, and pointing to the dark corner of the stage, says, "Over there."

"Then why are you looking over here?"

"Because, there is no light over there," replies the clown.[5]

Obviously, if the parties carry any hope for the arbitrator to find their precedential key, they must first shed light on the right places.

However, when the cited case of another party does strike on all fours, an arbitrator may utilize its reasoning for application to his case. In referring to a union-cited case,[6] arbitrator B. Meredith Reid stated:

> With the reasoning there, as far as it went, your arbitrator agrees and uses its principles to state this Board finds as fact and *thus overrules that portion of the company's position* which claimed the grievants herein were "temporary employees"; they were not ... [emphasis added].

The relevancy of prior awards, obtained in decided disputes between the same parties, is also determined by the similarity in fact situations between the prior and the present case. In a case where a company was having a lot of trouble with light bulb changing, an arbitrator in a prior case had ordered the company to pay an electrician call-out pay because a kiln operator had changed a light bulb. In a later case, arbitrator LeRoy Autrey denied a claim by another electrician for call-out pay because a maintenance mechanic had changed a light bulb. In the first case, the light bulb had been changed by an employee not authorized to handle electrical equipment, but the maintenance mechanic was so authorized. Autrey disregarded the prior award since the bulb change did not require any high degree of skill, nor did it present any safety hazards.[7]

Where the previous case has appeared to show good sense and reason after a fair hearing, arbitrators are cautious about rendering a new and different solution.[8] Carrying this principle another step forward, arbitrator Whitley P. McCoy came upon a situation in which he considered prior awards to have precedent value:

> Where a number of competing companies negotiate jointly with a union, and agree on identical contract provisions in order to avoid competitive disadvantages, it would seem the mutual intent of the several parties would be nullified if arbitrators should, by contradictory interpretations of identical language, destroy the identity of meaning.

So saying, McCoy ruled that a decision by one arbitrator under these circumstances should be followed by another unless it is clearly wrong. Having thus ruled, and finding that an earlier award had held salaried personnel entitled to a full 40 hours salary for any week in which they worked at all under this contract, he made the same ruling.[9] Despite their protestations to the contrary, arbitrators have been known to "go along" with prior awards, even those to which they do not wholly subscribe, thus giving them persuasive precedent value—for the sake of stability and certainty, between the parties, in their contract interpretations. Serving on a Special Board of Adjustment, chairman Jacob Seidenberg, expressing the opinion that had the case been found before him for the first time he might have decided otherwise, nevertheless ruled that a pay dispute had to be resolved in accord with prior awards on the same subject involving the same agreement.[10] In a similar case of greater complexity and wider ranging implications, arbitrator Robert W. Fleming decided it was not important whether he might have decided a prior case differently; although between another plant and another local of the union, but under the same national agreement, Fleming following the previous awards and denied the grievance.[11] This is not to suggest that arbitrators will not reverse a fellow arbiter when they feel he has erroneously interpreted a contract clause.[12] However, such reversals do appear to be a minority exception to the generally followed rule of not disturbing "good sense" prior rulings.

Although arbitrators usually minimize the importance of the precedent value of other awards, they do find sufficient merit in them to conduct their own private research to see how other arbitrators have ruled in similar cases.[13] On occasion they may even invite and encourage the parties to submit cited cases.[14]

As mentioned earlier, a factor affecting the weight given a prior award is whether a change has occurred in the contractual language since the previous award. Obviously if one party or the other finds a particular award so objectionable as to be motivated to change the applicable contract language, and if fact is so successful in collective bargaining negotiations, then the same case brought forth a second time, under changed language, may understandably bring a different ruling, even before the same arbitrator. However, a small language change may not be enough; it has to be "sufficient to change the meaning." In an International Harvester case,[15] an arbiter found that a contract language change had occurred, but in the final analysis was insufficient to change the meaning of the earlier clause. So finding, he awarded in accord with the prior ruling.

It appears that arbitrators are also fairly consistent in giving substantial weight to prior awards, where a negotiation has occurred since the previous ruling, and the contractual language has not been changed.[16]

All of the foregoing inspection has dealt primarily with the ad hoc arbitral system, and obviously the possibility of conflict between decisions of arbitrators is one of the risks of that arbitral process. It is partly to minimize this danger that parties sometimes enter into contractual arrangements for permanent rather than ad hoc arbitrators. Naturally under a permanent arbitration system the likelihood of conflicts between decisions is greatly lessened.

An example of the difference between the two systems can probably best be portrayed by reviewing a permanent umpire situation. An excellent example of this is the Chrysler-UAW arrangement.[17]

In summary, it can probably be safely said that the following of precedent in the usual ad hoc arbitration process rests upon the assumption that the precedent has a sound and continuing validity. But where a conflict in decisions results from a clear and supported conviction that the earlier decision does not reasonably resolve the issue, a given arbitrator need not abdicate to his predecessor that function of judgment for which he was engaged.

Although the doctrine of *stare decisis, et non quieta movere*—adhere to precedents, do not unsettle things—does not strictly apply to arbitration, nevertheless, the value of the predictability of decisions to parties in the contractual relationship when an arbiter has once again passed upon the identical issue, and the reluctance to unsettle established things, are desirable elements to be sought in arbitration.

It is obvious that one of the primary purposes of the arbitral system is to aid the parties in reaching a clear understanding of the meaning of their agreement as applied in practice in the plant. Re-litigation of decided issues (repeated attempts to persuade an arbitrator to change an established interpretation of the contract merely because one side or the other does not like it or refusal to accept arbitral decisions as the basis for settling disputes without arbitration) cannot fail to defeat this purpose.

Arbitrators can also make a positive contribution in this regard by laying a heavy burden of proof and persuasion on the party that claims a prior award was erroneous and should be reversed. And such burden must clearly be heaviest in cases involving the same contractual provision as the prior case, the same facts, the same parties, and no new evidence or argument. Where such cases are faced, prior awards must be accorded persuasive value in the interest of stability to the decisional process.

9

Avoiding Some Pot Holes

Now I will offer some suggestions for handling specific difficulties that the advocate might encounter in a case. While these suggestions may seem elementary, they are fundamental to the preparation and prosecution of any case. You'll notice that these suggestions include an emphasis on detail that may seem almost compulsive. There's a reason for that emphasis: Success is often dependent on paying attention to every detail.

Require Specifics; Define Grievances

Require the union to identify specific contractual provisions allegedly violated. Determine if the grievance deals with a matter that is a grievance as defined by the labor agreement. What is a grievance? Is it any dispute between the parties? Is it any complaint or problem raised by an employee? The definition of a grievance as found in the thousands of labor agreements has numerous variations. Typical of a broad and loosely worded provision is the following: "Any dispute, disagreement or difference arising between any employee or the union and the company may be presented as a grievance."

Such a clause is generally sought by the labor union since few unions regard the contractual definition, irrespective of its verbiage, as a prohibition or limitation to the union's legitimate presentation of any employee complaint. Typically, shop steward's manuals instruct the steward to obtain the answers to two questions in making his judgment as to whether an employee has a bona fide grievance. These typical questions are: 1 has the contract been violated? And 2 has the company treated the employee unfairly?

In the union's view, if the employee's complaint can fall within the purview of either of these conditions, it is a matter that should be processed as a grievance.

As representatives of an institution dedicated to employee representation, most shop stewards feel a compulsion to press any claim made by a member employee. As adversary representatives of their special interest group, they also feel an obligation to obtain every possible extension and expansion of the benefits and privileges already provided under the labor agreement. Granted, only cases meeting the criteria of question 1 will customarily be processed into arbitration if unresolved. But those disputes falling under question 2 also will often be pursued by the union on behalf of the employee. And once filed, such cases must be discussed and reviewed between the parties just as fully and thoroughly as a bona fide complaint dealing with a contract violation.

Modern and experienced industrial relations managers have come to agree that it is in the best interests of the company to have a narrower and more restrictive grievance definition. *Therefore, unless the union's grievance involves the interpretation, application, or meaning of a particular contractual provision, it should not be considered a valid grievance.* Basically, this approach is taken to prevent union attempts to further encroach on the managerial function. It is also taken to resist union efforts to obtain through the channels of the grievance machinery what they failed to attempt or failed to obtain at the bargaining table.

This view embraces the concept that the labor agreement represents a compromise arrived at between the parties. It springs from the management theory that the labor agreement is the only expression of those rights, privileges, and benefits to which the union and the employees are entitled as a matter of contractual relationship—and any additional conditions and benefits to be enjoyed by the union and the employees must be achieved only through the formal process of collective bargaining, not through the grievance machinery during the life of the contract.

Obviously, such a narrow grievance definition should not be employed by a manager as a shield to prevent him from exploring and resolving employee complaints that are *not* grievances as defined in the contract. The foreman must still view each employee problem with an understanding of the principles of human relations and thereby treat each instance of worker discontent as a serious matter. Although a trivial matter, such as a complaint over the malfunction of a coin-operated vending machine and other like problems, may not constitute a grievance, for the sake of continuing good employee relations the foreman should nevertheless treat such complaints as significant and effect a prompt solution.

What is not a grievance? *Presuming that the labor agreement does not provide otherwise*, the following matters are typical of those usually deemed to be within the exclusive province of management, and, therefore, not appropriate subjects for a valid grievance:

- location of plants
- selection and hiring of workforce
- size of workforce
- selection and control of supervisors
- maintenance of discipline
- establishment and elimination of jobs
- internal organization of plant
- type of product to be manufactured
- control of the methods of operation
- control of the quality requirements
- price setting
- sales practices and advertising
- control and protection of plant properties

Management generally adheres strongly to the proposition that "residual" powers rest with the company. Therefore, the foreman should always assume the position that he does not need to look into the collective bargaining agreement to determine what rights management has reserved for itself, but should look to the agreement only to establish what rights it has ceded to the employees and union. The best method for getting the union into the idea of assuming the burden of establishing its case is to insist upon answers to two questions relative to any processed grievance: (1) *What* provision is allegedly violated? And (2) *how* did the company violate this provision? Requiring the union to answer these questions has the following distinct advantages:

- It tends to contain the argument within the terms and provisions of the labor agreement.
- It keeps the discussion or meeting more disciplined and businesslike.
- If the union is unable to produce sound argument as to *what* or *how*, it may discourage further appeals. It may reveal to the union the weakness and shortcomings of its case and cause it to think twice about processing the case further.
- In arbitration, it enables the company to point out inconsistencies, if any, in union arguments. When arguing "*what* provision is allegedly violated" the union may first select a given contract clause in support of their contentions only to abandon it later in favor of another when the first takes them down a fruitless path. The change of argument may result in inconsistent or contradictory positions.

The same contradictions may result from the union's changed position on "How did the company violate this provision?" Such incompatible or incongruous positions may sometimes prove damaging to the union's case when the matter is fully explored before an arbitrator.

Remember the Union Is the Moving Party

Assuming the manager has no prior knowledge of a management violation of the contract when approached by the union steward, he should conduct himself as though he is innocent until proven guilty. In other words, it is incumbent upon the union to establish that a contract violation has occurred through its factual presentation of information and evidence. *On all but discipline cases, the union is the moving party,* the one asserting a claim, and it should make at least a preliminary or introductory presentation. The supervisor can fully explore the union's thinking on the issue, determining its position, its arguments, its logic, its case. In conducting this discussion, the foreman must be careful not to let the union put him on the defensive. As mentioned earlier, a typical union technique in arguing a case with the manager is to demand that he point to the particular contractual provision that gave him the right to take the action he did. This is putting the shoe on the wrong foot. The fact of the matter is, it is incumbent upon the union to identify some contractual provision that prohibits, restricts, or limits management's right to take the action. The supervisor's entire conduct must be motivated by the philosophy that management has all rights it possessed prior to the recognition of the union and the existence of the labor agreement and that the right to manage is restricted only to the extent that this is expressed in a provision of the labor agreement. Typical of the great majority of arbitrators on this point is the following view: "It is now a well established generalization that every employer continues to have all powers previously had or exercised by employers unless such powers have been curtailed or eliminated by statute or by contract with a Union...."[1]

If the union claims a violation, expect it to establish the fact by a clear presentation of the evidence. *If the matter isn't covered by the contractual agreement, then it shouldn't be treated as a legitimate grievance.* Regarding this approach, it is desirable to distinguish the substantive burden of proof from the procedural burden of going forward with evidence. The substantive burden of proof—whether in a court of law, or in an arbitration proceeding, or in a grievance processing—rests with the complaining party. The substantive burden of proof never shifts from one party to another. It may be defined as the burden on the complaining party to prove by a preponderance of the evidence the truth of his contentions.

The supervisor, as the responding party, merely defends by denying the affirmative allegations of the complainant union, which must assume the burden of proof. But when the supervisor's defense is to admit all of the essential allegations of the union and to assert affirmatively that his action is justified for some other reason, then the supervisor has used an affirmative defense and therefore must assume the substantive burden of proving the facts to sustain that defense.[2]

In discipline or discharge cases, it has been generally held that the substantive burden of proof is on the company to show that its action was for just and proper cause.

In an arbitration proceeding, the party with the substantive burden of proof, and this is usually the union, has initially the burden of presenting the evidence. If the complaining party establishes what is called a prima facie case, then the company must rebut that evidence. A prima facie case may be defined as support of the complainant's contentions by evidence that, if believed, would sustain these contentions. *In an arbitration proceeding, if the union has the substantive burden of proof, it must establish a prima facie case in order to transfer the burden to the company.*[3]

Determine If There Were Any Witnesses

If the dispute involves disciplinary action or a case of questionable facts and information, the matter should be discussed with other employees, hourly and salaried, who may have been eyewitnesses to the incident. It is advisable to interview them and get their views of the matter. In so doing, the motivation will primarily be to establish the company's innocence or the employee's guilt. But such investigation may also lead to discoveries of serious infirmities and contradictions in his own case, thus enabling him to reconsider his position before the matter is pressed further.

Most labor agreements provide that necessary witnesses may be called into grievance meetings to contribute facts and evidence that may further the understandings of the parties and permit better solutions. Typical of such clauses is this one: "Grievants and necessary witnesses may be called into Grievance meetings to introduce facts or evidence which may lead to a resolution of the Grievance." Of course the utilization of witnesses, particularly those who come from jobs manned in the bargaining unit, must be accomplished in a manner that does not interrupt or disrupt production operations. This is not to say that there should be unreasonable delays in grievance processing, but a common-sense approach can accomplish the dual purpose of accommodating both production and grievance commitments.[4]

In most cases a key witness in any grievance proceeding is the grievant himself, particularly if the individual has been the subject of management-imposed disciplinary action.[5]

Examine the Relevant Contract Provisions

If the contract language is clear and explicit, it may permit only one position. Typically, however, contract clauses are the product of draftsmen of varying skills, and, as a result, it is not uncommon to find ambiguous or unclear clauses. Hence, they may be susceptible to more than one interpretation, pointing in several directions, any one of which could be persuasively argued. Frequently, the clause in dispute has widespread application in many departments of the plant and may even have been administered in a different way from one plant section to another. It is even possible for the same contractual provision to be applied and administered differently within the same work department by the various shift foremen. If so, the advocate must establish how that provision has generally been interpreted by the parties. How has the company administered it? What is the thinking of the labor relations department? Perhaps the advocate did not negotiate the contract nor did he share in drafting its provisions. But in this situation, onto his shoulders falls the burden for interpreting properly the ambiguous product of someone else's negotiation efforts. He is in no position to gamble, hoping he has correctly interpreted and administered the provision in accordance with the true intent of the parties. He must seek counsel before answering in this case.

Determine If the Company Has Been Consistent

Any doubts about the meaning of contractual provisions should be resolved in favor of further investigation. Supervisors on other shifts in the grievant's work department can be interviewed to determine if they have administered the agreement in a similar manner. If they have not, were they consistent in their particular administration of the provision each time it has come into play? At one time or another almost every dispute, at least in principle or substance, has been raised before. How was the situation handled on these prior occasions? Has the company been consistent in its repeated applications of the provision? Are there any inconsistencies in the company's practices? If so, are they contradictory to the position taken by management in the current case? All of these questions arise when contract provisions are vague and unclear, and the advocate must obtain the answers before he can safely proceed.

Examine the Total Agreement and Make Interpretations Based on the Whole

The contract provision the union alleges was violated may or may not be relevant to the dispute. This does not mean that a contract violation has not occurred, nor does it mean that the grievance should be denied because of the union's erroneous selection of a contract clause. Although the clause cited may not have specific application, conceivably an examination of the agreement may reveal other contractual provisions that are pertinent.

It is a well-established rule of law, frequently invoked by industrial arbitrators, that a collective bargaining agreement, like any other written instrument, must be construed as a whole. Single words, sentences, or sections cannot be isolated from the context in which they appear and interpreted independently of the apparent purpose and understanding of the parties as evidenced by the entire instrument.[6]

In deciding on the proper contractual interpretation, the advocate should be mindful of such recognized canons of contract construction. These principles are supported by ample authority. In this connection, one arbitrator has remarked:

> It is a cardinal rule of contract interpretation that Agreement must be so construed as to give effect to all of its provisions. An arbitrator is not justified in reading a portion of the contract provisions out of the Agreement where it is possible to give effect to each provision therein included. There is also the well settled rule of construction that the "specific" provision and the specific provision must be given effect in the interpretation of the Contract.[7]

In their excellent book *How Arbitration Works*, Elkouri and Elkouri stated: "If an arbitrator finds that alternative interpretations of a clause are possible, one of which would give meaning and effect to another provision of the Contract, while the other would render the other provision meaningless or ineffective, he will be inclined to use the interpretation which would give effect to all provisions."[8]

The interpretation of any particular clause, if properly made, will reflect consideration of these rules. Avoided should be conclusions that adopt an inequitable construction of the agreement and result in an unwarranted general restriction upon the company's managerial discretions. His conclusions should not run counter to the principles of reasonableness and equity—two fundamental prerequisites to constructive labor relations. If examination of the entire agreement reveals that management's action violates other contractual provisions, the company should readily admit the error. On the other hand, the contract may be entirely silent on the disputed matter, bringing to the forefront management's position on residual rights. However, a silent contract does not necessarily dictate that such matters are automatically resolved in the company's favor. Contract language may cover a matter generally but fail to cover all of its aspects—that is, gaps sometimes exist. Or the matter may actually not be covered in any fashion by any contract clause. In such an instance, custom and past practice may constitute a significant factor in the dispute. It has been recognized that fixed and established practice may give meaning to vague and ambiguous contract clauses and put meat on the bones of the contract skeleton.

In the presence of unclear and ambiguous contract provisions, or in the fact of a silent agreement not covering the matter, the investigation should concern itself with determining the extent and the nature of past practices still in force. In determining if a practice in fact exists, the advocate must determine if it is *fixed* and *established.* In other words, has the practice been known to both parties and relied upon before in similar instances? How long has the practice existed, and has it extended over the term of more than one labor agreement? Are there any inconsistencies, contradictions, or deviations from the practice? Was it instituted unilaterally or bilaterally?

The advocate must realize that practices are not established by the employees, nor are they established by the union. Practices come into existence and continue from one application of the practice to another *by action or inaction of management.* Practice develops as a result of the foreman making decisions and taking actions as a member of the management team. Or, they develop as the result of the supervisor's acquiescence to union and employee conduct and behavior. Any such practices harmful to the company's interests, whether discovered during grievance administration or by other means, should be immediately reported and discussed with management's labor relations representatives.

Examine the Contract Negotiation Record

Whenever the question arises about whether language changes have occurred or whether prior discussions have taken place where a change of intent was agreed upon, the advocate must turn to the negotiation records or to participating individuals to fill in this void. His research will pursue the following:

- Is there a *new* or *changed* contract provision on the grieved matter?
- If a new provision exists, which party proposed the language and what were the reasons for seeking the change? In this regard, which party's language was eventually adopted?
- If the contractual provision has been *changed* from what appeared

in the prior contract, who proposed the change and what were the reasons? In this regard, which party's proposal was finally adopted?

- Were minutes of the negotiation meetings kept, and what do those minutes reveal regarding the discussions between the parties on the provision in dispute, irrespective of whether it is a new, a changed, or an unchanged clause?
- Who represented management in these negotiations and was present during discussions on the relevant provisions? Is that individual available and able to supply credible accounts of what the parties intended?
- Did the union attempt to insert language in the contract to cover an uncovered subject—but fail to accomplish it?[9]

Of course, subcontracting is not the only provocative issue for which arbitrators refer to prior bargaining talks to gain an inkling about a particular contract interpretation. Arbitrator Paul Prasow found himself in somewhat this type of situation in a case between Hitco and the Glass Bottle Blowers Association:

> It was recognized during negotiations that there would be differences in the qualifications and availability of employees, and the impossibility of absolutely equalizing overtime. Another subject of considerable discussion was the obligation of the Company to train employees. *The Union made a series of demands requiring the Company to train employees in connection with seniority, layoffs, and promotions. At all times the Company rejected such union demands and the Contract contains no provision in any section where there is any obligation to train employees* in connection with seniority, layoffs, promotions, or overtime distribution.[10]

Using this conclusion in conjunction with other imagined problems, I would like the manager to assume that this same negotiation history has preceded his receipt of a union grievance claiming that the company should have trained an employee and used him, instead of another, in an overtime assignment, or retained him in employment and laid off another employee. As pointed out earlier, it is not uncommon for the union to attempt to obtain through the grievance procedure what it attempted but failed to obtain in collective bargaining. The grievance just described is typical of such situations. Clearly, in such a case, the prior bargaining history is an essential missile in the supervisor's arsenal if he is to defend management's position that it justifiably did not, and was not required to, train employees in such instances.[11]

Thus, for the advocate to take the proper position in any dispute, he should inquire into, and be fully apprised of, the relevancy of prior bargaining discussions to current grievance matters.

Bear Burden of Proof in Discipline and Discharge Cages

The basic principles of industrial discipline that are accepted and respected dictate that management must run its plant efficiently if it is to remain competitive, and its supervisors must have the authority to eliminate the unfit from the workforce. On the other hand, and this is equally important, there are limitations on management's right to discipline under the "just cause" provisions of a collective agreement. The company's basic rights are not limited by this provision, but the principal difference between the old days, when the company could discharge by whim, and today is that collective bargaining constitutes a private system of law where the individual worker receives many of the traditional safeguards of the public court system with respect to his job.

The grievance procedure accepted by both parties guarantees to the worker the right to be confronted by his accuser, to be represented, and to be assured in the final decision that the punishment is consistent with the offense. If it is not, the grievance procedure guarantees his return to his job.

It is rather clear that the usual terms of a labor agreement impose upon the company the burden of justifying its right to discharge the particular employee against whom its action has been taken. If the company produced no evidence whatsoever, an arbitrator would have no choice but to reinstate the discharged employee with back pay.

The company should proceed "first" in discipline and discharge cases, since the party that holds the affirmative of the issue must produce the evidence to prove it; therefore, the burden of proof rests with the party who would be defeated if no evidence were given on the other side. This is so although the union, by virtue of filing the grievance that initiates the formal dispute, technically occupies the position comparable to a plaintiff in a judicial proceeding.

Therefore, in a discharge case, the burden of proof is generally on the company to establish that the grounds for discharge were valid and sufficient. By the same token, when a union alleges discrimination as the real motivation for discharge, the union has the burden of proving its charge. This must be so since the mere assertion that discrimination was the real motivation for the discharge does not establish it as such. The party who makes such an allegation must support this belief with specific, concrete evidence. The employee or the union must be prepared to state the basis for his belief and to support it, not by repeated or positive assertion, but by specific and understandable evidence that relates directly to such an allegation as well as to the circumstances surrounding the entire incident. Without such testimony and evidence in the record, an arbitrator is unable to evaluate the situation to determine whether the union's interpretation of the matter is the correct one.

The decision in a discharge case usually involves consideration of the quantum of proof required to sustain a discharge based upon the managerial right set forth in a collective bargaining agreement to discharge for "just cause."[12]

It is often said, sometimes uncritically, that discharge is the economic equivalent of capital punishment. Yet it is clear that in an area where there is a shortage of the particular skills possessed by the discharged employee, competitive labor conditions may largely redress the injustice (aside from seniority) of a mistaken or unjust discharge. Perhaps in such a case the application by an arbitrator of either the "clear and convincing" or the "reasonable apprehension" standards of proof would protect the rights of the grievant. But where the labor situation means an employee is not readily employable elsewhere, or where discharge is based upon an allegation involving moral turpitude that, if upheld, will blackball the discharged employee elsewhere, a rigorous standard of proof seems applicable. The consequences are then so drastic as indeed to be tantamount to economic capital punishment. In the context of a moral turpitude discharge, therefore, protection of an innocent employee against the injustice of industrial blackballing and social ostracism demands the most careful and exacting scrutiny to assure that the facts alleged as the basis for the discharge actually exist. That kind of scrutiny is embodied by the community in its criminal law under a standard so phrased to require that guilt be demonstrated beyond any reasonable doubt.

Therefore, in handling discipline and discharge grievances, the advocate should recognize his obligation to assume the burden of proving the company action as necessary and proper. All of this is not so much a shift in philosophy toward sympathy for the worker as much as it is merely an extension of scientific management to industrial relations. A company in its operational decisions is impersonal and objective; it carefully weighs decisions to be sure they are justified by the principles involved and the facts. Today the personnel and industrial relations function must be accorded the same intellectual emphasis. These are the facts of modern industrial life.[13]

Don't Treat as Arbitrable Claims Demanding Discipline or Discharge of Management Members

Occasionally, the conduct or alleged misconduct of a management representative will provoke a grievance demanding his discipline or his ouster. And sometimes a supervisor's attitude and demeanor may leave much to be desired by both the employees and management. This topic does not presume the eternal innocence of all management people thus charged, nor does it presume to sanction or condone behavior or remarks by such individuals that exceed the boundaries of reasonable and proper plant conduct. *It does presume that management should and will take the necessary and adequate steps, within its own organization, to censure and correct any instances of supervisory misconduct.* What this does deal with is the treatment to be accorded by management to grievances demanding the discipline or discharge of such supervisors who are charged with misconduct.

It is recommended that the company treat such grievances as nonarbitrable from the moment they are received. In the overwhelming majority of such cases put before an arbitrator and contested by management regarding their arbitrability, the arbitrator has most often ruled against the union *unless* the parties have agreed by contract or by submission agreement that the arbitrator has jurisdiction to decide the grievances on their merits.[14]

Less common, but not unheard of, is the grievance demanding the discipline or discharge of another member of the unionized bargaining unit. Arbitrator B. M. Selekman, in dealing with a case involving a foreman accused of name-calling, insults, and vilification of employees, touched on this second point in his ruling:

> In rendering judgment, I feel a distinction must be drawn between the alleged wrong against which this grievance is directed and the remedy and relief sought to redress it.... Nothing in this Agreement ... makes this remedy of discharge available to the Union. It is not only that foremen are expressly excluded from the coverage of all contract provisions; it is not only that the Union is barred from intervention into anything involving the status and tenure of supervisory personnel or the relations generally between top management and shop foremen. The barrier is even more rigorous than these restrictions would imply. The Union under the contract *cannot* demand the disciplinary discharge *even of a production employee.*[15]

Therefore, any such grievances received by management that demand as their relief or remedy the discipline or discharge of a management member or a fellow unit member should be answered along these lines: "Under the contract the Union cannot demand the discipline or discharge of a management (unit) member. This is not a valid subject for grievance redress. The grievance is not arbitrable. On this basis the grievance is denied."

Provide the Grievance Process to Nonunion Members

The majority of today's labor agreements contain elaborate provisions for union security, with the most prevalent clause being a "union shop" arrangement. Under such a clause, all employees must obtain and maintain membership in the union as a condition of continued employment. Presuming the agreement contains instead a type of union security clause allowing employees the option of joining or refraining from joining the union, some employees may choose the latter. However, irrespective of the union's preference in such a case, it has an obligation to represent *all* employees in the bargaining unit for the purpose of collective bargaining over wages, hours and other terms and conditions of employment—whether the employees are members of the union or not. Despite such a legal requirement, typically the union may give discriminatory representation, particularly regarding those employees who are hard-core holdouts.

The courts have held that unions must be accorded broad discretion in handling individual grievances.[16] But they are not entitled to absolute immunity. They do owe a duty of fair representation.[17] And a union can become liable in damages for breaching this duty.[18]

The duties owed by unions to employees in handling grievances are more fully examined by Hauslowe in "Individual Rights in Collective Labor Relations":

> It is arguable that, whatever the needs for flexibility and wide discretion in the negotiation of new or modification of existing collective contracts, no such flexibility is either needed or appropriate when rights under a contract are involved. The standards for judgment in this area have been less than perfectly formulated. In general terms they are frequently stated as follows: the Union's conduct must not be willful, arbitrary, capricious or discriminatory. The Union must not have declined to press the grievance out of laziness or prejudice, or out of unwillingness to expend money on behalf of non-members. Its decisions with respect to individual grievances must have been honest and reasonable.
>
> The rejection of a grievance by the Union must have been on the merits, in the exercise of honest discretion and/or sound judgment, following a complete and fair investigation. The rejection must not have been unjust in any respect. There must not have been bad faith or fraud. The bargaining agent must not have acted in a negligent manner.[19]

In any event, the company's approach to the handling and resolution of grievances involving nonmember employees whose claims may be mishandled by the union should be no different than that accorded the member employee. It should still use the labor agreement as the *only* basis for judging the issue and applying any remedy. Presuming the union's steward refrains from providing a full and fair representation to the nonmember grievant, the manager should proceed, advising the steward subsequently of the manner in which he handled the matter.

In handling the grievances of nonmembers, the manager should be aware of two particular provisions of the National Labor Relations Act with regard to the rights of employees. In Section 7 of the Act:

> Employees shall have the right to self-organization, to form, join or assist labor organizations, to bargain collectively through representatives of their own choosing, and to engage in other concerted activities for the purpose of collective bargaining or other mutual aid or protection, *and shall also have the right to refrain from any or all of such activities except to the extent that such right may be affected by an agreement requiring membership in a labor organization as a condition of employment* as authorized in Section 8(a)(3) [emphasis added].

The second provision of the Act that comes into play most often under this type of union security clause is Section 9(a):

> Representatives designated or selected for the purposes of collective bargaining by the majority of the employees in a unit appropriate for such purposes, shall be the exclusive representatives for all employees in such unit for the purposes of collective bargaining in respect to rates of pay, wages, hours of employment, or other conditions of employment: provided, *that any individual employee or a group of employees shall have the right at any time to present grievances to their employer and to have such grievances adjusted, without the intervention of the bargaining representative, as long as the adjustment is not inconsistent with the terms of a collective bargaining contract* or agreement then in effect: provided further, that the bargaining representative has been given opportunity to be present at such adjustment.

The grievance process must be afforded to nonmembers as well as union members and on the same terms and conditions. Any grievance should be viewed in the light of the basic standards established by the terms of the contract between the company and the union. All grievances, including those from nonmembers, must be limited to problems within the scope of this standard. Any relief or remedy applied must not violate or undermine this basic standard.

Under the management right clause, the company has retained the right to manage and direct the working forces. In so doing, its representatives must necessarily converse and discuss with employees, issue them instructions and orders, ask them questions, give them information. It may not "bargain" with them individually regarding their wages, hours, working conditions, and so on. It may not endeavor to enter into individual "agreements" with them covering such subjects.

Satisfy the Union's Right to Relevant Information

Since 1956, the courts and the National Labor Relations Board have effected extensions of earlier rulings in this "informational" area of the Act, which in substance require that the employer supply such economic data and information in a manner "sufficient to enable the union to bargain intelligently." Such material is further intended to enable the union to understand and discuss issues raised by an employer that are in opposition to union demands and *enable it to administer the contract.*[20] Concepts such as these have continued to be applicable through later affirmations in the courts and by the board.[21] As these concepts have evolved over the years, it has been determined that this "employer duty" is not necessarily restricted only to a period of contract negotiations between the parties. *Such "duty" has been construed to also continue beyond the "negotiation" period into the "administrative" life of the agreement.* This concept is intended to allow the union to administer its agreement more intelligently and effectively. The board has, almost invariably, ruled that "8(a) (5) [of the Act] imposes an obligation to furnish *all information relevant to the bargaining representative's intelligent performance of its function.* This obligation extends to information which the union may require in order to police and administer existing agreements."[22] *For the employer to offer the desired and requested information at arbitration—but withhold it beforehand—does not satisfy its "duty."* The board has said, "It is no answer to a request for information to state that the information will be forthcoming in the course of an arbitration proceeding. To sustain this would put the employer in the position to force the union to arbitration [and the expense connected] even in those instances where had the union had the information, it would have determined that the grievances were without merit."[23]

During the "administrative" periods of the contract, the most prevalent union request for information is in the area of time studies. In this connection, the board has held that not only are time studies required to be furnished to the union for its bargaining purposes but also the employer must permit the union to have access to the plant to enable it to make its own time studies of the disputed operations in pending grievances.[24]

However, such decisions do appear to require that the information sought by the union should be relevant to its task as a bargaining agent either in negotiating the contract or adjusting a grievance properly falling within the contract's purview. In a case involving Hercules Motor Corp.,[25] the union filed a grievance regarding the fairness of certain incentive-standard rates. The union asked to examine the employer's data that related to the disputed operations and also requested an opportunity to make its own time study. These requests were refused by the company on the grounds that the agreement did not give the union the right to grieve over the fairness of rates. The employer did indicate to the union that if this matter were found to be grievable by an arbitrator, it would then supply the requested information. The union chose to file 8(a) (5) charges with the NLRB; however, the board finally held that there was an issue of contract interpretation and, therefore, the case was not properly before the board. In this instance, the NLRB decided that this was not the simple case of a union seeking, and being denied, information pertinent and relevant to its role as a bargaining agent. Instead, in this instance the union was seeking information to support a grievance dealing with a matter which the company (perhaps properly) contended could not be the valid subject matter for a grievance.

It may also be held that the employer need *not* furnish information that the union can reasonably obtain from other convenient sources or from information it may already have.[26]

In cases involving charges of violation of the National Labor Relations Act, it has been held, even in cases where there was no contract provision to aid the union, that

- An employer is required to furnish a union on request with sufficient data on wages and allied matters.[27]
- This requirement includes original data on time studies.[28]
- The data must be furnished for the processing of grievances as well as for general collective bargaining.[29]
- As to relevancy, it is sufficient if the information sought is "related" to the issue.[30]
- Such data must be supplied even though the employer considers it confidential.[31]

Whether these cases illuminate this clouded area of labor-management relations is doubtful. What they may do, however, is to alert management to the danger inherent in arbitrary refusals of information requested by the union. *Perhaps the safest general rule of thumb is for management to consider carefully any request for data actually needed by the union to understand, prepare, or present facts and positions on any dispute covered by the agreement.* And if the request is reasonable and proper, management should grant it to the appropriate extent.

Don't Overlook the Precedent Value of Prior Grievance Settlements

Most members of management would like to make a distinction between "collective bargaining" and the "settlement and adjustment of grievances." Presumably, the former is the negotiation and establishment of the terms and conditions that govern the relationship between the parties, while the latter is merely the settlement of disputes, within the confines of those terms, which arise during the fixed period of the contract. Unfortunately, but understandably, that is rarely the case. In the vast majority of instances, the contract is somewhat widened and broadened during its life by the day-to-day negotiations occurring in the name of grievance adjudication. As each party resorts to whatever power it can apply to compel and particular settlement, the contract takes on new shape.

What shape it takes is usually determined by where the balance of power rested in the majority of settlements. The result is a contract more agreeable to the one party and less desirable to the other than was the case when it was initially signed. As mentioned earlier, the objective typical of most unions is to expand the original agreement through grievance settlements during its term by obtaining what they failed to attempt or secure during formal negotiations. The objective typical of most managements is not to surrender anything more during the contract term than they had found necessary to concede during the negotiations. Some cavalier managements even attempt to recover and recapture during a contract's term some of what they had presumably surrendered to the union during collective bargaining.

However, in the context intended here, it is assumed that (1) the company has engaged in good-faith bargaining in the development of the agreement, (2) it considers the agreement as fully embodying all of the agreements and understandings and terms that are to govern the parties during its fixed period, (3) it views the union and the employees as entitled to the full measure of the provisions of the agreement, and (4) it wants its supervisors to resolve grievances in good faith and in full accord with the terms and conditions of the contract but without making settlements that add to or subtract from its terms and do not further limit, restrict, prohibit, curtail, or compromise management's future ability to initiate action.

But, irrespective of the particular philosophy followed, one thing is certain—each time a grievance is settled between the parties it has some influence on that labor agreement. Either the grievance is resolved in absolute accord with that agreement under language which is clear and unequivocal; or the settlement provides clearer meaning to otherwise vague or ambiguous contract terms but is still in accord with the true intent of both parties; or the settlement in some manner and to some degree either adds to or subtracts from the agreement as it was originally intended by the parties. In any case, each grievance settlement builds a body of common law that surrounds the agreement and the relationship between the parties. And, as each grievance is resolved, the body of law surrounding that settled issue becomes firmer and stronger, and the precedent value of the parties' positions on that issue becomes more persuasive regarding other similar or same issues. Such settled issues can supply a great reservoir of tested experience that may prove invaluable to the advocate in choosing a direction to take. The importance given prior grievance settlements in the event of an arbitration hearing will probably turn on the degree of similarity of the issues in such prior cases.

A flavor of arbitral opinion in this connection may provide further insights. For example, in a case involving the Tennessee Coal, Iron and Railroad Company, the employer challenged the right of the union to file a grievance on the basis that it constituted an effort to open once again an issue that had already been decided between the parties. The arbitrator in the dispute first defined a "grievance" in this case as referring only to a particular complaint, and the "issue" as having reference only to the contractual question raised. He then gave his position in the following statement:

> (1) A grievance which has been settled in grievance meetings or in arbitration or which has not been appropriately appealed if the proposed settlement has not been accepted, remains settled. This grievance cannot be reinstituted. (2) An issue that is settled by the parties in grievance meetings remains settled. Such a settlement, if accepted by both parties, is equivalent to a separate, local agreement. (3) Either party may bring an issue to this Board (by the appropriate procedure) even though the party has not appealed the decision on a grievance incorporating the issue. (4) A grievance even though generally similar to a grievance which has been settled may be processed if it raises an issue which is in any way different from an issue that has been settled. (5) An issue which has been ruled on by an umpire prior to the constitution of this Board remains settled unless the ruling is in conflict with the ruling of other umpires entrusted with the same issue. In such a situation, either party is entitled to a ruling from this Board (by following the procedure prescribed in the Agreement) which will dissipate the conflicting arbitration decisions. Further, if the ruling by the umpire is not clear, either party is privileged to process a grievance to this Board so as to secure a clear ruling on the issue. Also, if the ruling of the umpire on an issue appears not to be in line with the rulings of this Board, a grievance dealing with that issue may be processed to this Board. Rulings by this Board on issues have precedence over the rulings made by other umpires. Issues ruled on by this Board shall remain settled and no grievance clearly confined to such issues may be processed to this Board.[32]

In this particular case, the grievance before the arbitrator was denied on the basis that the issue involved had been ruled on before.

It should be a generally recognized principle that the interpretation of contract language embodied in grievance settlements becomes a part of contract language. *As a matter of industrial reality, settled issues should be viewed as having "precedent" value until the parties change the labor agreement.* A central purpose of the grievance machinery is to terminate controversies so that the parties may know where they stand. The only way to achieve this end is to award some weight and influence to settled disputes. When a prior grievance decision involves the interpretation of the identical contract provision based on similar or closely related facts between the same company and the same union, every principle of common sense, policy, and labor relations demands that it should stand until the parties alter or annul it by a newly worded contractual provision.

Withholding Grievance Information

The matter here is not so much the legal requirement to furnish certain information to the union but the good-faith obligation as contemplated by the labor agreement. Much has been written on this "information" area of the National Labor Relations Act, to the effect that the duty of the employer to furnish such economic data and information must be furnished in a manner "sufficient to enable the union to bargain intelligently," to understand and discuss issues raised by the employer in opposition to union demands, and to administer its contract.[33] Such concepts continue to be an effective rule of law by reason of later affirmations by the National Labor Relations Board and the courts.[34]

Such decisions as referred to herein have also deemed that such a "duty" is not always limited to the time when the parties are engaged in collective bargaining *but extends also into the term of the agreement to enable the union to administer that agreement intelligently.*

The fact that laws governing these issues are on the record does not necessarily dictate that such questions shall be decided by the NLRB or the courts. *Actually, the great majority of disputes involving issues of this type are not decided in those forums but are ruled upon in arbitration hearings.* The concern here is not worry over compliance with legal requirements but that of meeting one's contract obligations in a good-faith and contractually proper labor relations fashion.[35]

In this next grievance, the company refused to give the union certain information from the company's records during the processing of grievances protesting the promotion of a junior employee. From the outset, the company argued that the grievances were untimely filed and refused to explore the merits of the dispute. It placed all of its eggs in the "timeliness" basket, protesting to the arbitrator that due to the procedural defects of the grievance, he should rule that the grievance was not arbitrable on its merits and thereby be precluded from determining the propriety or impropriety of the company's promotion of the employee it selected. The final outcome was a ruling that the grievance was untimely filed thus barring consideration of it on its merits, but the arbitrator did make some remarks relevant to the question of the company's obligation to supply its promotional records. An examination of these comments is critical to full understanding of the "information" decision.

> On the basis of these fundamental considerations it seems to the Impartial Arbitrator that in a promotion case of this kind where the Company has

> based its entire position on the fact that the grievances were not filed in time, it is not incumbent upon the Company to state its position on the merits if it does not desire to. It is true that when the Company bases its position entirely on the question of the timeliness of the grievances, then it does so at its peril. It cannot later in arbitration argue the merits of the case. It is therefore apparent that when the Company refused to reveal to the Union certain information from the files of the promotion board it did not violate any of the cited sections, inasmuch as the Company was resting its case on the question of the timeliness of the grievance.
>
> In view of this finding, it would be unnecessary for the Impartial Arbitrator to rule on whether or not the contract requires the Company to make certain promotion board data available to the Union. However, in view of the importance of this question, and in view of the comprehensiveness with which the parties argued this matter in their briefs, the Impartial Arbitrator believes it desirable to rule on this question at this time. It should be noted that there is no specific contract obligation on the part of the Company to reveal any information regarding the proceedings of the promotion board to the Union.
>
> Conversely, good faith requires the Company, in the processing of a promotion grievance, to set forth the basis of its action in promoting a certain employee. In the opinion of the Impartial Arbitrator, the Company can meet this obligation in various ways. It is not essential that the Company reveal information from the files of the promotion board if in its opinion its relations with its employees or the integrity of its promotion procedure are endangered. However, where it does not choose to reveal such information, it cannot rely on this information in its defense in the arbitration proceeding. It would be manifestly unfair for the Company to deny the Union information in the grievance procedure and then attempt to make it available to the Impartial Arbitrator without the Union having an opportunity to adequately investigate and rebut this information. It follows from the above reasoning that the Company must make its choice. If it desires to rely on the promotion board records in any way in arbitration, in the event there is arbitration, then it must submit that information to the Union during the processing of the grievance.[36]

Although the line drawn in this case may be a fine one, it is nevertheless clear and understandable. In essence, the arbitrator has said that the company took a calculated risk by placing sole and complete reliance on its procedural arguments. For if the arbitrator had found the grievance to be without time-limit defects and had proceeded into an examination of the matter on its merits, the company would have been in an awkward position indeed. Conceivably, the arbitrator would have foreclosed the company from introducing any information or evidence into the arbitration record that was refused the union. This just goes again to highlight one of the dangers inherent in a refusal by management to supply relevant and meaningful information on a grievance to the union.[37]

Maintain Records

This has been covered elsewhere, but because it is essential, I will repeat myself: The maintenance of records of all types and in a variety of forms is one of the essential requirements leading to successful labor relations for management. A company can be assured that a knowledgeable and sophisticated labor organization will be maintaining a wide variety of records to enable it to police the agreement, to insure that management's actions are consistent and in accord with the contract, and to support and defend its position in any dispute it may face with the employer. It will maintain such records as seniority lists, overtime rosters, wage rate changes of employees, layoff and recall rosters, employee transfers, changes in employees' job classifications, grievance settlements, arbitration awards, and a host of others. It is at least as important that management does so also. For unless it does, it is clear that it will be at the mercy of the union if the union is the sole record keeper. Naturally, the types of records maintained by the company will be very much like those kept by the union. In this category are a number of records each manager should maintain that relate to his particular operating department. Numbered among these are the obvious ones of overtime lists, seniority rosters, absenteeism records, and the like. Of equal importance, however, are others he may refer to on only an intermittent basis but which may be of great significance. Among this type we can list copies of any disciplinary letters he may have issued, copies of any written grievances he may have handled and answered, copious notes he may have made pertinent to some dispute or significant labor relations incident, and so on. Although the significance and relevance of maintaining such records may not be instantly apparent and although the passage of time may further seem to diminish their importance and consequence, the absence of them when they are suddenly or unexpectedly needed will immediately make their essential nature obvious.

Arbitrator Harry J. Dworkin rendered the following award. Under this contract, a grievance was processed in April 1954. The union carried this matter through step three of a four-step procedure and was denied by the employer in this third step. The union did not appeal the grievance into step four nor did it appeal the matter to arbitration as the final step of the grievance procedure. Pertinent language of the agreement provided that "the grievance shall be considered settled on the basis of such decision and shall not be eligible for further appeal." This was the contractual disposition of a grievance not appealed to arbitration by the union and, where the union elected not to so appeal, it was deemed settled on the basis of the decision indicated by management. Subsequently, in August 1954, the union instituted another grievance of different phraseology but one which resubmitted the identical issue in another form. After explaining the logic and reasoning behind his award in a comprehensive manner, the arbitrator concluded:

> It is the Arbitrator's holding, under the facts involved in this case, that the election on the part of the Union not to proceed to arbitration with reference to the prior grievance is conclusive of the rights, questions and facts in issue in all other grievances concerning the same and identical subject matter. The final disposition of the previous grievance constitutes a bar to the arbitration of the latter grievance, and is conclusive between the company and the union where it involves the same matter which was dealt with in the former dispute.[38]

Here again is an example of the great value of the maintenance and preservation of records by management: *the company's its presentation to the arbitrator of a prior grievance with all of the accompanying facts and circumstances enabled its contentions to be sustained.*

As mentioned earlier, one of the essential records that must be maintained is that related to the employee's personal conduct and performance. As discussed in an earlier section, the prevalent arbitral view toward the imposition of discipline and penalties for employee wrongdoing turns on a concept of corrective discipline: progressively more severe penalties applied, culminating in a discharge action. Each of such disciplinary actions imposed by the employer should be carefully documented and recorded. Their presentation to an arbitrator to demonstrate the evolving history of the employee's conduct will be a key factor in persuading that arbitrator to uphold management's action. Discipline matters are perhaps the most arbitrated issues between the parties—and the arbitration journals contain the thousands of published and recorded cases of this type.

On this matter of past work record, an employee was discharged for failing to carry out orders to pump ore slurry from one basin into another and falsifying his report thereon to his laboratory. Here again it was determined that this incident in and of itself might not have been sufficient, if taken alone, to justify discharge. But as it was a part of a pattern of unworkmanlike performance, the discharge could be justified. The union objected to the company's introduction of the employee's past work record into the arbitration hearing. The arbitrator's comments in this particular case are particularly worthwhile of consideration:

> While the Company contends that V_____ had not carried out his written orders to pump 3 inches of iron slurry into Basin No. 2 and had falsified his report to the Laboratory, his past work record played a role in his discharge. Mr. McBride, the Plant Superintendent, testified that he discharged the Grievant after receiving the facts of the incident of March 19, 1962, as well as reviewing his past unsatisfactory work record. The attorney for the Union strenuously and ably argued that the past work record of the Grievant

should not be considered but that the Arbitrator should look only to the reasons given on the discharge slip, i.e., "failure to carry out orders and falsifying report to Laboratory."

While all arbitrators have not agreed upon this matter of past work records, some consideration is generally given to the past record of any disciplined or discharged employee. Thus a good past record may result in the mitigation of an offense and a bad past record may aggravate it. An employee's past record may often be an important factor in determination of a proper penalty for an offense. (See Elkouri and Elkouri, *How Arbitration Works*, BNA, rev. ed. 1960, at 428.) Thus the so-called "final incident" may not be sufficient if taken alone to justify discharge, but where it is part of a pattern of unworkmanlike performance, discharge may be justified. (See Phillips Chemical Co. 61–1 ARB para.8181.) Of course, this requires the careful examination of the past work record in order to determine its effect upon the penalty. On pages 10–14, the Company in its Brief gives in detail the past work record of the Grievance, which was buttressed by the testimony of Mr. McBride. Not only are there numerous instances of unworkmanlike conduct of varying degrees of seriousness, but warnings were given to the Grievant and discussions were had with Union representatives concerning his unsatisfactory work record with a request that the Union representatives work with the Grievant to improve his job performance.[39]

A final example of a case perhaps illustrative of the improper authorization of personnel records involved a company that had discharged an employee who was found asleep on the job. In the arbitration hearing, the company presented records of five employees previously discharged for similar offenses, none of which had been protested by the union. Also introduced were the grievant's own personnel records, which showed two prior warnings for suspected sleeping on the job. There were also records offered that he had been absent from work on several occasions and that he had been reprimanded or warned at least three different times for being away from his work place. Although the arbitrator upheld the discharge action, he was critical of the fact that the company had failed to provide offending employees charged with rules violations with copies of the written notices of any reprimands and disciplinary action that the company had entered on their records. In this connection, he remarked as follows:

The use of M_____'s past record as part of the basis for his discharge is another weak part of the Company's case and a very troublesome matter. If these were really secret records there would be more danger in their use than in setting aside a discharge penalty, but, in all conscience, it is not felt that these are the kind of secret records deserving such treatment.

The Company would be on much safer ground if it gave each employee written notice of any reprimands and disciplinary action entered on his record, in addition to making the records available for inspection as they now are.

These are not the kind of secret records used in the arbitration cases cited by the Union. In the Consolidated Vultee Aircraft Corporation case (10 LA 907) there was no evidence that employees were ever invited to inspect the records or had any reliable information about their existence. Only by rumors and word-of-mouth reports did employees learn that records of their misdeeds existed. The issue in the Harshaw Chemical Co. case (32 LA 86) was whether employees were entitled to copies of certain new forms developed by the company. The arbitrator ruled that they were, if the records were to be used as a basis for future disciplinary action because the forms were actually records of reprimands which should be known to the employee. Since the records had not yet been put into use we cannot discover how secret they might have been.

At Purex new employees are supposed to be informed at the time of employment that records are kept of rule infractions on their part. It was more difficult to determine whether, in fact, such information was passed on to new employees, but evidence was quite convincing that it was. Mr. W_____, a Checker Lead man, testified that he knew a reprimand given him had been entered on his record. More significant, Local Union President T_____ stated that in cases where employees are disciplined by Company representatives above the foreman level, they are aware of the entries that go on their record, even though they may not be aware of such entries after a foreman speaks to them. M_____ stated that he knew that the records were kept, and Production Superintendent D_____ stated that during a meeting the M_____ on his past performance entries on his record had been referred to, and, indeed, the entire record was used. That meeting took place about July 1960.

This evidence convinces the Chairman that the records of Purex should not be regarded in the same way as the secret records pictured in the Union's post-hearing brief. Employees not only knew of their existence, they were invited to inspect the records. The Company did not attempt to hold back information about prior disciplinary action in order to spring it on the employee at some future date and surprise him with situations he could not explain. One may—and should—condemn the Company for not issuing written notices of reprimands and discipline, but one should not rule that its records are so secret that they cannot be used to establish an employee's past conduct.[40]

The common thread throughout each of these cases is that in every instance the outcome of the case turned on the introduction of records maintained by the company. *Had these records not been maintained so that they were available for presentation, the outcomes would have been substantially altered—that is, the companies would not have been upheld.* Whether these records are maintained by individual supervisors or in some master location is not usually of great consequence; the essential point is that they be maintained somewhere and by someone in management. However, it is evident that certain records are unique and peculiar to a manager's own departmental operations and, therefore, should be maintained and preserved in that location irrespective of their existence in any other department.

10

Procedures for Selecting the Arbitrator

This is where the arbitration process begins.

A grievance has been processed through the contractual dispute resolution machinery. The parties have met and discussed the issue in the progressive grievance steps stipulated in the contract. The respective levels of management have met with the various officers of the union hierarchy. Viewpoints have been exchanged; arguments have been proffered and, it is hoped, weighed and considered by each party. The bargaining history has been explored; witnesses and principals in the dispute have been heard relevant records examined and pertinent contract language scrutinized and interpreted. But the parties are unable to reach a mutually satisfactory settlement of their disagreement.

The matter is now being moved toward its last step, an arbitration hearing. What happens next?

First of all, let us examine the mechanics – that is, the instrument or means by which the issue is led into the final and binding process.

Contractual Provisions

A review of typical contractual arbitration provisions will illustrate how some parties have made their prearbitration arrangements. For example:

> Arbitration – If the grievance shall not be satisfactorily adjusted through the above steps, the matter may proceed to arbitration, providing the Union notifies the Company of its desire to arbitrate and names its arbitrator within three (3) working days after the date of the regular Union meeting following the Production Manager's reply in Step Three. If the Union fails to notify

> the Company of its desire to arbitrate within the time stated, the grievance shall be considered dropped.
>
> If the grievance is carried to arbitration as set forth above, the Company shall designate its arbitrator within five (5) working days or the grievance shall be considered granted. If the two arbitrators named in the manner set forth above fail to agree on a third arbitrator within fifteen (15) days of the Company's designation either party may request the Director of the Federal Mediation and Conciliation Service to appoint a panel of five (5) impartial, disinterested members. Each party shall have the right to challenge two members of the panel. The remaining member of the panel shall act as the Chairman of the Arbitration Committee. The written decision of the majority of arbitrators shall be final and binding upon both parties. The expenses and compensation incident to the service of the third arbitrator shall be determined in advance and paid jointly by the Company and the Union.[1]

A brief analysis of this provision may provide helpful insights. First, in the initial paragraph, the time period within which the union shall notify the company of its intent to arbitrate appears to be a fluctuating period, dependent upon how close the date of the union's next regularly scheduled meeting is to the third and last grievance step. Further, at one point, the provision requires that the union shall "name its arbitrator" and, at another, that the company shall "designate its arbitrator." Presumably, this sets the structure for functions; the union- and company-appointed "arbitrators" operate as advocates for their respective parties and are certainly not neutral third parties.

In the second paragraph, the language provides for the two appointed arbitrators (union and company advocates) to attempt to mutually agree on an infirmed, neutral third party, a bona fide arbitrator. Failure to agree is anticipated, in which case the selection process is to devolve on the Federal Mediation and Conciliation Service (FMCS). Interestingly, the wording could present potential problems to the parties. It does not appear to be incumbent on a given party to accept the obligation and responsibility of making a request to FMCS. Problems could result if neither party was moved to do so. Problems could result if each argued that it was the obligation of the other. Also, there does not appear to be a stipulated time period within which a party (which one?) is required to forward a panel request to FMCS. Problems could result if such panel requests were long delayed—particularly if one party alleged that the delay of the other was undue and thereby raised a threshold issue of arbitrability, based on the claim of untimeliness of the request, causing alleged procedural defectiveness.

Still another point is that the second paragraph of this provision does not clearly spell out how the parties shall remove names from the FMCS-submitted panel. It merely says that "each party shall have the right to challenge two members of the panel." It does not stipulate that the parties shall alternately, and in turn, remove a name until only one of the initial five remains. It could be inferred that a party could remove any two names it wished, simultaneously. In any case, the contract does not indicate which party shall be first to remove a name or names, before the other party is afforded such opportunity. Nor does it provide a means, such as a coin flip, for determining which party shall scratch the first name or names.

To suggest that any of the foregoing is nit-picking or tilting at windmills is not to face industrial realities. These have been real problems on numerous occasions. The labor arbitration research volumes contain hundreds of cases of this type of dispute—all issues precedent to the actual issue in the case.

One last point before leaving this provision: Its conclusion provides that the parties determine in advance the expenses of the arbitrator, which could be interpreted to mean that he should be paid in advance. Nevertheless, this requirement to determine full arbitral costs prior to a hearing is a rather unusual arrangement and often could be difficult to strictly adhere to.

Let us now look into another contractual provision, one which is more explicit about the movement of grievances into arbitration and toward the selection of an arbitrator.

> Step 4: Arbitration. If no settlement is reached in Step 3 within the specified or agreed time limits, then either party may in writing, within ten working days thereafter request that the matter be submitted to an arbiter for a prompt hearing as hereinafter provided in 19.6 to 19.9 inclusive.
>
> Section 19.6. Selection of Arbiter—By Agreement. In regard to each case reaching Step 4, the parties will attempt to agree on an arbiter to hear and decide the particular case. If the parties are unable to agree on an arbiter within ten work days after submission of the written request for arbitration, the provisions of 19.7 (Selection of Arbiter—From Arbitration Panel) shall apply to the selection of an arbiter.
>
> Section 19.7. Selection of Arbiter—From Arbitration Panel. Immediately following execution of this Agreement the parties will proceed to compile a list and agree upon a Corporate Panel of five arbiters. If a case reaches Step 4, and the parties are unable to agree to an arbiter within the time limit specified in 19.6, the case, irrespective of location, shall be heard and settled by an arbiter on the Corporate Panel if available. Assignments of cases to arbiters on the Corporate Panel shall be rotated in the alphabetical order of the last names of those available. An available arbiter is one who is available to conduct a hearing sixty days (unless mutually extended) after expiration of the time limit specified in 19.6.
>
> Section 19.9. Procedure Where Corporate Panel Not Available. In the event, as to any case, that there is no available arbiter on the Corporate Panel, the parties shall jointly request the American Arbitration Association to submit a panel of seven arbiters. Such request shall state the general

> nature of the case and ask that nominees be qualified to handle the type of case involved. When notification of the names of the seven arbiters is received, the parties in turn shall have the right to strike a name from the panel until only one name remains. The remaining person shall be the arbiter. The right to strike the first name from the panel shall be determined by lot.[2]

The draftsmanship of this provision is clearly superior. The language is neither vague nor uncertain in outlining the overall procedures to be followed. However, even this excellently written contract clause presents one potential problem to the parties—that is, presuming they do not already have an established practice or understanding. The last sentence reads: "The right to strike the first name from the panel shall be determined by lot."

First of all, what is "lot"? Presumably, in the context of this agreement, as in countless numbers of labor contracts, the term refers to some type of drawing or other determination by chance. But what type of determination? What form does it take? What if one party perceives this term to mean one kind of game or contest of chance, while the other considers it to be something quite different? What if each is stubborn or irresponsible—or what if only one party is either of these? What if one of the parties merely wishes to be disagreeable in order to prevent or frustrate the orderly processing of the claim to arbitration? Any or all of these problems can result.

Vagueness in the terms of the contract may be a source of disagreement between two parties. But that is not the extent of the problem presented by the above-quoted contractual language; it can be even more complicated, as it has been for various other parties.

Let us assume that the parties can agree on the game of chance they will engage in. Let us assume that they draw straws from a vessel containing straws of various lengths, with the understanding that the one who draws the longer straw is considered the winner. Let us assume further that the company representative draws the longer straw. Then who strikes the first name from the list of arbiters? The implication of the contractual language is that the winning party shall strike the first name. However, that is merely an inference a reasonable person might make.

But why all this fuss about which party strikes the first name? Why is it significant, or even relevant? The answer is that many labor-relations practitioners, representing either labor or management, consider that the party that does not strike the first name from an odd-numbered list of arbitrators is at an advantage when the list is ultimately reduced to only two names. Consider the example below:

Arbitrator A—Company strikes
Arbitrator B—Union strikes

Arbitrator C—Company strikes
Arbitrator D
Arbitrator E

This is a simple example of five names. The company has struck the first name, A in the example; the union has struck arbitrator B; and the company has again struck, this time arbitrator C. It is now the union's turn, now that only two names remain. By virtue of not having struck first, the union has the "final" choice between the two remaining names.

The potential for problems to arise because of vague terminology becomes more discernible when viewed in the light of the above example, and many have been the parties who have argued over such an issue. Many problems may be avoided by the use of precise contractual language. In the following example, the provision specifies the party to go first:

> The parties shall first attempt to agree upon an impartial arbitrator. If they cannot agree within five (5) working days the parties shall jointly request the Federal Mediation and Conciliation Service to submit a list of five (5) names of possible arbitrators. First the Union, then the Company, shall alternately strike names from the list until only one (1) remains, and this person shall act as the arbitrator.[3]

Apparently the two parties who designed the above contract clause resolved the question of which one was to strike the first name on the arbitral list during the course of their collective bargaining. In any case, it is a settled issue, and the union always strikes the first name.

Sometimes it is not specified which party is to strike first on each and every instance of arbitral selection. Nevertheless, the contractual provision may enable the parties to reach such determination. One such example follows:

> 7.02. If the parties cannot agree upon the selection of the Arbitrator then the Party demanding arbitration shall, within five (5) working days following the above-mentioned meeting, upon written notice to the other, request the Federal Mediation and Conciliation Service (address, Office of the General Counsel, Dept. of Labor Building, Fourteenth Street and Constitution Avenue, N.W., Washington, D.C. 20427) to submit a list of seven (7) qualified arbitrators, each of whom must be currently a member of National Academy of Arbitrators.
>
> 7.03. Within three (3) working days of receipt of said list, the Parties will meet, and alternately and in turn strike a name until each Party has eliminated a total of three (3) names from the list. The Parties shall flip a coin to decide which Party strikes the first name and the losing party shall strike the first name. Such procedure shall apply in each case. The Party demanding arbitration shall, within two (2) working days thereafter, with written notice to the other, advise the arbitrator of his selection.[4]

What should be noted first here are the contractual time limits that appear in these clauses. Time limitations, particularly ones as brief as these, enable the parties to move their disputes along expeditiously to a conclusion. This is one of the ways in which parties may remedy delays.

More, as to the reason for citing the above clause: The author was personally involved in the bargaining that led to its adoption. In these particular negotiations, representatives of both parties, company and union, were concerned about the question of which one would strike the first name from an arbitration list. Each party considered it a disadvantage to strike first, and such is reflected by the contractual language.

Procedures

Arbitrators are generally selected on either a case-by-case or a permanent basis. Where the arbitrator is chosen for each case, the ad hoc method we have been reviewing, a wide variety of procedures have been adopted for determining who is to be the impartial umpire. Some parties prefer to leave the selection to an agency such as FMCS or the American Arbitration Association (AAA). While these agencies quite willingly perform such service, they most prefer that the parties themselves make the choice.

Still another method that has been popular with many parties for several years is one that operates as follows: Each party is supplied with a list of names. Each, independently of the other, eliminates from the list names that are unacceptable to it. Usually, more than one name will not be acceptable, for a variety of real or imagined reasons, and more often than not, one or more will be acceptable. If two or more names are acceptable to the party, each name is numbered in the order of preference. When compared, the lists may show something like the following:

Union List	*Company List*
~~D. Adams~~	1. A. Adams
5. M. Easy	~~M. Easy~~
~~F. Hard~~	3. F. Hard
L. Baker	~~L. Baker~~
1. S. Smith	5. S. Smith
~~W.-Jones~~	~~W.-Jones~~
2. H. White	2. H. White
4. C. Black	~~C. Black~~
3. B. Brown	4. B. Brown

In this example, H. White, S. Smith, and B. Brown are acceptable to both parties, the others having been cancelled by one or the other. By adding the respective ratings, H. White would be the top man on the basis of having received the lowest numerical total (2 + 2 = 4), with S. Smith in second place (1 + 5 = 6), and B. Brown in third place (3 + 4 = 7). The lower the total score of the arbitral candidate, the higher his level of acceptability to both parties, since each party has numbered the candidates in the order of its preference, beginning with 1. Thus the appointment as to arbitrator would first be offered to White, after which, if he declined or was otherwise unable to serve, the parties would offer the post to Smith and Brown, respectively.

Obviously, there are shortcomings in this system, just as there are in the others cited. In the procedures previously discussed, the parties are more or less stuck with their own selection made by alternately striking names from a pre-established list provided by those agencies. Of course, such lists may be returned to the agencies, by mutual agreement of the parties, if all names listed thereon are wholly unacceptable to either. However, this is a relatively rare occurrence, primarily because of the care and professional approach of FMCS and AAA in their construction of arbitration panels. Usually the parties will merely proceed to check off names.

In this procedure there are a few potential problem areas. There is always a good chance that the parties will coincidentally strike names in a manner that precludes selection from a particular list, that is, each could strike the names that are acceptable to the other and such a happenstance would necessitate a second list and a repetition of the above-described process, all of which imposes lengthy delay upon the ultimate selection of an arbitrator. Naturally, the same result would occur if either party checked all names on the list. Also, in theory at least, it could happen over and over. The answer to this dilemma may lie in the parties' agreeing to limit themselves to a maximum number of exclusions, say, three names each from a panel containing seven.

As previously stated, the parties may elect to set up permanent machinery for the determination of disputes. An example of one such arrangement follows:

> Within thirty (30) days after the date of this Agreement, representatives of the parties thereto will obtain from the American Arbitration Association a list of Arbitrators, and will agree upon a panel of three arbitrators, obtaining additional lists, if necessary. The parties shall furnish said Association the names of the arbitrators so selected. Thereafter the Association shall designate one of said arbitrators to hear each grievance that may be referred to arbitration but no one arbitrator shall hear more than three grievances. If said panel shall be exhausted, representatives of the parties shall in the same manner select a second panel of arbitrators to hear grievances arising thereafter, each of whom may hear not more than three grievances.[5]

Permanent arbitrators or systems providing for them are more frequently found in large enterprises with long collective bargaining histories and which have a large number of cases going into arbitration.

Several arguments are put forward by those favoring permanent-arbitrator systems. It is contended that a permanent arbitrator comes to know the peculiarities of the business better; he understands the features of the relationship which makes it unique to the given parties; his rulings have conformity, continuity, and uniformity, which simplifies enforcement of the contract; and his awards set precedents that form a set of guides and rules supplementing the contract and enabling smoother labor relations.

However, the permanent-arbitrator system is not without its opponents. Labor relations practitioners may oppose it on the grounds that (1) the arbitrator tends too often to play the role of mediator; (2) he eventually tends to supplement or supplant management in the determination of industrial relations policies; (3) he may, because he must please both sides or come to feel that he should, have a tendency to decide the issue on the basis of the trend of decisions instead of on the merits of each particular case; and (4) his presence often acts to promote the number of grievances pushed into arbitration.

If one elects to secure a permanent arbitrator, several considerations are advisable. First, one should be extremely thoughtful and thorough in researching and selecting the individual who will serve. It is easier and less painful to avoid making a mistake in selection than to undo and outlive mistaken decisions rendered. Second, one should stay with ad hoc arbitration at least until one is quite acquainted with the process, how it works, and how various arbitrators reason and function during hearings. Exposure to different arbiters may assist in the later selection of a permanent arbitrator. Third, one should have a clear understanding with the selected permanent umpire regarding fee arrangements. If a yearly retainer is required, one should take into account the frequency of arbitral cases in the past. What are the charges of the arbitrator? How available is he? Will he readily give his time without unreasonable delay? These are a few of the primary questions that will have to be answered satisfactorily. Fourth, even if a permanent arbitrator is decided upon, one may wish to consider keeping provisions in the labor agreement which would enable the use and selection of temporary arbitrators and would specify that such clause should apply when the office of the permanent umpire is vacant or when he cannot serve for any reason. It is much better to have taken this precaution before an emergency arbiter absence occurs, rather than trying to cope with it at the very time the need for arbitral help is greatest.

The fifth consideration is only applicable to some parties, whose investigation it merits. In a multi-plant, or multi-division, operation, one may wish to consider using the same permanent individual under each of several agreements. To pursue this thought one step further, if the industry has an employers' association, one may wish to consider joining with others to select and retain a single umpire, especially if each member of the group feels the need for an arbitrator who understands the peculiarities of the particular industry. As a result, a group may be able to attract and finance, with a more sizable retainer, an arbiter of wider experience and national reputation. When such arrangements are made, often the parties will name several alternates to serve in the absence of the permanent selection.

There are a few more reasons why careful selection of a permanent arbitrator is so important. He may conduct a hearing in any manner peculiar to his particular philosophy and style of personality. He may run a tight or a loose hearing. He may rule on objections raised against testimony or procedure, disallowing and precluding their admission, taking it "for whatever it may later prove to be worth." He may be a strict constructionist in his interpretation of the agreement, ignoring consideration of any factors or matters outside of contract language. Or he may give weight to the customs and practices of the parties, previous arbitration decisions, previous grievance settlements, and the history of collective bargaining discussions between the parties.

It is advisable that mattes such as these, and others to be mentioned later, be taken into consideration in the selection of an arbitrator, whether for permanent duty or for ad hoc service.

Arbitration may be conducted either by a single nonpartisan arbitrator or a tripartite board, composed of an equal number of employer and union representatives, with an impartial member acting as chairman. A few agreements allow the parties the option of having either a single arbitrator or an arbitration board. In some contracts, the partisan representatives first attempt to settle the disputed issue. Only after they have been unable to agree on a final decision does the board become a tripartite board, with the impartial man added to make a decision possible. Most often, all members of an arbitration board, including the impartial chairman, are selected before the arbitration hearings start, and the board functions as a tripartite board at all times.

Arbitration may be conducted by an individual or a board newly chosen each time a dispute arises, or by a person or board named in the contract serving continuously for the duration of the agreement.

Agreements calling for permanent arbitration usually specify a single arbitrator, rather than a tripartite board. In some instances where a board is provided, only the impartial chairman serves on a permanent basis, while the company and union representatives are selected for each dispute.

Whatever the prescribed procedure, when one is trying to agree on an arbitrator, only the requirements of the labor contract limit the selection. Naturally, if the contract specifies that the arbitrator chosen must come from panels of FMCS or AAA, or be a member of the National Academy of Arbitrators, such a requirement, usually mutually waived, dictates at least the source. Otherwise, the company and union may choose anyone they wish to arbitrate for them, and they often obtain their neutral third party from other sources. It is not unheard of for a priest, minister, rabbi, mayor, or other public official—even a governor—to decide an issue for an employer and a union. Parties may even agree upon an apparently partisan person, if such a choice is mutually acceptable. But remember, the quality of the arbitrator may eventually prove to be as significant as the merits of one's case and the quality of one's presentation at the arbitral hearing.

11

Researching the Arbitrator

We are now ready for the next step.

A list of names of arbitrators has been submitted to each party by the Federal Mediation and Conciliation Service (FMCS) or the American Arbitration Association (AAA), or perhaps has been obtained from some less frequently used source. The list typically contains seven names or five names or some other odd number requested by the parties from one of these services.

The list lies before one of the parties on his desk. Perhaps, if he is lucky, one or two of the names are familiar to him. He may have previously used one (or more) of the arbitrators listed and thus have already had some actual experience with him. He is therefore familiar with the arbitrator's style, and the manner in which he conducts a hearing. He has at least some notion of the kind of rationale he employs in arriving at conclusions. If one is fortunate enough to be in this situation, the research chore of sifting through the potential arbiters is somewhat minimized. Those who go to arbitration often, or on a fairly regular basis, have an edge over others in their familiarity with the professionals in the business of deciding disputes as neutral third parties.

By virtue of their having appeared on previous lists, perhaps one has some knowledge of the background, experience, qualifications, and general reputation of certain names appearing on the list. Presumably, if their names have appeared on previous lists submitted, the arbitrators may have already been checked on in the past. If so, the research chore is further diminished and one-fifth or one-seventh or more of the basic questions have already been answered. But if all the names are unfamiliar, what then? Or worse yet, if one does not know what steps to take in order to determine to his satisfaction the arbitrator's qualifications, what then? This chapter will attempt to answer the most basic questions in this regard.

Qualifications

In order to serve the parties fairly, an individual must have certain qualities of character. For the moment, this discussion will lay aside other desirable arbitral qualities, such as experience, knowledge, or education. These will be reviewed shortly.

Among the qualities of character the parties are entitled to find in their selection, none can be considered more important than that of impartiality. It is a fact of life that everyone is possessed of certain biases and prejudices, on an endless variety of matters. It is not possible to find a human who is not. At the same time, it is not unreasonable of the parties to expect to have an individual who will discipline himself to decide the issues on their own merits. Sentiment or bias for or against the issue, a particular party, or the conditions of the parties' labor agreement is a factor that must be divorced from the decision-making process. From the opening of the hearing until a decision is rendered, an open mind is not merely desirable, it is essential, not only to provide equity and impartial justice to the parties and their relationship, but also for the preservation of an honorable arbitration profession. There is no implicit suggestion here that arbitrators are not impartial and fair; quite the contrary. The absence of these essential qualities is definitely the exception; that is why arbitration and its neutral professionals have flourished for so many years. Without these qualities of character, found in the overwhelming majority of practicing arbitrators, they, and the process they serve, would never have endured. This is not to say that an arbiter does not, or even should not, call the shots as he sees them. He must exercise his own best judgment, which sometimes results in the rendering of an unpopular decision. If such an award is the result of his judgment, and not the consequence of partiality or favoritism, he has still provided a valuable service and has not been guilty of violating one of the basic and essential precepts of his office. An arbitrator is not engaged in a popularity contest. Accordingly, while one or both parties may be displeased with a particular decision, they will not lose faith in the fundamental benefits of the process so long as they are convinced that awards are the consequences of judgment impartially exercised.

The integrity of the arbitrator is equally important. The arbitrator does not seek to serve the parties, nor is he elected to the position he holds. As a consequence, he does not serve or operate at the sufferance of either party. He has not, nor should he have, any vested interest in, or allegiance to, representatives of either faction. His post has not been a political appointment. His integrity has hopefully been established and is discernible to the parties through his prior business and personal dealings and affiliations.

To many practitioners in the labor-relations arena, the fact that an arbitrator has previously gained considerable experience in representing exclusively either labor or management gives the kiss of death to the desirability of his serving as a neutral. However, it simply does not follow as night follows day that previous partisan service renders the individual incapable of impartiality and integrity in functioning as a true neutral. In this respect, labor arbitration is somewhat akin to other fields of endeavor. Many of the best defense lawyers were previously district attorneys. Many referees with unquestioned integrity were formerly players in the same game—baseball, football, basketball, hockey, and the like, and some even performed for the same teams they later render judgments for and against. A more reliable determinant of whether the arbitrator's feelings of partisanship still prevail would be the public record of the cases he has decided and the manner in which he has decided them. In fact, that prior partisanship may have been the very instrument by which he has gained the depth and breadth of insight and experience that enables him to appraise the issues and circumstances with greater understanding. Some of the ablest and most informed neutrals practicing as labor arbitrators today, with impeccable reputations in the eyes of both parties, came out of the labor movement, or from the ranks of management.

Whether a certain experience or education or training is necessary for all arbiters is questionable. No two possess exactly the same kind or amount of background attributes, but they must possess the essential qualities of character which enable them to render decisions impartially and to serve with unchallengeable integrity.

Let us turn now to another area, that of actual experience and qualifications. There are a few helpful indications.

If the individual is a member of the National Academy of Arbitrators, he is an experienced neutral who has met several high standards imposed by his own peers. Perhaps there are no harsher critics than one's own peers, and, if he has passed the scrutiny and investigation of the membership committee of the Academy, the odds are substantially good that the arbitrator will possess the desired necessary credentials.

The Academy, however, does not include all of the individuals who have accumulated impressive qualifications and capabilities as arbitrators. The Academy, founded in 1947, takes in relatively few new members, so that not being on its roster does not necessarily indicate any lack of ability or proficiency. Arbitrators on the panels of FMCS and AAA have also been investigated prior to their acceptance by those agencies. In fact, both agencies require that the individual provide a number of references from the ranks of both labor and management who will attest to his acceptability, knowledge, and character. In addition, his application for membership on these rosters must exhibit sufficient labor-management exposure to qualify him for consideration. Therefore, arbitrators whose names are furnished on such panels have already been screened for impartiality. The rules of non-partisan arbitration agencies forbid an arbitrator to serve in a case in which he has any financial or personal interest or is related to any of the parties, that is, unless the parties expressly waive this condition in writing.

The qualification of arbitrators becomes doubly important when it is realized that they have been deemed to be judicial officers and share certain immunities from suit by parties, since arbitrators "must be free from the fear of reprisals" and "must of necessity be uninfluenced by any fear of consequences for their acts."[1]

It is not uncommon to hear disparaging remarks, from both management and labor, about the integrity of arbitrators, their principles, and their biases. This contributes to the unusually troublesome problem of selecting an arbiter. The usefulness of arbitration in the field of industrial relations is largely the result of the quality of the arbitrators, their personal and professional integrity, their intimate acquaintance with the varied facets of industrial life, and their judgment. The parties themselves are mostly responsible for whatever undermining of arbitration there has been. In their eagerness to win cases, they contribute materially to reducing the usefulness of arbitration and to breeding attitudes of cynicism vis-à-vis arbitration on the part of companies, unions, and the public generally. The foundation stone of successful arbitration is the confidence of the parties in the fairness and competence of the arbitrator.[2]

As mentioned earlier, sometimes the parties will specify certain arbitral qualifications in their labor instrument. For example, an agreement between New Jersey Bell Telephone Company and the Electrical Workers (IBEW) contained this clause among its arbitration provisions:

> (3) At the same time that written demand for arbitration is served upon the other party, the American Arbitration Association shall be requested in writing to appoint an impartial chairman. The Impartial shall not be an officer, director or employee of the company or of any company in the Bell System, nor shall he be a member, officer, official, employee, representative, attorney or counsel of the Union or of any other Union or labor organization.

It is doubtful that such a restriction on AAA need be spelled out in the labor agreement. It is not conceivable that that agency would knowingly submit a panel containing the names of persons from the contractually prohibited categories. However, for whatever reasons, these parties felt more assured after taking the expressed precautionary measures.

More often, the parties specify in their contract the qualities sought in the arbitrator rather than listing those that would be unacceptable. An example of one such provision follows:

> Within two (2) working days thereafter, the Parties shall jointly write to the Arbitrator selected and request hearing dates. Neither party shall deliberately delay the setting of a hearing date.
>
> 1. Such arbitrators must be technically qualified to resolve disputes and have skill, knowledge and/or experience relating to measurements of standards of work.
> 2. Such arbitrators must have prior arbitration experience in regularly deciding issues relating to measurements of standards of work.
> 3. Any arbitrator selected by the above procedures must be currently a member of the National Academy of Arbitrators.[3]

The above language appears in a contract that contains two grievance and arbitration provisions, one dealing with disputes outside the "wage incentive plan," and the other quoted in part, dealing with disputes about the administration and implementation of an incentive standards program. It is evident that an attempt has been made here to engage only arbitrators who have industrial engineering-type expertise, education, and/or experience.

Only relatively few contracts specify eligibility qualifications for arbitrators. In the above example, only engineers or other technically trained and experienced persons may be allowed to arbitrate disputes involving time-study and incentive systems. Appointment of public officeholders is occasionally prohibited and, in the case of tripartite systems, lawyers may be precluded from serving either party. To prevent selection of an individual whose judgment might somehow be prejudiced from association with the parties involved in the dispute, persons living within a specified distance of the enterprise may be declared ineligible for service as arbitrators. The reverse situation may sometimes be found also: A person familiar with the particular industry may be preferred and so specified by the contract.

There can be no question that substantial arbitration experience is of considerable benefit, both to the arbitrator and to the parties he serves. However, the absence of experience as an arbitrator can be materially compensated for if he possesses a keen and analytical mind and has the capabilities to quickly grasp and perceive new subject matter presented to him. Competence may be acquired during the course of hearings where parties have adequately prepared and intelligently presented the facts upon which the determination is to be made. The most experienced arbitrator cannot fully understand the issue and the circumstances surrounding it unless these are clearly articulated to him during the proceeding. Of course, the quality of integrity either exists or does not exist. When the least question arises about his integrity, the arbitrator's usefulness ceases. This ingredient is the equal of maturity or judgment, and both are indispensable.

There are occasions when special knowledge is required about the matter to be decided. Such instances are in the minority, and a few have been previously mentioned. In the vast majority of cases, general experience in industrial matters, however obtained, will enable an arbitrator to relate to the issues at hand.

The question of whether an arbitrator needs legal training in order to function adequately and successfully arises frequently. The answer is no. It is true that many arbitrators have been trained in law, just as many practioners in labor relations have been. It is also true that such training usually operates to the benefit of such individuals. The process of training in legal affairs provides a neutral discipline that promotes objective and analytical thinking. It teaches the evaluation of facts and information, with limitations on personal prejudice. It disciplines toward the elimination of extraneous matters and the consideration of relevant and pertinent factors only. It is also true that several of the ablest established arbitrators have law backgrounds. However, it is equally true that many of the most able, best established, and most reputable arbitrators have not had legal training. Finally, it has to be recognized that not all legally trained individuals make good arbitrators. It was stated earlier that legal training usually operates to the benefit of the individual. But not always. The arbitrator's legal background may, in some circumstances, even be a hindrance to a full and open hearing of all matters. The arbitration process is only quasijudicial, and strict rules of evidence, testimony, and procedure do not apply. One of the virtues of the process is its availability and adaptability to the parties as a fast and relatively simple means of resolving their difference. The introduction of too much "legalese" into the system may actually complicate it unduly for those it is intended to serve. It may stifle both the informal presentations of their cases and their dispositions toward the subsequent use of the process. How a person reasons and exercises good judgment, how he analyzes and evaluates situations, and how much objectivity and adherence to facts he demonstrates are far more important considerations than what formal education he may have obtained. How the parties determine the presence or absence of these essential qualities will be reviewed next.

Evaluation of Arbitral Candidates

The Bureau of National Affairs (BNA) (1231 25th Street, N.W., Washington, D.C.) publishes *Labor Arbitration Reports*, which are designed to provide accurate and authoritative information about arbitration awards.

They also contain information about particular arbitrators, including their names, addresses, telephone numbers, birth dates, training, positions, affiliations, and publications. Access to these volumes, or to those provided by other such reporting services, is an invaluable tool to the practitioner wishing to examine the published decisions of certain arbitrators. One word of caution is in order. Not all decisions of all arbitrators are published; only a very small percentage of decisions are. Not all decisions of any particular arbitrator are published for public review. Arbitrators choose only certain cases to submit to the publishing services. These reporting services must also be selective in the cases they publish. The factors of expense are obvious determinants. In addition, the arbitrator must obtain permission from the parties before submitting a report to one of the publications. Therefore, published arbitration reports are somewhat like an iceberg; only a small portion of the total cases is visible to the examiner. The great majority never get into print, primarily because of the limiting factors mentioned. Nevertheless, a sizable number are available to the interested and diligent researcher.

The increasing frequency of arbitration awards, both in number and significance, led BNA to a decision to segregate the text of all court decisions relating to labor arbitration into separate volumes. It devotes the space saved thereby in *Labor Arbitration Reports* to increased coverage of labor arbitration awards. These volumes and the *Index-Digest*, particularly, contain the aforementioned "Directory of Arbitrators." This publication also furnishes a full listing of the unions involved in the reported cases, providing the popular name of the union and the official name of the national or international union and its subordinate branches.

Such service is merely the launching pad for someone wishing to learn more about a prospective arbiter. Consulting these publications is one of the essential steps to be taken if a thorough and comprehensive job of research is to be accomplished. There are other equally productive sources.

Additional information regarding arbitrators' qualifications may also be obtained by turning to the *Who's Who of Arbitrators* put out by Prentice-Hall, Inc. (Englewood Cliffs, N.J.). From this source one can learn the potential arbitrator's age, address, education, occupation, affiliations, experience, books or articles written (often informative and insightful as to labor-relations concepts and philosophy), awards published, and a variety of other miscellaneous information.

Commerce Clearing House (CCH) (4025 West Peterson Ave., Chicago, Ill., 60646) is another major publisher of decisions. Its volumes, entitled *American Labor Arbitration Awards* (ALAA), provide a comprehensive reporting of hundreds of awards. This series is not a duplication of the BNA service. True, cases published by CCH may also be found in BNA's *Labor Arbitration Reports*, but there are many reported by one which are not necessarily published by the other.

Both services are equally impressive, and parties generally choose between them on the basis of which is more appealing in terms of reporting style and ease in locating desired matters therein. If both sets of volumes are available, the dedicated researcher may find it is well worth his time to examine in each the reported cases that pertain to his particular potential arbitral candidate. The panels maintained by AAA and FMCS contain the names of hundreds of qualified arbitrators. Whenever either of these agencies receives a request for an arbitrator, or a panel of arbiters, a listing is submitted. Such a list includes several pertinent particulars on each of the individuals offered. A hypothetical sample of the type of biographical data included follows:

NAME: Harold Decisive

OCCUPATION: Professor Economics and Chairman, Department of Economics

ADDRESS: (Bus) Ohio State University, Columbus, Ohio

(Res) 1050 Treelined Street, Columbus, Ohio

ARBITRATION EXPERIENCE: Arbitrator since 1992. Majority of working time devoted to teaching, with balance spent in arbitration. Has experience in arbitration of wages, fringe benefits, grievances concerning management prerogatives, overtime and premium pay, job specifications, seniority, discipline and discharge.

OTHER EXPERIENCE: Fourteen years teaching experience. Labor relations consultant, Atomic Energy Commission, 1984–1987. Mediator, U.S. Conciliation Service, 1975–1977. Corps of Engineers, U.S. Army, 1972–1975.

PROFESSIONAL AFFILIATIONS: Arbitration Association, Industrial Relations Research Association, American Economics Association.

EDUCATION: B.A., M.A., Ph.D.

DATE OF BIRTH: March 6, 1942

PER DIEM FEE: Not exceeding $150.

This hypothetical data sheet, representative of the type and form of material that both AAA and FMCS forward to requesting parties, is taken from the format of FMCS.

Some parties with arbitration pending make their determinations on arbiters on the basis of these sheets. While they are helpful and informative in themselves, the data sheets should only be the basis for further investigation. At this point, one of the recommended things to do is to turn to the aforementioned publications of BNA and CCH. At the same time, one may wish to ask AAA or FMCS for the names of parties who have been previously served by the arbitrator's performance. Employer associations and chambers of commerce, too, can sometimes furnish lists of cases decided by arbitrators of the locality. One should find out how many times the same parties have chosen their particular candidate; "repeat orders" are a strong endorsement.

As many as possible of the people who have advocated cases before the arbitral candidate should be contacted. A suggested list of questions is given below. One should try to pin them down to specific good or bad qualities, remembering, nevertheless, that anyone who has lost a case may be inclined to blame the arbitrator. On the other hand, a recommendation from the losing party or a criticism from the party given the award should have special weight.

After the prospective client has talked with other parties and read opinions, he should judge the arbitrator on the general quality of his work, not on how many cases he has decided for one side or the other. If the majority of his awards favor the union, this does not necessarily indicate a pro-union bias, since a great many variables enter the picture.

There are many questions that may be raised with parties who have already had experience with the arbitral candidate under consideration. The following are merely a few of the more pertinent ones:

- How soon after the close of the hearing was the award submitted? Was it within the preferred 30 days? If not, was there a justifiable reason for it taking longer?
- What was the issue decided?
- Did the arbitrator consider only the relevant contractual provision, or did he give weight to other matters, such as the practices and customs of the parties, the history of collective bargaining on the disputed clauses, and so on.
- Did the arbitrator prefer a transcript of the hearing and the use of a court stenographer, or did he record the events of the hearing by making his own notes?
- Did the arbitrator follow the concept that management rights are residual, that all rights and privileges of managing the business continue to reside with the employer except to the extent they have been abridged or compromised by provisions of the contract?
- How did he conduct the hearing? Was it informal or legalistic?
- Did he rule on objections, or did he accept all evidence and testimony proffered by the parties?
- Did he ask many questions of the company, the union, and their witnesses—or did he simply let what was given him suffice?
- In the "opinion" portion of his award, were his remarks pertinent and on point with the issue to be decided, or did he delve into extraneous and foreign matters that were not submitted or intended to elicit his opinion?
- Was his opinion and award clear and understandable?

- What were his money charges? Were they considered reasonable in light of the length of the hearing(s) and the complexity of the case?

The reason for asking most of these questions is fairly evident. They deal with the arbitrator's promptness, style, objectivity, analytical ability, rationale, and fees. These are all important considerations. Merely learning this much about an arbitrator may give one party a decided edge on the other if it has not been equally resourceful. It may have an influence on the approach to be taken and style to be followed, enabling a party to prepare its witnesses as to what to expect. It may provide insights into an arbitrator's personal idiosyncrasies. The arbitrator may be more expensive than anticipated, although other positive determinations may outweigh this factor. It may be discovered that he is inclined to go far afield in his "opinion," even when he renders a favorable award. Such a discovery may lead to the realization that one could "win the battle, but lose the war." Needless to say, one may decide to reject a candidate for a particular case. Despite such a decision, he may still be considered acceptable for some other future issue.

Whatever the findings at the end of the research, they should not be disposed of. Instead, an arbitration file should be developed and maintained in order to accumulate all of the information pertinent to the selection, evaluation, and qualifications of arbitrators. Some candidates' names will subsequently appear time and again on lists. If one wants others in the labor-management community to share opinions with him, the willingness must be reciprocal. If a party has justifiable cause to be dissatisfied with the service of a particular arbitrator, he should share his concern in a fair and objective manner with the agency providing his name. If criticism is constructively expressed and intended, the agency will be grateful for the report. If it sees an appraisable pattern of comments from different parties, that will enable it to determine appropriate reaction if necessary. Preserving the results of research can save one the considerable time, trouble, and expense of later having to duplicate his efforts. **Although there are many settled and well-established concepts endorsed by the majority of arbitrators, there are other areas where some difference of opinion persists, even among the best known, most reputable neutrals. Once this is realized, additional reasons, which are perhaps more important that those already cited, emerge for researching a prospective arbitrator.**

12

Preparing Your Case

Thorough preparation of cases for arbitration is of paramount importance. Ordinarily most or all of the arbitrator's knowledge and understanding of the case is based upon evidence and arguments presented at the arbitration hearing. Moreover, a party must fully understand its own case in order to communicate it effectively to the arbitrator, and full understanding depends upon thorough preparation.

What is necessary for thorough preparation of any given case will depend largely upon the nature of the case. In some cases the facts are especially important and each party will concentrate upon proving, largely through testimony of witnesses, that the facts are as that party sees them. In other cases the facts may be less important or not disputed, the controversy being centered upon some other matter, such as the proper interpretation of the collective agreement. Here, each party's case may be devoted largely to arguments about how the agreement should be interpreted. In still other cases, economic and statistical data may be especially important.

Thus, the advocate should consider nature of the case in determining which items of the following "preparation" checklist should be emphasized in any particular case (no significance lies in the order in which they are listed):

- Review the history of the case as developed at the prearbitral steps of the grievance procedure.
- Study the entire collective agreement to identify all clauses bearing directly or indirectly on the dispute. Also, compare current provisions with those contained in prior agreements; the comparison might reveal language changes significant to the case.

- To determine the general authority of the arbitrator, and accordingly the scope of the arbitration, examine the instruments used to initiate the arbitration.
- Talk to all persons (even those the other party might use as witnesses) who might be able to aid development of a full picture of the case, including different viewpoints. You will thus better understand not only your own case but your opponent's as well; if you can anticipate your opponent's case you can better prepare to rebut it.
- Interview each of your own witnesses (1) to determine what they know about the case; (2) to make certain they understand the relationship of their testimony to the whole case; and (3) to cross-examine them to check their testimony and to acquaint them with the process of cross-examination. Make a written summary of the expected testimony of each witness; this can be reviewed when the witnesses testify to ensure that no important points are overlooked. Some parties outline in advance the questions to be asked each witness during the hearing.
- Examine all records and documents that might be relevant to the case. Organize those you expect to use and make copies for use by the arbitrator and the other party at the hearing. If needed documents are in the exclusive possession of the other party, ask that they be made available before or at the hearing, preferably before.
- Visit the physical premises involved in the dispute to better visualize what occurred and what the dispute is about. Also, consider the advisability of asking at the hearing that the arbitrator (accompanied by both parties) also visit the site of the dispute.
- Consider the utility of pictorial or statistical exhibits. One exhibit can be more effective than many words, if the matter is suited to the exhibit form of portrayal. However, exhibits which do not "fit" the case, and those which are inaccurate or misleading, are almost certain to be ineffective or damaging to their proponent.
- Consider what the party's past practice has been in comparable situations.
- Attempt to determine whether there is some key point upon which the case might turn. If so, it might be to your advantage to concentrate upon that point.
- In "interpretation" cases prepare a written argument to support your view as to the proper interpretation of the disputed language.
- Research the party's prior arbitration awards and the published awards of other parties on the subject of the dispute for an indication of how similar issues have been approached in other cases.
- Prepare an outline of your case and discuss it with other persons

> in your group. This ensures better understanding of the case and will strengthen it by uncovering matters that need further attention. Then, too, it will tend to underscore policy and strategy considerations that may be very important in the ultimate handling of the case. Use of the outline at the hearing will facilitate an organized and systematic presentation of the case.

Thorough preparation involves the use of ingenuity to illuminate all the possibilities of the case. Certainly, the arbitrator needs a full picture of the case, and he will be interested in all its possibilities to aid him in reaching a sound decision.

The most successful and outstanding arbitral advocates do the preparation themselves. If a case is sufficiently important to be sent to arbitration, they deem it advisable to prepare it personally, or at least to direct every step, to interview the witnesses, to study every document, to read every relevant case, and in every way to have firsthand knowledge and complete mastery of the facts and the law of the case to be tried. Certainly, until the advocate can afford one or more excellent assistants on whose preparation he can rely thoroughly, he should prepare the case himself from beginning to end. Not only will the mastery of the case improve his chances of success, but the insight he will gain into the practical problems of preparation will give him the ability to guide and direct preparation by others when he becomes too busy to do all the work himself.

The advocate who starts his career with the idea that small cases are not worth thorough preparation is not likely to get more important cases to prepare and try. On the other hand, the advocate who prepares his minor cases thoroughly will not only win more cases (thereby attracting more notoriety and praise) but will also acquire experience and confidence which will enable him to succeed with the more important cases that are likely to follow in the wake of success.

The preparation of the case should be started as soon as the grievance is filed. Every grievance filed should be treated at the outset as though it were preordained for arbitration. *If all grievances were handled that carefully and considerately, we might be surprised by a significant decrease in cases going all the way to arbitration.* We might also be enlightened by seeing how many more of those that reached arbitration were ruled in favor of the diligent and dedicated party so handling them.

There is a serious danger in postponing the preparation of a case until shortly before the hearing. Not only should all the facts be inquired into and checked, but all the available evidence should be in the hands of the advocate at the earliest possible date. Early preparation is a protection against possible loss of valuable evidence. It prevents the advocate from going off in the wrong direction in his theory of the action or of the defense. Incorrect or incomplete evidence at the hearing can be seriously damaging. Even if the evidence is amended at the trial, a competent opponent will find opportunity to point out its insufficiency or the shift in the advocate's position. So, too, careless or uninformed questioning of witnesses can produce disastrous results even when handled by the most able and intelligent advocate.

Preliminary Interview of Witnesses

Of first importance in any action are the facts—the exact facts and all the facts. As you, the advocate prepare, it is generally advisable to let the witness tell his own story while you listen. If you shut him off and insist on getting only answers to specific questions, you may screen out some important point, for you cannot possibly anticipate all the facts in every case. After getting his story, you will most likely have to ask questions to sift the relevant parts, to emphasize the salient features, to fill in important gaps, and to help the witness see the outline of the total case, as you see it, and as you develop it from the facts before you. If the witness can be made to understand your thoughts and the theory of the case, he may tell you facts which he otherwise would have inadvertently overlooked or consciously and erroneously discarded as immaterial. In other words, you must probe the subject and get your witness to give you assistance which will be more valuable because it is intelligent.

In questioning the witness you must be a friendly but nonetheless searching cross-examiner. It is your task to learn all the good and all the bad points of the case, to help the intelligent marshaling of evidence, the proper preparation of arguments, and the avoidance of unpleasant surprises at the hearing. Advance knowledge may enable you to explain or minimize unfavorable facts and to weaken the effect of your adversary's cross-examination, or of some of his direct evidence by anticipating those facts in your direct examination.

A witness, party to arbitral litigation, can hardly be objective about his case. Consciously or otherwise, the good points will be exaggerated, the bad minimized. Self-interest or bias may lead to fabrication or omission; faulty observation or poor memory to distortion and confusion. Infrequently there may even be a deliberate or psychopathic invention of a story which has little or no foundation in fact. An early investigation of the purported facts will save an advocate a great deal of woe in some cases.

Experienced advocates have learned that even an honest and rational witness, who will not invent facts, may nevertheless suppress facts. Simplest to cope with is unconscious suppression, caused by a lack of understanding as to what is important. It is the advocate's task to elicit all the important facts. One can generally overcome this type of suppression by detailed questioning of the witness. Somewhat more elusive is subconscious suppression, psychologically induced by the witness's wish to put his best food forward, or by nature's trick of inducing forgetfulness of what one does not like to remember. This type of suppression may also be overcome by detailed questioning, but it must be handled more delicately than the first type and requires a keen observation of psychological reactions. Every trial advocate can benefit from the study of practical psychology.

In any case, you must find a way to make your witness realize the importance of his confiding in you so that you will not be faced with any surprises at the trial. A fact that is damaging will be all the more so if it takes you unaware.

Not only is frankness by the witness essential, but frankness of the advocate with the witness is also advisable. Some advocates have a tendency to assume an optimistic attitude which is apparently intended to encourage their party and its witnesses at the early stages of the case. There is danger, however, in too much optimism. A fair approach to the problems involved in the litigation is not only the ethical approach but is also, in the long run, the best insurance against disappointments and dissatisfaction. If there are weaknesses in a case, they should be discussed candidly so that the client will understand the difficulties. Sometimes this understanding will help the client to render intelligent aid in the preparation of the case. At other times it may be more advisable to effect a compromise settlement when the opportunity is presented, or to create an opportunity for that purpose. Furthermore, if the case should go to an arbitral hearing and be lost because of the weaknesses which were glossed over, it would be rather late to make excuse for a failure incompatible with the earlier enthusiasm and optimism of the advocate.

Some advocates fail to take detailed notes of the facts related by their party and its witnesses. They either make a few cryptic notations, understood only by themselves, or depend entirely on their ability to remember the related facts. This is a dangerous and unwise practice. No memory is so good as to assure the advocate that he will recall all the necessary details at the right moment. Moreover, it is useful to preserve an accurate record of the facts as they are recalled while they are fresh and in the minds of the witnesses. Then, too, there always is the possibility that the person who confers on the case at the outset may not be available at a later time. The records in the file should, therefore, always be in such condition that any other advocate called into the case on short notice will be in a position to study the file and understand the case quickly and fully.

All witnesses should be interviewed as early as possible. One of the essential facts to ascertain from the witness to any occurrence is how he happened to be in a position to see or hear what he relates. If he says he was a witness, it is important to ascertain where he came from, where he was going, exactly where he was, and what he was doing at the moment of the occurrence, and his position with respect to what he says he saw or heard. It is also important to ascertain whether there were any stationary or moving intervening objects, so that you may determine for yourself whether the witness could have actually seen or heard what he says he saw or heard.

There may be a few times when it is important to obtain a signed statement from the witness. A sworn statement is most effective in holding the witness in line at the time of the hearing. If the witness prepares the statement in his own handwriting, he will be unlikely to repudiate it. If it is not in his handwriting, it is helpful to have him sign a statement that he has read each page signed or initialed by him, and that the facts stated therein are true.

The importance of obtaining such statements in certain particular cases cannot be overemphasized. An employee may leave or be discharged before the hearing and either lose interest or become hostile, or he may be too concerned about his new job to go to the arbitral hearing willingly. A friend of your side today may become your foe tomorrow. A witness who evidences an interest at the time of the occurrence of an event may sometimes lose it later and even be unwilling to take time from his business or work.

Final preparation for the hearing should include a review of all documentary evidence in the case—not only of those exhibits which you intend to offer in evidence but also of those which you know the opposing party may offer. The exhibits should therefore be sorted and arranged for ready use at the hearing. And remember, you will need three copies at the hearing: one for the arbiter; one for the opposing party; and of course, one for yourself.

If there are only a few exhibits, they may be arranged in a special folder simply in the order in which you expect to use them at the trial. A separate folder should hold correspondence and other documents which you do not intend to use but which may be called for by the other side, or for which a need may otherwise arise at the trial. If such documents are not too numerous, the simplest arrangement is to keep them in chronological order.

In some cases it may be helpful to prepare special exhibits. It may be desirable, for instance, to enlarge photographs for more effective view by the arbiter. In an accounting case which involves extensive testimony by accountants based on voluminous books and records, it is desirable to have an accountant prepare such visual aids as balance sheets, operating statements, comparative statements, and summaries for introduction as exhibits. Such exhibits would greatly aid in the arbiter's understanding of the accounting testimony which you will offer.

Certainly complicated cases need, and those of substantial importance deserve, an even more careful and detailed preparation.

Final Interview of Witnesses

Even though you have prepared the case thoroughly up to this point, the careful advocate will not go to trial without having had *final* interviews with all the witnesses, or at least all who are available to him.

Final preparation should include a preview with each witness of the facts to which he will testify on direct examination, or about which he may be asked on cross-examination.

After the final interview, after the facts have been reviewed, the witness should be questioned in the same manner in which you expect to ask the questions at the hearing. Your hearing-room manner should be simulated as much as possible, so that the witness may feel at ease when you question him during the arbitral proceedings.

The witness should be shown, and familiarized with, any exhibits which he will have to identify, interpret or testify about during the course of his examination. It is always advisable to have the witness be fully oriented about the hearing room. He should understand the importance of each link of the chain. Telling a witness that certain exhibits will be introduced at a certain point is more effective if accompanied by an explanation of why the exhibit will be offered.

To have a witness memorize his testimony is a horrible mistake. The memory may falter and the witness may collapse, figuratively. Memorized testimony can often be detected and the fact that the story may be true in all particulars will be crushed under the burden of the psychological handicap. Furthermore, if all witnesses use the same language, the arbiter will naturally be suspicious, no matter how truthful the witnesses are.

The lay witness should be informed that it is the substance of his testimony rather than the exact language which is important, unless, for example, the exact wording of an alleged abusive, threatening or slanderous remark, or the like, is vital to the case. He should understand the aim of the examiner, the purpose of the questions, and the nature of the answer which each of the questions seeks to elicit. He will not only be a more intelligent and cooperative witness, but also a more effective one, if he knows what he is talking about.

After you have finished the questions you expect to ask the witness at the hearing, and he has given you the answers, tell the witness that you are going to assume the role of opposing counsel and that you will cross-examine him in order to accustom him to cross-examination by your opponent. If you know the style of your opponent, it might be helpful to imitate him as closely as possible. If you cross-examine in a mild manner and the witness gets the impression that mildness is what he is to expect, he may receive a disconcerting shock if the cross-examiner at the hearing shouts or bullies, uses a sarcastic tone, or adopts some other manner calculated to create discomfiture for the witness.

You cannot possibly conceive of every question that your opponent will ask, but you can anticipate some of the important ones if you train yourself to be objective and critical of your own case. If you are sufficiently objective, you will find the weaknesses in the story told by the witness, or in the omission from his story, and you will concentrate on those weaknesses in your "cross-examination."

Cross-examination preparation should also concentrate on the weaknesses of the witness as distinguished from the weaknesses of the testimony. For instance, the pecuniary interest of the witness in the case, his friendship for another party, his bias, the nature of his position, or any other factor which may influence his testimony (i.e., his hostility to another party) should be covered in preparing for cross-examination. Of course, if the witness has something in his background which may be subject to attack, you cannot afford to spare the feelings of the witness in your office and subject him, without preparation, to a far less friendly probing at the hearing. You must go over the facts, so that the witness will not, under the influence of shock, excitement, or embarrassment during trial, suppress the truth to "protect himself" and ruin his own credibility and your chances of success. The witness must be impressed with the importance of his telling you the truth so that you can anticipate attack and make the effect of any attack milder.

And now let's turn our attention to the kind of advice an advocate should give to his would-be witnesses in preparing them for their appearance in the witness chair. The following paragraphs are addressed to potential witnesses.

For the Witness—Do's and Don'ts

Being a witness in an arbitration proceeding is often not a comfortable experience. You are perhaps understandably worried or anxious about your testimony. You know you will be cross-examined, plus the arbitrator is likely to ask you questions. Naturally you want to make a good appearance and leave the arbitrator with a favorable impression. You naturally are concerned that during cross-examination the opposing advocate will attempt to discredit your testimony, to cause you to contradict yourself and thereby sound inconsistent or untruthful.

The purpose in covering these do's and don'ts of witness conduct is several-fold: The suggestions are designed to help you to be as comfortable as possible, to be aware of how arbitral proceedings are conducted, to know what to expect and how to comport yourself. Equally as important, they will enable you to get your truthful story across in a manner which makes it believable to the arbiter. It is for these important purposes that the following do's and don'ts of witness conduct are presented to you.

- *DO sit erect and comfortable.* How you sit in the witness chair can influence the arbiter's perceptions of your credibility. Sit fairly erect but comfortably so. Don't slouch, change positions frequently, fidget or wave your arms about. Your objective is to appear cool, calm, confident, self-assured—in other words, to enhance your credibility.
- *DON'T volunteer information.* Answer the opposing advocate's questions honestly and directly. Answer only the question asked of you. If a yes or no answer is all that is solicited, don't give an answer which provides the requested information plus more information which was not solicited. If there is something you've left untold which could be helpful to your case, it is the responsibility of your advocate to bring it out during re-direct examination. Remember, you are not on the witness stand to try the case: that responsibility rests with your advocate. You are only there to answer the questions asked of you.
- *DO answer all questions asked of you, no matter by whom, in the same courteous, forthright and honest manner.* In addition to your own advocate asking you questions, you will also be cross-examined—plus the arbiter may also ask you questions. Answer them all in the same tone, in the same manner, with the same demeanor—honestly, forthrightly, courteously. Don't use a different manner or tone with one than you do with another.
- *DON'T argue with the opposing advocate (or the arbiter).* It is the legitimate job of the other party's advocate to try to upset you, get you angry or irritated, to attempt to discredit you or cause you to contradict yourself. He may use harsh tactics or an aggressive manner, but don't play into his hands. Don't get angry, sarcastic, smart-alecky, pugnacious, or in any way emotional. Remember, you're not responsible for his behavior—you're only accountable for your own. You want the arbiter to leave there with an impression favorable of you.
- *DO tell the truth.* Tell the truth on the witness stand. Also, tell *all* of it—not just some of it, or most of it, but all you know about the case, both good and bad, to your advocate when he's preparing the case for trial.

- *DO be alert and attentive to all other witness testimony.* If you are in the hearing room during other testimony, listen carefully and attentively. If something comes out which provokes your recall of something relevant you forgot to mention to your advocate, quietly pass down a note telling him of it. You can be very helpful to your side in this manner.
- *DO watch the arbiter.* You may sometimes tell how the case is going by watching the arbiter. His body language may communicate his attitude. Watch when he picks up his pencil and makes a note. Has something significant just happened which caused him to want to make a special note of it? If so, was it something helpful to your case, or had something damaging to your case just been brought out? In the former instance you may realize an opportunity to beef up a strong point favorable to your side; in the latter instance, you may realize a need to shore up against a weakness in your case. If you notice such development while not testifying, by being alert and observant, you can quietly pass a note or a whispered comment to your advocate of what you've observed and thus be helpful to him and to your side of the case.
- *DON'T patronize the arbitrator.* Be courteous and polite in your reactions to the arbiter. Don't be overly friendly or patronize him in any way. If you treat him in an exceptionally friendly manner, and the opposing side observes any of this, the arbiter is placed in an awkward position for a neutral third party. Being human, he may feel he must compensate for this in some way to demonstrate to the other party that he has not been prejudiced by your actions or words.
- *DO consider each question before answering.* Questions should be answered unhesitantly, without long pauses or undue reflection on the part of the witness. However, don't let the cross-examiner set the pace for your answers. He may fire questions at you at a rapid pace in an effort to cause you to answer too quickly and without due reflection. Think before you answer.
- *DON'T be afraid to say "I don't know."* If such is an honest answer, don't be afraid to admit you don't know about something. No witness is expected to know all there is to know about any given subject. Don't offer opinions or conjecture in reply to a question which you simply don't know the certain answer to. If you have answered other questions in a straightforward manner—giving certain and specific answers to questions you know the answer to with certainty—you will actually enhance your credibility when you say "I don't know" to questions about which you don't have certain knowledge, avoiding speculative or opinion (guessed-at) answers.

- *DON'T answer a question you don't understand.* If you don't understand a question, because it is ambiguous or unclear to you, don't guess at what is being asked of you and proffer an answer based on your guess. You may be mistaken in your interpretation of what the question is asking. Ask the questioner if he will please repeat the question (or rephrase it if need be) as many times as is necessary for you to clearly comprehend the question. The question may have been deliberately phrased to be susceptible to more than one interpretation. If you answer without being certain what is being sought, you may guess wrong or differently than it was interpreted by the arbiter; thus you may be supplying an answer misunderstood by the arbiter who is looking at it another way.
- *DON'T deny you've reviewed your testimony with your party's advocate.* Occasionally the other party's advocate may ask you if you've gone over your testimony with your advocate prior to the arbitration hearing. He may even make it sound as though you're guilty of wrongdoing if you admit you have done so. Tell the truth. If the answer is yes—and rarely will it be otherwise—readily admit to it. There is nothing wrong with such practice. It is routine and commonly done. The arbiter will assume that you have. It will reflect negatively on the total of your credibility if the arbiter believes you are dishonestly denying you've gone over your testimony with your advocate beforehand. Tell the truth on this and in all answers you give to all questions.
- *DO be prepared to take an oath.* In adversary proceedings such as arbitration the swearing of witnesses is often preferred, whether required by statute or not (it is not required under the common law). If either party requests the swearing of witnesses, the arbiter will ordinarily oblige them. In swearing witnesses, the arbiter asks the witness if he solemnly swears that the testimony he is about to give in the case is the truth, the whole truth, and nothing but the truth, so help him God. The witness, with right hand raised, answers "I do."
- *DON'T repeat questions before answering them.* To do this gives the appearance of hedging or stalling to buy time to conjure up an answer that will best serve your interests—an answer concocted, rather than the truth, which could be stated with more spontaneity.
- *DON'T stall, or delay, or fuss and fidget.* Try to answer questions with reasonable promptness, and try not to wiggle, squirm, or fidget while in the witness chair. Such mannerisms and behavior merely cast suspicion on your honesty and credibility.
- *DO be neatly groomed if possible.* It is recognized that this is not always possible. But if it is, at least be neat and clean. It is not necessary to be in a suit and tie, nor dressed up in any way—it is merely

desirable that where it is practicable, you appear clean and as neatly groomed as you can be under the circumstances.

- *DON'T mumble.* Speak clearly and forthrightly. Your testimony is of value only if it is heard and understood by the arbiter. Also, he may interpret your unclear utterances as a form of evasiveness in your response to questions.
- *DO sit quietly if objections are raised by your advocate.* If you are testifying, probably being cross-examined, and your advocate raises an objection, hush up, take a deep breath, sit back and relax. Don't continue testifying until the arbiter orders you to, or has ordered a resumption of the hearing. The reasons for your advocate's objection may not always be very clear to you, but you can be sure it is intended to be in your best interests and those of your side. Under no circumstances should the witness continue testifying in disregard of his advocate's objection being raised.
- *DO keep your hands away from your face.* Preferably hold your hands still or fold them comfortably on your lap. Don't cover your mouth with them or otherwise fiddle with your face. It conveys an impression of nervousness, tension, anxiety, worry, uncertainty, or evasiveness, all of which behavior reflects poorly on the witness's honesty and credibility.
- *DO advise your advocate of all pocket memos, diaries, notes, etc.* If you have any such notes you previously made at the time of the grievance occurrence, which are relevant to the case, review them with your advocate when he is preparing the case for trial. Don't surprise him by pulling them out of your pocket at the hearing. He may or may not elect to use them when reviewed in advance. Under certain circumstances they may be useful in supporting or corroborating your oral testimony.
- *DO quietly advise your advocate if you hear testimony which provokes your recall of a relevant matter.* No one has a perfect memory or perfect recall. You may unintentionally overlook some point you know about the case, and thus fail to so advise your advocate. If something unfolds at the hearing which provokes your recall of a previously overlooked and relevant matter, pass a note or quietly whisper about it to your advocate.
- *DO quietly suggest a recess to your advocate if you consider one will be beneficial.* Be alert—listen carefully and watch attentively. If you hear or see something occur which has not been seen or heard by your advocate, or you fear it has not been, pass a note or quietly whisper to him suggesting a recess. Remember, however, whether he calls for one is within his province, for he is the strategist, tactician and quarterback for your side.

- *DON'T deny you are being paid while testifying.* If you are on salary, you will probably be receiving pay while testifying. If asked if you are, readily admit it. You are not being paid a sum of money to induce you to give certain favorable testimony—but that is what such a question tries to imply. Be truthful. Don't worry about honest admissions. Your advocate will clarify the point with the arbiter if any confusion follows your honest admission of being paid and why.
- *DON'T look to your advocate for answers to questions.* This is a no-no. The answers to questions asked of you must come from you. If the arbiter sees you getting signs or nods or head shakes from someone else, it will merely cause him to discredit all or most of your testimony.
- *DON'T unduly hesitate in answering questions–or contradict yourself.* Arbiters believe relative spontaneity accompanies honest replies. Don't unduly hesitate or procrastinate over an answer. Under normal circumstances, repeated undue hesitation in answering questions will result in arbitral suspicion about witness veracity. Also, a witness who contradicts himself always leaves the arbiter with some doubt about his testimony, at least with respect to those questions he answers contradictorily and perhaps with a residue of doubt about his whole testimony. If the other side then testified clearly and certainly on the same points over which you have been inconsistent or contradictory, the arbiter may well resolve his doubt in favor of the other party.
- *DO realize the scope of cross-examination is not limited to direct examination subjects.* Since the arbitrator has paramount interest in securing all of the facts, he may refuse to restrict cross-examination to matters brought out in the examination-in-chief, and he can be expected not to place strict limitation upon the number of re-cross or re-direct examinations. As to the first of these points, arbitral consensus appears to be that reasonably wide latitude should be permitted in cross-examination. While the parties are allowed considerable latitude in cross-examining witnesses to reveal conflicts in their testimony and to challenge credibility, arbitrators will not condone use of personal invectives against witnesses.
- *DON'T contact the arbitrator before or after the hearing.* Before a hearing has been held and after it has been closed, the arbiter should not be contacted except by the principals who handled the case for the respective parties. Witnesses who are going to or who have already testified should not be in contact with the arbiter.
- *DON'T bring prepared lists of questions into the hearing room.* In preparing the case, the company advocate may prepare a list of

questions he intends to ask you, and/or a list of the questions he anticipates you may be asked on cross-examination, to merely further your familiarization with such questions and its procedure. Don't bring such lists of questions with you into the hearing room.

- *DO control your emotions, remarks, demeanor.* It is the legitimate role of the cross-examiner to try to upset you, make you lose your temper, cause you to make emotional or intemperate remarks, to get you confused or contradict yourself. You are not responsible for his behavior; you are only accountable for your own. Don't respond to his baiting. Be calm, cool, self-assured, and in control of your actions and words. The arbiter will be evaluating you, your answers, and your demeanor. You want him to leave the hearing with a positive impression of you and your credibility.
- *DO realize witnesses may be excluded from the hearing room when not testifying.* One of the traditional methods for preserving the purity of testimony, the rule that witnesses may be excluded from the hearing chamber during the reception of others' testimony, frequently is invoked in arbitration. Whenever it is sought by either party, it is invariably granted by the arbiter. This is often considered an effective safeguard against the possibility that one witness may be influenced in his testimony by what he has heard someone else say. It also highlights the importance of each witness telling the truth so each account coincides with each other witness's account.
- *DO understand that an interested party has a right to be present.* The arbiter customarily has authority to require witnesses (except those who are direct parties) to leave the hearing room during the testimony of other witnesses. However, direct parties or interested parties (e.g. the grievant or aggrieved individuals) do have the right to remain in the hearing room during all testimony that is taken from all witnesses.
- *DO bring a note-pad and pencil to the hearing with you.* You may be of assistance to your advocate by being alert and attentive to all that transpires during the hearing. You are free to quietly make notes and pass them to him so long as you don't interrupt or interfere with the ongoing proceedings.
- *DON'T you as a witness raise any objections.* A witness who himself objects to questions and tries to avoid answering them will create an impression that he is biased and unwilling to make a full and frank disclosure. An exception to the instructions against objection by the witness must be recognized as to matter that is the subject of a personal privilege—a privilege that must be asserted by the witness. If such matters are anticipated and the privilege is to be asserted either under your advocate's advice or upon the independ-

ent decision of the witness, it should be certain that the witness and the advocate have a common understanding of the procedure for asserting the privilege.

- *DO understand that the grievant need not testify.* A question sometimes arises as to whether an employee may refuse to testify in arbitration by the exercise of a privilege against self-incrimination. The answer is that he may so refuse, but of course at his own risk. The individual grievant is often able to cast light upon the dispute, and he ordinarily does take the witness stand. It is not unexpected that the failure of a grievant to appear and testify at the hearing of his grievance has in some cases been one of the factors leading to the arbitrator's conclusion that the grievance lacked merit. However, arbitrators sometimes have expressly stated that the failure of a grievant to testify creates no inference against him, but even so, an arbiter may pointedly note that the grievant's failure to testify has left the case against him unrefuted. The latter situation assumes, of course, that the company has adequately established its case by probative evidence.
- *DO study carefully any contract provisions applicable to the case.* You are not expected to be an expert on the contract. However, you should at least have a working knowledge of the provisions relevant to the arbitrated case if you were instrumental in interpreting or applying them in connection with some decision you made, or action you took.
- *DON'T speak out or otherwise interrupt the hearing while you're not testifying.* This type of conduct is a no-no. It reflects negatively on you and on your side. Arbitrators are only human. Don't knowingly engage in conduct which will prejudice him in any way against you or your side of the case.
- *DO realize the arbiter may also ask you questions.* The arbiter is also privileged to ask questions of witnesses. He may do so to clarify a point, or to obtain information additional to that proffered, or even to inquire into new areas not previously covered on either direct or cross-examination. Witnesses should convey the same demeanor in their answers and conduct as they do on direct and cross-examination, namely, they should be courteous, honest, and forthright in the answers they provide.
- *DO realize the cross-examiner may use harsh or aggressive tactics.* It is important to realize the potential objectives of cross-examination, which may be classified into four groups: (1) discrediting the testimony of the witness being examined; (2) using the testimony of this witness to discredit the unfavorable testimony of other witnesses; (3) using the testimony of this witness to corroborate the

favorable testimony of other witnesses; and (4) using the testimony of this witness to contribute independently to the favorable development of the cross-examiner's case. Accomplishing one of these aims may require an entirely different method of dealing with the witness from that appropriate for another aim. It is not uncommon for the cross-examiner to use an aggressive manner or even harsh tactics. Don't let this get to you, or upset you; be calm, cool and self-assured. Remember, the arbiter is carefully evaluating you, your behavior, and your remarks.

- *DO realize that leading questions (ones so worded to suggest a desired answer) made to you during cross-examination are permissible.* Leading questions asked during cross-examination are not improper. A question is leading if it suggests to the witness the answer the interrogator desires. The witness must listen carefully and give a considered, intelligent, and honest response, even though it may be (as it most often is) different than the suggested and obviously desired answer. Don't be drawn or seduced into an answer which you don't basically agree with, in an effort to be agreeable with the questioner.
- *DO realize the cross-examiner may shift the subject of inquiry suddenly and frequently.* The theory of the "hop, skip, and jump" method of cross-examination is that the witness is kept so busy shifting his thought processes from one subject to another that he will not have time to formulate answers to fit some dishonest scheme, or that if he does so, they will be so artless that the cross-examiner will be able to expose them. You needn't worry about such a questioning technique if all of your responses are thoughtfully considered and are honest in context.
- *DON'T offer speculation or conjecture.* Stick to the facts you know about. Don't proffer opinion evidence. Tell only what you saw or what you heard. If you don't actually know the answer to a question, don't forward an answer which can only be speculative at best. It waters down the rest of your otherwise factual account.

Use of Witnesses

Witnesses will be and should be used only if they are essential for the production of certain information which is not otherwise available through records, documents, files, etc.

Witnesses are potentially the weakest link(s) in the party's case, where they are used. Witnesses are invariably exposed to cross-examination. There's no such thing as a perfect witness—though there are many occasions where a witness leaves the stand unscathed and his party's case is not injured by his testimony. But the reverse potential is always present—and too often such potential is realized to the detriment of the party he intended to benefit. Witnesses should only be used, but certainly should be used, where there is no other way to bring forth the information they possess except to put them on the witness stand.

13

Arbitration and Advocacy

The Advocate

Two experienced labor relation practitioners may meet identical situations with wholly different methods and each may achieve success. One may be dramatic and witty, while another appears equally successful with low-key methods designed to emphasize the earnestness of the appeal. Each has developed a distinctive talent for presenting his cause persuasively. Undoubtedly those who become the most effective arbitration trial advocates begin with native ability to think accurately under pressure and to speak extemporaneously, but this is only a beginning. Other practioners with less native ability may prove to be more effective advocates because they prepare more thoroughly and give greater attention to discovering and applying methods most suitable to their own peculiar talents and limitations.

Very few persons have the ability to effectively assume numerous different roles. Your attempt to assume a demeanor that is unnatural will usually result in creating the impression upon the arbitrator that you are trying to put something over on him, rather than trying to persuade him to agree with the position you sincerely advance. Whatever the particular method you may be considering, avoid it if there is a serious danger that it will create or contribute to an impression of want of sincerity. Use only those roles you can actually live.

Probably you will be at your best as an advocate when you cause the arbitrator to believe that the decision you are urging him to reach is the decision you would reach yourself.

The beneficial effect of your apparent sincerity may be lost or greatly reduced if you seem willing to use any means available, fair or unfair, to advance your cause. It is understandable that an advocate is often more intent upon winning than upon getting a fair hearing, though usually the two seem to the advocate to be synonymous. An advocate's bias is expected and usually excused, though not ignored; but the advocate's methods may be viewed more critically. An appearance of desiring a fair hearing—no less and no more—generally produces a more favorable and sympathetic response from an arbitrator. This is particularly true if there is an apparent contrast between the attitudes of the opposing advocates in this respect; the one who resorts to methods that may be regarded as unfair, or to contentions that may be regarded as technical or tricky, rather than being founded on merits of the controversy, incurs disfavor.

From a long-range point of view, as distinguished from concern with the immediate case only, you have an interest in avoiding customary use of methods designed to win cases on grounds that may be regarded as unfair, though perhaps technically proper. A reputation for this type of practice becomes a handicap to you in presenting your side in future cases.

To be an effective arbitration advocate you must maintain perspective. Consider each case problem in its proper relationship to the development of the case as a whole. In each instance, let your decision on whether to make a certain point—to ask a certain question of a witness, to raise a certain objection, or to use a certain technique—be guided not solely by whether you have a technically sound basis for doing so and will realize some immediate advantage, but also by your appraisal of the effect that your making a point may have upon the arbitrator's consideration of all the other aspects of the case. Likewise, let your choice of the time for raising the point be guided by the effect of timing upon the reactions of the arbitrator.

And last but not least, there is no substitute for thorough preparation of each case for trial. This means preparation of contract, argument and facts. It means not only knowing and planning the presentation of your own side of the case but also knowing the other side well enough to anticipate your adversary's evidence and case theories. It means discovering the weak points as well as the strong points of the case. In short, your aim should be to know the whole case.

Direct Examination

For their contribution toward the ultimate aim of winning the case, these more immediate aims of direct examination deserve your attention: to present evidence sufficient to raise each claim or defense, to complete a record of testimony that will support whatever arguments you may wish to urge in the hearing, and to convince the fact finder, the arbitrator, of the truthfulness and accuracy of all the evidence supporting your claim or defense.

Although effective direct examination is usually less spectacular, more cases are won by evidence on direct that by than on cross-examination.

In the ordinary hearing, the original development of all elements of the claimant's case depends almost entirely upon direct examination. As the claimant's advocate, you may plan to use cross-examination of the other side's witnesses to support the case presented in direct examination of your own, to the end that the arbitrator will be persuaded. But do not rely on cross-examination of your adversary's witnesses to supply any element of the claim that you are able to supply by direct examination of witnesses whom you can safely call to the stand on your own.

You may appropriately place somewhat greater reliance on cross-examination in planning a defense than in planning the development of your own case. The defense is often a denial, rather than an affirmative assertion. When you are dealing with a nondiscipline case (one involving contract interpretation), your problem is one of convincing the arbitrator that vital elements of the opponent's case are unsupported in fact, or of convincing the arbitrator that some vital element of fact is entirely omitted from the other party's proof. Also, you have the opportunity to cross-examine their witnesses before you call your own witnesses; if your plans to use cross-examination go awry, you have an opportunity to change plans. With respect to an affirmative defense, it is better in your precise planning not to rely upon cross-examination for developing any element of your defense; at the least, you should prepare an alternative plan for developing each element by your own witnesses in the event the cross-examination does not go according to plan.

Using Cumulative Witnesses

Usually the problem concerning use of corroborative testimony or cumulative witnesses is purely tactical. Calling cumulative witnesses is one of the most dangerous practices in trial technique. If they testify alike, the case is subject to the charge that the testimony is suspect because people do not observe and remember events in exactly the same way. If they differ, the case is subject to the charge that the witnesses are poor observers, or otherwise unreliable. Of course, you may answer the discrepancies on irrelevant matters, merely vouch for the honesty of your witnesses and your case, but you never know whether the arbitrator will be convinced. More important, however, is the danger that contradictions on important maters will arise, especially when the witnesses are subjected to skillful cross-examination.

Determining Order of Witnesses

A problem encountered early in planning your direct examination is determining the order of witnesses. Your decision on this matter may be influenced by practical factors such as the time of availability of particular witnesses whose convenience you must serve to secure their cooperation. Such factors as these influence the order of witnesses to the detriment of most effective presentation of the case; but through careful planning you can usually eliminate their influence and almost always you can reduce it.

A logical progression in the story of the case, as it develops through the testimony of the witnesses, is an asset. It aids the arbitrator in understanding and remembering the testimony.

The opening and closing witnesses often have positions of special prominence. The arbitrator is sometimes more alert at these times, and especially so at the time the opening witness testifies. Most observers agree that first impressions tend to last; once an impression is formed in the mind of an arbitrator, the burden is on the one who seeks to change it. For these reasons it is desirable to present a strong and favorable witness as the first witness in the case.

At the other extreme, the last witness occupies a special position because the memory of what he says is freshest in the mind of the arbitrator during his formal deliberation. It is especially damaging if that freshest memory is one of a weak witness, and helpful if it is the memory of a strong and favorable witness. Accordingly, it is usually advisable to use a strong witness first and a strong witness last, allowing other factors to govern the particular order of the witnesses in between.

This special importance of the opening and closing witnesses is but one aspect of a broader proposition that the timing of evidence may materially affect its influence upon the arbitrator. Through careful planning, unfavorable evidence can be offered at a time calculated to reduce the notice it receives, and favorable evidence can be offered at a time that will invite special attention to it and give it greater emphasis.

The necessity of laying a predicate by one witness for some part of the testimony of another influences the order of witnesses Your failure to consider this factor may result in delay and the necessity for recalling witnesses, and can even result in failure to secure admission of material evidence because you were unable to get an essential witness to return for the sole purpose of providing a predicate.

The need for a logical presentation of the theory of your case may be served by your using effectively the right to make an oral statement of the claim before any evidence is offered. Also, in your selection of witnesses for appearance on the stand, you may give your weaker witness the opportunity of observing the other witnesses at the hearing proceedings. He may thereby become more at ease in the surroundings and less nervous when he takes the stand so that he can state his case more effectively. The danger of damaging mistakes in one of your witness's testimony is reduced when he has the opportunity to hear the testimony of his supporting witnesses and to observe the techniques of the opposing advocate on cross-examination before he takes the stand.

Preparing an Outline of Testimony

A spontaneous statement is the most convincing statement. If you could know that the spontaneous, unplanned direct examination would produce only favorable statements, you would avoid anything suggestive of a plan or outline for fear of interfering with the convincing spontaneity of the witness's testimony. Unfortunately that condition can never exist. Direct examination without planning is, therefore, a gamble. Direct examination may still be a gamble after the most thorough planning, but at least the odds are more favorable. There may be the rare combination of witness and advocate capable of presenting effective direct examination without specific advance preparation, but preparation is necessary for most advocates and helpful to all. The goal is a type of planning that will cause the least possible interference with the spontaneity of the testimony consistent with reasonable assurance that it will not develop unfavorably in substance. A conflict exists here between the interest in encouraging a convincing manner of testifying and the interest in assuring that the substantive content of the testimony is favorable. A compromise between these conflicting interests is necessary; the degree to which one interest is favored over the other in a particular case must be a matter of judgment in light of the circumstances.

The early interview of the witness while the facts are fresh in his mind, the written or recorded statements, the investigation of contract and past practice to determine what facts must be proved to support a cause of action, the comparison of the witness's statements with physical facts and other expected testimony—all of these, as well as the final witness interviews, are, in a sense, merely steps in the planning of the direct examination of the witness.

An arbitrator is no doubt favorably impressed by spontaneity of answers of the witnesses. However, they do not expect or credit spontaneity in interrogation. They know that trying arbitration cases is the labor relation practitioner's business and that any good practitioner plans his work. Accordingly, it is no disadvantage before the arbitrator that the course of interrogation reveals to him that it has been carefully planned. The advantages of outlining the examination of each witness are many: your presentation is more logical and orderly; less confusion and waste of time results; you can check your outline of the examination of all witnesses against your outline of the essential fact elements of your case theory; you are less likely to omit some vital evidence in the stress of the hearing; and you can more easily anticipate and provide against objections to your important evidence. You will usually find it worthwhile to make a detailed outline of the proposed direct examination and cross-examination of every known witness. The more experience you gain, the more of this planning and outlining you can do mentally and rapidly, without reducing it to writing.

Whether the outline is a written one or a mental one, it is not final. It is merely a tool to be used in the hearing, and not an invariable pattern to be slavishly followed. Variations from it will be demanded in light of the actual developments in the hearing.

Another advantage of outlining the examination of each witness in advance is that it enables you to open and close the testimony of the witness on the stronger points and in other ways to arrange the timing of evidence for the greatest tactical benefit.

Preparing Questions

Particularly for direct examination, you can anticipate accurately the subject matter you will cover with each witness, and you can frame your questions in advance, at a time when you can consider and test each question as to whether it is leading or not. In due course, that practice will help you to develop good habits of framing questions, so that your phrasing of even your extemporaneous questions will tend to meet the requirements of proper interrogation. In short, the suggestions that follow admittedly can give you little help in phrasing a question during the course of a hearing, because there is then insufficient time to think of a proposed question and subject it to tests such as these, modifying or abandoning it pursuant to the results of the tests. These suggestions are intended for advance preparation of specific questions and for use in developing good habits in the phrasing of questions.

- *Ask only one question at a time, and not a question with several parts.* Compound sentences are sometimes hard to understand. Answers to compound questions are worse; they are likely to be incomplete, ambiguous, or both.
- *Avoid negatives in the question if possible.* Consider this exchange: Q—"You do not know whether Jones was there?" A—"Yes." Did the witness mean "Yes, I know" or did he mean "Yes, it is true that I do not know," or did he mean "Yes, Jones was there"? If you notice it, this doubt can be cleared by another question and the loss is simply that of delay and a slight danger of confusion; but if you failed to call for clarification after an exchange such as this, you may have lost a vital point by having the answer interpreted differently from what you yourself know that the witness meant.

- *Make the question brief.* Both the witness and the arbitrator must understand all the question in order to understand it correctly.
- *State the question in simple words*—those used in everyday conversation. You want the arbitrator to understand both the questions and the answers, and this requires the use of words that will be common to him and, therefore, understood. This is not a recommendation for use of slang or bad grammar, however; that practice, unless it comes naturally with the advocate, probably will be recognized and resented as talking down to the arbitrator.
- *In summary, make the question clear.* It is not enough that you and the witness understand each other's questions and answers, though of course that is important. Understanding by the arbitrator is also important. The arbitrator is the one whose understanding is your primary interest. He is less familiar with the facts and circumstances than either you or the witness. It is no reflection on the intelligence of arbitrators that simple questions are best.

Leading the Witness

The effect of a leading question cannot be erased by objection or instruction. The vice of the question is telling the witness what the advocate wants him to say. Having received the message, the witness can then answer a nonleading question in the desired way, even though the leading question is stricken. Consequently, you may sometimes be tempted to ask a leading question deliberately, realizing that an objection to it will be sustained. You are then, in effect, coaching the witness by a leading question.

However, there are occasions when leading questions will be permitted:

- Questions as to preliminary matters which set the stage for inquiries relevant to the material disputed issues in the case;
- Questions that the witness has already answered;
- Questions addressed to an adverse or hostile witness;
- Questions on cross-examination of a witness called by the adversary;
- Questions to a witness of limited understanding;
- Questions to a witness whose recollection has been exhausted but who is supposed to know additional facts material to the case;
- Questions to a witness who is being asked to contradict statements previously made by another witness.

A question is leading if it suggests to the witness the answer that the interrogator desires. Pursuing inquiries by leading the witness may cast a cloud of suspicion not only upon his particular statement but also upon other testimony of this witness and even upon still other evidence you later offer. Whether you should take that risk will depend upon how important the evidence is to the case.

The use of leading questions has tactical disadvantages. If objected to, the practice will result in repeated rulings of the arbitrator probably sustaining the objections and perhaps reprimanding the advocate who is doing the questioning. Although labor relations practitioners in arbitration generally prefer to avoid objections for fear of impressing the arbitrator unfavorably, most of them consider that objections of this character, sustained by the arbitrator, are more damaging to the interrogator than to the objector. Certainly the practice of leading witnesses causes an unfavorable reaction from the arbitrator. Furthermore, even if no objections are being made to the leading questions, it is dangerous to assume that the interrogation is developing favorably.

The rule against leading questions is no more than a rule of common sense; if you want the witness's own story, instead of the advocate's, you must depend on the witness's memory and statement of it, and not on the advocate's. This is the commonsense rule that arbitrators are likely to apply in their judgment of the credibility of the testimony if the practice of leading witnesses is so persistent that they notice it. Of course, your adversary may frame objections so as to help the arbitrator reach that conclusion.

Expert Witnesses

Experts (persons with special training or skill in a particular field) may not only testify as to facts but may also give their opinions on matters pertaining to their field. Their special qualifications and knowledge tend to make their opinions trustworthy and enlightening. A company official, a highly skilled tradesman, an engineer, a medical man, and many others may have such special skills, training, and experience as to qualify them to state opinions on technical matters in their respective fields or to demonstrate a method of procedure.

When using witnesses of this type, you should prove their qualifications as an expert. This serves two distinct purposes: it lays the predicate for admissibility of opinion testimony of the expert, and it persuades the arbitrator that the findings and opinions of the expert are accurate. It may be that your adversary will suggest a waiver of the proof of qualification of the expert witness, particularly if his qualifications are outstanding, on the theory that this tactical move will prevent the arbitrator from hearing an impressive array of evidence that the expert's findings and opinions are credible. When such a waiver is offered by your adversary, you are not necessarily bound to accept it and desist from proving the qualifications of your expert. If his qualifications are impressive, you should consider proceeding nonetheless with offer of proof of his qualifications.

Of course, laboring over insignificant details of his background and experience will merely bore the arbitrator and perhaps lead him to the impression you are trying to build up the witness beyond what the facts justify. There is also a possible advantage in omitting some of the nitty-gritty detail so the witness may have something further to offer in the event your adversary chooses to cross-examine him regarding his qualifications. Try to avoid inferences to the arbitrator that he is a professional witness whose testimony can be bought for a fee or that he is biased in favor of one group, which group includes the party calling him.

Demonstrative Evidence

The traditional way of proving a fact is by asking a witness who knows. Some hearings conclude with no type of evidence having been offered other than what the witnesses say. Yet a moment's reflection will suggest to you that this type of evidence is in most respects the least convincing type of evidence you can offer. It is subject to all the frailties of human error and observation, memory, expression, and integrity. It is common knowledge that two witnesses standing side by side to observe the same event, if interrogated separately, will differ in their statements concerning what occurred. Arbitrators who are not already aware of these facts can usually be converted to believe in them with moderate attention to the question in the advocate's argument. The advocate who has more real or demonstrative evidence than his adversary has a distinct advantage in the contest of convincing the arbitrator. Some, though not all, of the chances for error are absent or reduced in the case of demonstrative evidence.

Generally, you should make use of all the favorable physical or demonstrative evidence that is available to you, and careful attention and some imagination in searching for such evidence will disclose that more is available than is customarily used in the trial of cases.

Oral testimony has not only the weakness of possibilities for human error in memory, observation, and statement, but also the weakness of inadequacy to convey information accurately and completely. Although a diagram made by the witness is no better than his observation, memory, and ability to draw, a diagram by one with average ability and drawing skills is superior to his mere statement of the information because he may more accurately convey to the arbitrator the idea that is in his own mind. A diagram or other type of drawing has another distinct value—the preservation of the expression of the idea, so that the arbitrator may turn back to it for study and comparison and to refresh his own memory of the testimony. However, you should never ask a witness on direct examination to prepare a drawing or a diagram unless you have previously made this same request and determined if the witness is able to do it reasonably well. Some witnesses are so poor at drawing, and particularly at keeping a reasonably accurate scale and relative position of various objects, that more harm than good will be done by asking that a drawing be made in the presence of the arbitrator.

If you plan to use a map prepared by another during the testimony of a witness, you should show the map to the witness in the prehearing conference with him. A hurried study for the first time on the witness stand may confuse the witness. Take care, however, in discussing the map with your witness, to prepare for the possibility that he will be asked on cross-examination if you showed him where he should place certain marks on the map. A wholesale denial of talking with you about placement of these marks by a witness uncertain about the propriety of such a conference would be almost as damaging as proof that you actually told the witness where to place the particular marks.

When using a drawing, should you ask that it be prepared on a blackboard or on a paper, and should you ask the witness to start from a blank or should you furnish a skill drawing of background objects already authenticated by previous evidence? An advantage of the drawing on paper is that you can offer it in evidence when it is completed, and the arbitrator who is permitted to take exhibits with him then may carry it with him for his ultimate deliberations.

Cross-Examination

The Art of Cross-Examination

To excel in cross-examination you must have native ability. If you are interested in arbitration work, however, it is probably a safe assumption that you have this kind of ability in some degree at least. You can develop your native ability by practice and experience just as one can develop a talent for music. But the talent for cross-examination, in this sense, is the lesser part of the secret of effective cross-examination. Nearly all effective cross-examination is planned, to one degree or another. Through adequate planning you can often achieve effective cross-examination even before you have any substantial arbitration experience. As you gain experience, your success in cross-examination will continue to depend on your diligence and thoroughness in preparing. The following material concerns the methods customarily used in effective cross-examination and ways of preparing to use them.

The potential aims of cross-examination may be classified into four groups: (1) discrediting the testimony of the witness being examined; (2) using the testimony of this witness to discredit the unfavorable testimony of other witnesses; (3) using the testimony of this witness to corroborate the favorable testimony of other witnesses; and (4) using the testimony of this witness to contribute independently to the favorable development of your own case.

Accomplishing one of these aims may require an entirely different method of dealing with the witness from that appropriate for another aim. A method of cross-examination designed to serve one aim may defeat another. Adequate planning requires an appraisal of the relative advantages associated with each of these aims, since this is a factor bearing on the choice of methods.

Your selection of methods of cross-examination of the witness will depend also on the type of witness you face; among other things, the age, education, and mentality of the witness are important factors. The most ignorant witness is often the hardest to cross-examine because you cannot set him up for a fall. Also, you must exercise great care to avoid creating arbitrator's sympathy for him because you are exposing his ignorance or illiteracy. Your aim is to condemn his testimony as unreliable without condemning the witness for being ignorant. If you inflict personal ridicule on an important witness, or treat him sarcastically, the arbitrator may think you are taking an unfair advantage of the differences in intelligence and education between yourself and the witness.

Give some thought to your general attitude and demeanor toward the witness. Should you let your contempt for a given witness be obvious for the arbitrator to see, if you feel that way about him, or should you be the paragon of courtesy? Usually it is best to adopt an attitude of courtesy toward the witness, for although the arbitrator expects you to be an advocate, he may very quickly develop sympathy for a witness whom he thinks you are badgering unfairly. It is quite possible to be very polite and yet convey to the arbitrator your distrust of the witness's testimony.

Aids to Cross-Examination

Begin your preparation for cross-examination at the same time you begin your investigation of the case. Obviously, the kind of investigation by which you know your adversary's case and evidence as well as your own is essential to the maximum success in cross-examination. Knowing what the witness probably will say is important not only for deciding what to ask but also for deciding what not to ask.

Thorough investigation provides the background information essential to your instantly realizing, during your adversary's direct examination, the implications of the questions and the answers; also it provides tools for cross-examination. Among these tools are written statements, documents and records, information concerning actions and statements of the witness to which other persons will testify. With due consideration for the aims of your cross-examination of each witness, the aids available, and the subjects of inquiry, you should prepare an outline of the proposed cross-examination of each witness whose use by your adversary you are able to anticipate. More variations from the outline are to be expected than in the case of direct examination of your own witness, but the previous consideration that you have given to anticipated problems will be most helpful to you during cross-examination even though you do not follow the outline closely

The Decision to Cross-Examine

Should you cross-examine each witness? Many lawyers' stories concerning cross-examination tell of the brilliant cross-examination that won the lawsuit. Others tell of the inept cross-examination that lost it. Although both types of yarns are commonly influenced by a recognized license like that of the poet and the fisherman, they are founded on truths.

The following are some of the risks you incur in cross-examination:

- Confronting a witness with a prior written statement inconsistent with his present testimony may result in proof of other facts recorded in the statement and not previously proved.
- Confronting the witness with inconsistencies between his testimony and that of your own witness may result in impeachment of the testimony of your own witness.
- An attempt to prove or even actual proof of bad character of the witness may provoke the sympathy of the arbitrator for the witness and the case he supports.
- The cross-examination intended to reveal indirectly the bias of the witness by committing him to an untenable extreme may result in strengthening the direct examination.
- The cross-examination intended to bring out matters about which your adversary failed to inquire, in the belief that the answers will be favorable to your client, may result only in more evidence favorable to the adverse party who called the witness.
- Calling on the witness to repeat and elaborate his testimony, as a foundation for proof of prior contradictions or inconsistencies, may emphasize and strengthen the witness's testimony if he has a plausible explanation for the apparent inconsistencies.
- Cross-examination intended to show bias from animosity associ-

ated with termination of employment may provoke sympathy for the discharged employee.

- Asking a "why" question in the belief that the witness can have no reasonable explanation may result in his stating prejudicial arguments that would have been clearly inadmissible in the absence of the invitation by the open question.
- Insistence upon a clear answer from an evasive witness may lead to an unexpected and unfavorable disclosure.
- Cross-examination of an expert concerning his qualifications may serve only to bolster less adequate proof of those qualifications during direct examination.
- Methods of cross-examination intended to exact disclosures from an unwilling witness may be harmful because of the arbitrator's feeling that they are unfair methods.

For each of the risks of cross-examination in this illustrative list, a corresponding possibility of gain is present. These are risks that you incur even though your cross-examination is carefully planned to achieve one or more of these gains. Proceeding blindly into cross-examination without an aim and a plan would involve many such risks without corresponding hope of benefit.

The plan for cross-examination need not be and should not be inflexible. Neither should the cross-examination be haphazard. Even those who use the hop, skip, and jump method of cross-examination—changing the subject of inquiry frequently and suddenly—do so with a purpose; they hope that the truth will come out because the witness does not have time to anticipate the next question and fabricate an answer other than the truth, or else that his quickly conceived untruths will be so artless that they can be exposed.

Careful planning may reduce but will never wholly eliminate the risk of harm to your own cause by your cross-examination. The decision whether or not to cross-examine a particular witness, and to what extent and with what aims and methods, calls for appraising the advantages and disadvantages and accepting a calculated risk. This weighing of risks is something that as an arbitration advocate you must do frequently, not only with respect to cross-examination but also in determining whether to use other methods, and even in considering the broader question whether to proceed to arbitration or to settle.

That cases are sometimes lost in cross-examination is reason enough to beware of an unyielding rule that you cross-examine every witness. It is also possible, however, that failure to cross-examine a witness may lead the juror to conclude that you concede that his testimony is correct, or that you have no way of disputing it though you might wish that you could do so. In rare instances the testimony of your adversary's witness is so favorable or so sound and undisputed that you are willing to adopt it, and you may even smile warmly as you say, "We have no questions." When you are not willing to adopt the witness's testimony, it probably is a sound rule of thumb not to release a witness without some cross-examination unless this possible inference of acquiescence in the testimony of the witness can be met successfully with an argument that either is apparent or probably will be accepted by the arbitrator when it is pointed out in the course of your argument to him.

Assuming that you have decided to cross-examine to some extent, you are also faced with the problem as to length and content of the cross-examination. Most of the individual questions discussed in this material are relevant to that problem, though of course not all of them can be presented in a single situation. Also, the potential use of re-cross-examination, in the event your adversary uses re-direct, deserves consideration; the tactical implications in this respect are substantially identical with those involved in determining when and how to use re-direct examination.

Using Inconsistent Statements

Should you confront a witness on cross-examination with inconsistencies between his testimony and his prior oral and written statements? When and how should you use a written statement for impeachment?

The beneficial ends you may serve by confronting a witness with inconsistencies include emphasizing the contradiction in the mind of the arbitrator by bringing together at one time contradictory evidence that appeared at different times during the course of the hearing (the impeachment of the witness in this way casts doubt on the value of his testimony on other subjects as well as that relating to the particular subject of the contradiction) and upsetting the witness and thus improving your chances of obtaining admissions on other subjects.

These ends are best served by confronting the witness with self-contradictions—inconsistencies between the answers of the witness on direct examination and those on cross-examination, or between testimony at the hearing and a prior statement (sworn or unsworn, oral or written), or between his testimony on the one hand and on the other hand his pleading or his demand or his formal claim. You may serve the same ends in some instances, however, by confronting the witness with inconsistencies between his testimony and that of other witnesses.

Against the potential of beneficial results from using inconsistencies, and from the timing of your use, you must weigh some risks of harm. The problem is well illustrated by the inconsistency between testimony at the hearing and a prior written statement. The first question faced is whether any use of the statement is advisable. The fact that the witness's written statement in your possession contains matter directly contradictory to his testimony on direct examination does not necessarily indicate that you should use the statement.

Here's an example of the risks and disadvantages that may be involved in using the statement: It may contain other matter that is favorable to the party who called the witness and has as yet not been proved; using the statement would probably result in proof of that matter by independent questions of opposing counsel even if that part of the statement itself should not be received in evidence over an objection. If the overall effect of the statement is less favorable to your client than to the witness's testimony, it will usually be advisable not to use the statement despite the fact that it would show contradictions in some particulars. Unless the contradictions are on important matters, the value of proving them is outweighed by the harm from contributing to your adversary's case in other respects.

How should you use the statement? Indeed you must consider the various ways you might use the statement in order to reach a sound decision on the question whether any use of the statement is advisable. Two distinct methods of use are possible: using the statement in cross-examination and introducing the statement separately after the witness has left the stand. It is sometimes inadvisable to authenticate a written statement by a person other than the one whose statement it is. This factor, when present, strongly supports the decision to use the statement on cross-examination or not at all. Also, it is usually more effective to get an admission from the witness that this is his statement than to depend on someone else's identification of his signature and of the statement. Another consideration is that the arbitrator probably would wonder why the witness himself had not been asked about his own statement and given an opportunity to explain. Finally, since it is a case of self-contradiction by the witness, you probably will achieve more dramatic effect by confronting the witness than by producing the contradictory statement after the witness is off the stand and beyond the observation of the arbitrator. In most instances you should use the statement on cross-examination rather than solely by introducing it separately. If the witness repudiates the statement on cross-examination, however, either in whole or by contending that he did not read it over and that it contains errors, you should consider authenticating the statement by testimony of the witness to the statement or of the person who took it.

Assuming that you have decided to use the statement on cross-examination, you then must determine in what manner you will lay the predicate for it and produce it. Should you produce the statement and ask the witness to identify it first, as a predicate for the questions about the statement and its contents, or should you postpone production of the statement until you have asked questions about the subject matter and about the circumstances of taking the statement?

You may have seen a lawyer in a courtroom sometimes hold a witness's statement in his hands as a means of frightening the witness, or as a method of conveying to the jury the impression that the statement contains certain comments as implied by the questions. The practice of holding such a statement in view though not referring to it verbally is sometimes used when the advocate does not want to introduce the statement itself, because of some risk of harm. Even this use of a statement that you do not want in evidence involves a risk, however. For example, if you attempt to use a statement in this way, your opponent may call upon you to produce the statement; if you withhold it or object to its being placed in evidence by your opponent, the arbitrator may draw an unfavorable inference from your conduct. It might be suggested that you could evade the problem by refusing to produce the statement for your adversary to see in the absence of an agreement in advance that it can be received in evidence—of course, with the expectation that your adversary will not so stipulate. But that attitude is more likely to cause unfavorable reaction to your methods than to your adversary's refusal to make the agreement with respect to some statement your adversary has never seen.

Usually the use of a contradictory statement in cross-examination is more effective if you are able to remember it well enough to get the witness thoroughly committed on all material points before you produce the statement. There is also a greater likelihood that you will catch the witness so completely off guard that the arbitrator can see it in his demeanor or in his answers. He has less time to steel himself for the blow than when you have been looking at the statement while asking questions.

Should you confront a witness on cross-examination with inconsistencies between his testimony and that of others?

In deciding whether to confront a witness on cross-examination with inconsistencies, you should consider the relative advantages and disadvantages of that method as compared with other possible uses of the same materials. The best answer will depend to some extent on the identity and relationship of the witnesses, the nature of the evidence of inconsistency, and the reason for its significance in the case. If the inconsistency is between the testimony of two witnesses, both of whom were called by your opponent, confronting either witness with the inconsistencies serves at least the purpose of emphasizing in the mind of the arbitrator the fact of contradiction. The degree of benefit you realize from the cross-examination will depend upon how serious the contradiction is, but usually there is no better method of making the most of it.

Rarely will much be gained by confronting a party with an inconsistency between his testimony and that of his adversary. His answer is obvious: The adversary is wrong. It may be desirable, however, to point out the inconsistency in a manner that, without forcing the issue on the witness, gives him the opportunity to call his adversary a liar. If he is the type who might do that, calling another a liar is more likely to harm the speaker's cause than to help it.

If the inconsistency is between the testimony of your opposing party or his witness and your witness, it is a two-edged sword. It may be construed by the arbitrator as reflecting unfavorably on the testimony of your own witness rather than the one you seek to impeach. If the witness being cross-examined offers satisfactory support for his own version when pressed about the inconsistency on cross-examination, the effect will be exactly the opposite of what you intended. Before pressing the witness about such an inconsistency, therefore, you should be prepared to meet this contingency with corroboration for the version of your own witness or with other evidence tending to impeach your adversary's witness. If you have neither of these at your disposal and the inconsistency does not relate to a crucial point in the case, it is probably wiser for you to ignore the inconsistency as long as your adversary is content to do so.

The nature of the inconsistency and the reasons for its significance have an important bearing on whether you should point it out, and if so, when. If you try to make much of obviously trivial matters, you will probably bore the arbitrator or amuse him at best, and at worst you may cause him to infer you are trying to confuse the issues in the case rather than seeking a fair and sound disposition. With this exception and that noted previously, the problem is primarily one of choice as to timing. If the inconsistency is one of observation, memory or expression and not upon his integrity, usually the best way to use the inconsistency is to confront the witness with it on cross-examination. On the other hand, if the inconsistency probably reflects on the integrity of your opposing party or a key witness, you may make more dramatic and effective use of it by merely laying a predicate during cross-examination and introducing at a later time your convincing, independent evidence of the falsity of the testimony.

Inquiring into Source of Knowledge

Should you cross-examine the witness regarding the source of his knowledge of matters to which he has testified?

Careful inquiry will often disclose that things the witness says as if they were his own observations are actually only repetition of what some other person has told him. If you ask a person unfamiliar with evidence rules whether he can state a fact "of his own knowledge," he may think the correct answer is "yes" if he has been informed of the fact by someone whom he considers reliable. Although arbitrators have not adopted a philosopher's definition of "knowing," their definition is more restricted than the ordinary layman's understanding. In the language of the arbitration hearing, the witness is not able to speak of his own knowledge if he is merely repeating what he has been told, regardless of the reliability of the informant. His testimony that the informant made the statement, when offered to prove the truth of the matter stated, is excluded by the hearsay rule unless some exception applies. His repetition as his own statement of the matter he heard is excluded because of his want of knowledge of the facts stated. A showing of a personal knowledge of certain facts may also be essential as a predicate for the admissibility of opinion evidence.

Inquiring into New Subjects

Should cross-examination touch upon subjects not mentioned in direct examination?

The possibility of independent contribution to the favorable development of your own case by the cross-examination of your adversary's witnesses is an important function of good cross-examination. Occasionally a witness called by your adversary will be the only possible source of particular evidence favorable to your case. Still more often, your adversary's witness will furnish a potential source of cumulative evidence corroborating other evidence that you've produced or will produce through your own witnesses.

You need to be concerned with purely tactical considerations in determining whether to open a new subject on cross-examination. Is it a subject as to which probably the answers of the witness either will be favorable to your client or else will lay the predicate for effective impeachment of your adversary's witnesses? Or, on the other hand, is it a subject as to which the particular witness on the stand will probably answer unfavorably to you? Or is it a subject that though producing favorable answers will probably lead to other inquiries producing unfavorable answers more than counteracting any benefits gained? Will the testimony on the subject finally be of more harm than benefit to your case? Will opening the matter possibly furnish proof for your adversary that he omitted, either from hesitancy about inquiring into the subject or from oversight? The competent arbitration advocate views his immediate problem with a perspective that places emphasis on the most effective presentation of the entire case and sacrifices any temporary triumph that is inconsistent with that emphasis.

It follows that although advantages to be gained by opening new subjects on cross-examination are obvious, there are some tactical limitations on using such cross-examination. You should not ask any question of your own witness on direct examination without having asked him the question previously, unless by some other means you have real assurance of what his answer will be: The risk of an unfavorable surprise answer is too great. Although this rule cannot be applied to cross-examination, the same risk of unfavorable answers responsible for the rule exists in the case of cross-examination.

In cross-examination the risk is less serious in that the unfavorable answer from your adversary's witness does not make as great an impact upon the arbitrator as the same answer from one of your own witnesses. It is a risk more serious in that the witness, particularly if unfriendly toward you, is more likely to answer unfavorably in both manner and substance. If you can anticipate well before the hearing that your adversary will use the witness, you may reduce the risk greatly through your preparation for cross-examination. One significant advantage of this preparation is learning what questions not to ask. Though this need for caution exists, often you can think of new questions to ask with confidence about what the witness will answer, and sometimes you will be able to think of new questions for which the witness has not been prepared by your adverse counsel. Working such virgin soil is one of the most fruitful and delightful phases of cross-examination.

Usually you will gain little if anything by extending your new inquiries to matters that are irrelevant, either to the issues in your case or to bias, interest, corruption, skill, or source of knowledge of the witness, since as a general rule arbitrators will not permit such impeachment on collateral matters.

Asking for Repetition and Added Details

Should you call on the witness to repeat or state more details concerning matters touched on in direct examination?

It seems to be a natural tendency of neophyte arbitration advocates to ask a witness on cross-examination to repeat testimony given on direct examination interspersing here and there a few inquiries calling for greater details than were stated on direct. Perhaps one reason for the tendency is that this procedure comes naturally to one who feels the need to cross-examine but has no specific goal or plan. The only thing that comes to mind at the moment is to ask the witness to repeat in the hope that some inconsistency will develop. Though occasionally that hope is realized, usually such cross-examination serves only to emphasize and strengthen the direct testimony. In view of the obvious likelihood that repetition and elaboration of the direct testimony will improve the effectiveness of the witness's testimony in the absence of contradictions, you should not follow this procedure without some specific aim and reasonable basis for supposing that you may realize an advantage.

When you have evidence of contradiction or inconsistencies between the witness's testimony on direct examination and statements made by him at other times, your first step in the effective use of such evidence is laying a firm foundation for its use—a foundation that prevents the witness from formulating a plausible explanation of the apparent inconsistency. In framing the questions, you should attempt to anticipate each possible excuse of explanation for the apparent inconsistency and get the witness committed to a contrary position before you point up the inconsistency. Otherwise, an apparently plausible excuse conceived by the witness may not only rob you of effective impeachment but will also make the net effect of your cross-examination worse than none. This first step is essential even if you propose to offer the impeaching evidence independently rather than on cross-examination.

Although the cross-examination in which you make the more detailed inquiries and call upon the witness to repeat and confirm his position serves temporarily to emphasize and not weaken the witness's testimony, this is part of your overall plan of giving greater emphasis to the impeaching evidence when you ultimately offer it later. With sufficient emphasis the impeachment on one point may cast suspicion on the witness personally and thus on all other things the witness has said. When you are using cross-examination for this purpose, however, it is generally not advisable to call upon the witness to repeat the entire story or most of it; rather you should single out the points in which you have impeaching evidence available and develop them only. These points then receive the emphasis.

Shifting the Subject of Inquiry

Should you shift the subject of inquiry on cross-examination suddenly and frequently?

The theory of the hop, skip, and jump method of cross-examination—shifting of inquiry suddenly and frequently—is that the witness is kept so busy shifting his thought processes from one subject to another that he will not have time to formulate answers to fit some dishonest scheme, or that if he does so they will be so artless that you will be able to expose them. In practice, however, this method generally does not work effectively. The arbitrator may have the same difficulty as the witness in shifting thought processes. In fact the arbitrator's difficulty may be greater because he may have less familiarity at that point in the hearing with the background of the case than does the witness. Furthermore, if you catch the witness in some inconsistency, the arbitrator may be more likely to accept the excuse of the witness that he did not understand your questions than if you proceeded in a logical, organized pattern of questions. As in the case of cross-examination during the course of the hearing, the witness's excuse of misunderstanding is often more acceptable if the question to which he was responding came out of context.

Using "Why" Questions

On cross-examination should you ask the witness "why"?

When an adverse witness takes an unreasonable position, you may have to repress an urge to ask, "Are you crazy?" and you may be tempted to ask him, "Why?" The latter question is usually as impractical as the former. The adverse party called the witness to the stand and probably, though not necessarily, the witness is sympathetic with that side of the case. Under proper questioning, however, you can limit his opportunity to help establish that side of the case by holding him to stating facts called for by questions. If you ask him why he makes a certain statement, you open the door to a full explanation which may be argumentative without being nonresponsive. In short, the "why" question removes all barriers of inadmissibility and allows the witness to state any kind of opinion, argument, or inadmissible fact he chooses to state in explanation. Though an arbitrator might permit you to interrupt the answer to restrict the witness to matter that is not subject to exclusion, your interruption of a responsive answer may be as damaging as the answer itself.

The temptation to ask the "why" question is based upon the assumption that the witness has no explanation that would seem reasonable to you or to the arbitrator. If you actually have the witness in that circumstance, the question might be more effective in catching him without an explanation or with such a poor one that it will certainly be recognized as such. The risk of harm in the event that you are in error in thinking the witness cannot offer an explanation is so great, however, that it is a sound rule of thumb not to ask the "why" question.

Using Argumentative Questions

Should you use argumentative questions on cross-examination?

Some advocates (regardless of the type of witness under cross-examination) customarily use the opportunity to pose an argumentative question. They recite the cross-examiner's theory of the case, barely nodding toward the theoretical purpose of cross-examination by clothing the statement with the phrase "isn't it a fact that...." Though this use of argumentative questions has some tactical value in aiding the arbiter to understand and remember the advocate's position, it is a crude way of doing what generally can be done more effectively through other means. Long before cross-examination you have ample opportunity to present your theory of the case to the arbitrator at times when you are not laboring under the handicap of having to phrase the theory in the form of a question. Perhaps there is value in repeating your theory as often as possible. Bear in mind, however, that the arbitrator will realize that only what the witnesses say, and not what the advocates say, is evidence. Only to the extent that you can get answers from the witness that support your theory of the case, or aid in the impeachment of some part of your adversary's case, are you generally justified in continuing cross-examination; indulging in further cross-examination for the purpose of stating your theories in the form of questions is more likely to be detrimental than beneficial to your case.

This is not to say that you should never use an "isn't it a fact that" question. Frequently this form of question is the best way of committing the witness positively and in a way such that the arbitrator realizes it clearly. Particularly is this so when the question is one that the witness should be expected to answer affirmatively.

If the witness is argumentative, something more can be said for arguing with him a little, although most labor relation advocates would advise you not to do that generally. Actually a well-turned question is a better argument than a statement—if you are able to put your finger on the weakness of his argument with a question. The ideal is to bait the argumentative witness enough that the arbitrator will get the idea that he is arguing while you are simply trying to get him to answer some questions of fact. Furthermore, the argumentative witness is one you may catch in an untenable extreme.

Demanding Clear Answers

Should you insist on a clear answer from an evasive witness?

It is often possible for a witness to frame a seemingly implausible evasion of a single question. One of your very important tasks as cross-examiner is on-the-spot analysis of the evasive answer so that you may follow up with further inquiries that pin down the witness to one position or another on material questions. Requiring a clear answer from the witness serves not only the purpose of producing this testimony, however; it also serves incidentally the aim of revealing the witness's bias or his efforts to conceal relevant facts about which he is asked.

In determining how far to press an evasive witness for a clear answer, consider the materiality and importance of the original question asked, the nature of the answer that the witness will probably give if forced to a showdown, and the probable reason for the witness's reluctance to answer directly. If the original question is not important, the principal possibility of an advantage from pressing the witness is to demonstrate his reluctance to answer your questions frankly. It is not likely that you can succeed in this aim while questioning the witness on a relatively unimportant topic, except to the extent that this may contribute toward an overall impression of evasiveness if the witness reacts similarly to other questions, including some relating to comparatively important topics.

The mere fact that the witness is evading your question on an important subject does not conclusively demonstrate that you should press him on the matter. If the evasion is apparent, you have already gained some advantage from it because of the unfavorable reflection on the reliability of the witness's testimony. You may lose this advantage and may even suffer more harm if you press a witness whose evasion is caused by something other than a desire to hurt your case or favor your opponent's case. The answer when finally extracted may be unfavorable to you.

If you have determined that the risk of a harmful explanation of the witness's evasion is slight and worth taking, what means should you adopt in pressing the witness for an answer?

Make your questions simple and pointed, and break down and attack item by item any qualified or conditional answers so that you eliminate, or at least reduce to a minimum, the opportunities for plausible evasion. If in the face of a simplified question the witness is still evasive, you may decide to drop the matter after the cross-examination has proceeded to the point that the evasion by the witness is apparent to the arbitrator. Other possibilities exist—for example, should you request the arbitrator to instruct the witness to answer the question? Most often such instruction produces an answer. However, the witness cannot properly be required to answer a question that he does not understand or the answer to which he does not know, nor can he be required to give a categorical yes or no answer without explanation if such an answer would be inaccurate or misleading. If you asked a question that cannot be answered categorically, your request to the arbitrator for an instruction to the witness would doubtlessly be denied, and with detrimental effect upon your cross-examination generally. Although you consider that your question is not of this type, if there is room for doubt about the matter, it is generally better not to take the risk of asking the arbitrator for an instruction to the witness because of the possible detrimental effect of an adverse ruling by the arbitrator.

Responding to Questions from the Witness

What should you do when the witness asks a question?

Occasionally a witness will ask you a question as you are cross-examining him. If the question is one seeking an explanation or clarification of the question you have asked him, you should readily give any explanation necessary to make your question clear and unambiguous. Any other attitude on your part may give your cross-examination the appearance of being more a game than a search for the truth. If the witness's question is rhetorical or argumentative—and usually such questions will be tacked on the end of the witness's answer to some question of yours—the problem is more difficult. In favor of your answering the question is the fact that usually you will have at the tip of your tongue an answer that at least seems to you to be logical and convincing. Your preparation of the case has included consideration of all contentions that you think might be raised by your adversary and all questions that he might be expected to ask of any of your witnesses. This has, incidentally, prepared you for answering any question that is likely to be asked you unexpectedly by the witness you are cross-examining.

Another factor favoring your answering any question such as this is that it may be difficult for you otherwise to avoid the appearance in the eyes of the arbitrator of evading an embarrassing question. On the other hand, there are tactical disadvantages in answering the witness since this may encourage more questions from him and more interruptions and interference with the direction and purpose of your cross-examination. Furthermore, such an interchange may lead to a running argument with the witness in which he is on equal ground with you if he, too, is allowed to ask questions. You have a great advantage over him in the privilege of asking questions while he must give answers. You should not surrender that advantage lightly.

Discrediting Testimony of Other Witnesses

Should you attempt to use cross-examination of the witness to discredit unfavorable testimony of other witnesses?

Unfavorable testimony may be discredited by independent evidence from other sources as well as by cross-examination of the witness who gave the unfavorable testimony. Whatever its nature may be, independent proof used to discredit unfavorable testimony of other witnesses is more effective if it comes from witnesses your adversary calls rather than those you call. If the difference in statement is only one of lack of the degree of certainty and emphasis that another witness whom you can afford to call to the stand would express, you will usually profit by bolstering the testimony of your own witness with admissions from a witness your adversary has called. On the other hand, if the difference between the testimony of the witnesses is more substantial, your decision as to whether you should go into the subject with the adverse witness must depend upon your appraisal of the probable arbitrator's reaction to your witness's testimony, neither corroborated nor directly contradicted, compared with his favorable reaction to the combination of the testimony of your witness and the less favorable testimony of the adverse witness on cross-examination. Ordinarily it will be advisable for you to cross-examine on any subject as to which you expect that your adversary will question the witness later by recalling him in the light of testimony that you offer. The risk of unfavorable testimony, both as to substance and as to form of expression, is greater if your adversary has time to confer with the witness and prepare him for specific inquiries than if you cross-examine him before such preparation.

Inquiring into Opportunity to Observe

Should you cross-examine the witness as to his opportunity and ability to observe matters concerning which he has testified?

Proof of poor opportunity for observation is one of the customary methods of discrediting the testimony of the witness. Ability to observe in the sense of personal capacity is less often an issue but involves many of the same considerations. Whether you should cross-examine on poor opportunity or ability in particular instances will depend on the principal purpose of your cross-examination and the probable effectiveness of this method as part of the cross-examination.

Frequently more harm than good is done by cross-examination because it merely reinforces the direct testimony. This observation applies to an attempt to get the witness to admit facts showing poor opportunity to observe when the witness is not subject to effective attack on this ground. The provable circumstances as to his opportunity do not necessarily indicate that you should avoid inquiry on this subject. You may be able to discredit him by committing him to an extreme position that is either patently absurd or clearly inconsistent with the actual circumstances proved by other convincing evidence. On the other hand, if the actual circumstances reveal a reasonably good opportunity for observation by the witness, the fact that the witness is inclined to be conservative in his statement—i.e., the type who will say only that the horse was white on the side he saw and not that it was a white horse—does not necessarily indicate that he should be cross-examined on the subject of opportunity to observe. The effect may be only to improve your adversary's argument that the witness was entirely disinterested and careful to be fair and accurate in everything he told the arbitrator.

Will your effort to prove poor opportunity for observations interfere with the more important purpose of your cross-examination? If, for example, your primary purpose in the cross-examination is to develop evidence favorable to you on a subject not touched in the direct examination, proof of poor opportunity to observe the subject of the direct testimony might incidentally have the effect of proving also poor opportunity to observe the other subject on which the witness gives testimony favorable to you. You must weigh the advantages of weakening the adverse testimony against the disadvantage of weakening the favorable testimony. Also, if the favorable effect of the testimony on the new subject on cross-examination has been striking, it may weaken the overall effect of the cross-examination to add to it a showing of merely doubtful opportunity to observe.

Proving Bad Character

Should you prove bad character of an adverse party or witness to impeach him? If so, should you do it on cross-examination or by independent evidence?

Evidence of bad character of a witness or party may bear directly on the issues of the case, but more often it has no direct bearing on the issues and is admissible merely on the theory that it affects the credibility of the witness. The sense of justice in the mind of an arbitrator often includes the principle that mudslinging regarding matters not before the arbitrator for decision is improper. Of course, in a legal way of thinking, the character of every witness is an issue to some extent because it affects the credibility of his testimony.

Arbitrators, however, do not necessarily agree that any evidence of bad character that is admissible is material to the case. They may regard the use of such evidence as unfair and they may, consciously or subconsciously, weigh that factor against the party offering the evidence. Because of these considerations, it is usually inadvisable to offer this type of evidence if its admissibility is doubtful. Even if it is clearly admissible, you should give careful consideration to the question whether the person sitting as arbitrator, deciding the matter of admissibility, will regard the evidence as so closely bearing on the credibility of the witness's testimony in this case that its use is justified. The decision as to whether you should use such evidence, therefore, involves an appraisal of how directly the evidence bears on the credibility of the witness and what attitude the arbitrator has brought with him into the hearing.

Objections to the Form of Questions

Should you object to your adversary's questions in leading or otherwise improper form?

Every advocate asks some improperly leading questions inadvertently, if not by design. With some adversaries you could spend a major part of the time objecting to their leading questions. Obviously, if you do not object, your adversary may succeed in leading the witness into much more favorable testimony than otherwise would have been given. Your objection also serves the purpose of calling to the attention of the arbitrator this unfair method by which your adversary is obtaining favorable testimony.

The major vices of the leading question—coaching the witness and getting something before the arbitrator that they might not otherwise hear—are already accomplished before the opportunity to object to the leading question arises. Your reasons for objecting are related not so much to exclusions of the anticipated answer as to restraining the further use of leading questions and calling to the arbitrator's attention the use already made and its bearing on the credibility of the evidence.

As against an adversary who persists in asking leading questions, the generally preferred practice is not to object to every such question, but to call the matter to the attention of the arbitrator by periodic objection pointing out that the practice is being followed continuously and that the arbitrator should be allowed to hear the witness tell his own story instead of hearing the advocate's version of it. After the practice has become persistent, you may also request and obtain an instruction by the arbitrator to your adversary not to lead the witness.

Another instance in which it is sometimes wise to object to questions on the ground of form is the case of a question calling for an answer regarding knowledge, as a preliminary fact supporting admissibility—e.g., when evidence of custom is being offered, a witness who is asked to state whether or not he is familiar with the custom regarding a specific matter, who usually replies by stating what he thinks the custom to be rather than answering yes or no to the question. If you consider that there is reasonable hope of getting the witness to admit that he is not familiar with the practices of others generally, but only with the practices of a few individuals so that his idea of what the custom is would be based upon insufficient knowledge to make it admissible, you should object or else move that the arbitrator instruct the witness to answer the question only yes or no.

If, on the other hand, you know that the witness will testify so as to qualify himself, your objection or request for the instruction, though sustained, would serve no useful end. It would be better under these circumstances to refrain from objecting and develop by cross-examination any weakness in the degree of familiarity of the witness with the question.

Opening the Case

An opening statement is intended to acquaint the arbiter with the essential facts of the case. It should primarily be an outline of the cause of action or the defense, but a skillful opening will be more than that. It will also present background and create a favorable atmosphere for the reception of the evidence to be offered and for the position taken by the party.

An opening statement should be brief, clear and direct. It should tell the story in logical sequence. Generally, chronological order can be followed most easily by the arbiter. There should be no argument and no peroration, but in the development of the story the important facts should be emphasized. The advocate should address himself to his own proof and not tell the arbiter what the other side cannot prove.

There should be no overstatement; it is dangerous to mention anything which you are not positive you will be able to prove. It is much safer to promise less rather than more. In the opening it is preferable to follow the example of the proverbial understatement. Reserve the strong statement for your summation. It is desirable also to reserve some of the details of the evidence for development on the witness stand so that the interest of the arbiter may be sustained. That does not mean, however, that any of the essential facts should be kept in the background.

The opening statement should be planned prior to entering the hearing room; it should not be improvised. Having prepared his own opening in advance of the hearing, the advocate is free to listen attentively—as he should—to his adversary's opening so that he may know what to expect in the way of proof by the other side.

You should know your case so thoroughly that you can tell it with flowing continuity, without notes or stammering pauses or coattail-pulling by an associate. It does not matter how long or how complicated your case may be. It is your duty to know every detail of your case backward and forward. If you do not, you will start off your opening, and the whole hearing, on the wrong foot.

You cannot inspire confidence and engender faith where you have none yourself, and you can have none if you do not know your case thoroughly. This is such a fundamental principle, not only for opening statements, but for the whole case, that it should be impressed deeply in every trial advocate's mind.

In this regard, this is specifically analogous to trial lawyers in courts of law. We hear of some trial lawyers who boast that they require no preparation and have the capacity to pick up the case as it goes along. Do not admire or emulate them. All the best known trial lawyers of this country achieved success in court largely by downright hard work before they ever took their cases to court, and when they got there they knew in detail every fact. The outstanding trial attorney boasts of how hard he has worked in the preparation of his case, not on how little he has worked. The outstanding arbitral advocate boasts of how hard he has worked in the preparation of his case, not on how little he has worked.

The thorough knowledge of every fact in your case will give you the calm and the poise which are so important in the hearing room. Your mind will be completely at ease and you will be relaxed because you are entirely free from haunting uncertainty and doubt. You cannot have poise, confidence, and an active presence of mind when you are inwardly beset by misgivings and doubts.

It is not enough to know your case thoroughly. You must also know how to present it in simple, understandable fashion. An advocate may know his case thoroughly but lack the ability to explain it so another can understand; as in the telling of any story, there must be a definite continuity. In every case without exception, the arbiter must be fully acquainted with what the issues are, i.e., what is involved and what questions he must decide. Keep to the chronological sequence of events as much as possible. This is an easy way to tell your story and a simple style for the arbiter to follow. In cases where there are many separate events, spaced at varying intervals, and where dates are important, it is almost imperative that a chronology be followed. By this method your story will hang together, and the various events will stand in proper relationship to each other.

Effective presentation obviously involves a consideration of the manner in which the case as a whole should be handled.

We are all aware of the favorable reaction which understatement produces in our everyday conversation. It carries within itself an implication of fairness and strength and develops a feeling of confidence which exaggeration destroys. Arbiters also have imagination and can draw the most favorable inferences from a framework of understatement.

A good case may be lost because of exaggerated statements which an opposing advocate can demolish by cross-examination or by testimony offered upon his own case. Similarly, exaggerated claims which cannot be supported by testimony result in an apparent failure of proof, and the opposing advocate may build upon it. Moreover, understatement of claims provides a better background for the testimony of witnesses because the proof develops even stronger than the arbiter may have expected.

Final Argument

The final argument, or summation, at the close of the evidence is of particular importance to the advocate because the responsibility for the presentation of this position rests upon him alone. The presentation of final argument cannot be undertaken intelligently unless the advocate has closely observed and absorbed all developments occurring during the entire course of the hearing.

The scope of the final argument is limited by the factual and contract law issues in the case. In most cases the resolution of conflicts in the evidence depends in some measure on reasonable inferences, deductions, and conclusions. These may be offered to the arbiter in final argument. Sometimes the inferences and deductions speak louder than the testimony of witnesses and are afforded greater weight.

The bulk of the argument will, of course, relate to the evidence and exhibits in the case and the reasonable inferences, deductions, and conclusions which may be drawn there from. These constitute the principal working material in every case. Absence of evidence or failure of proof is also a proper subject.

In some cases the conduct of the parties, as the same appears in evidence, is a particularly noteworthy subject for final argument, as, for example, where a party has been deceptive, inconsistent, or contradictory in the assertion of his claim or defense.

So, too, comment may properly be made about the fact that a party failed to produce evidence or testimony under his control or available to him. Thus, attention may be invited to a party's failure to produce books and records or other possible exhibits in his possession or under his control.

The credibility of witnesses may always be discussed in final argument. However, vituperative or inflammatory language should not be used in commenting on the lack of credibility of the witnesses for the other side. Not only may the credibility of the opponent's witnesses be attacked, but the credibility of one's own witnesses may also be urged. This may be done by reference to the reasonableness of the testimony and the support which it receives from the circumstantial evidence in the case.

The advocate may properly refer to the contract law and relevant precedent applicable to the case, and the relationship between the evidence and the pertinent authority.

Proper presentation, entailing familiarity with all aspects of the case, an analysis of the evidence and contract, a review of the witnesses and the testimony which dissects the opponent's case as well as one's own, and a simplification of the issues, will reduce the controlling issues to a minimum. Toward these few issues the argument should be directed. Argument on immaterial matter is a waste of time and effort. If there is but a single controlling question in the case, the argument should be confined largely to that issue.

Few cases will be found which do not have both strong points and weaknesses on each side. Not only should one's own strong points be emphasized, but those of the opponent should not be overlooked. The same is conversely true of weaknesses, i.e., the opponent's weaknesses should be stressed and one's own should not be ignored.

The astute advocate will shun the psychology of the ostrich and not close his eyes to his problems. The strength of the opponent's case should be recognized even though not expressly acknowledged, and an attack should ordinarily be directed at it. Similarly, weak phases of one's own case should ordinarily be bolstered by all the implications which the evidence affords. If the advocate fails to do this, his opponent will be quick to take advantage.

The suggestions as to the treatment of the opponent's strong points and one's own weaknesses are not inflexible. If satisfactory arguments are not available, either by direct attack or by confession and avoidance, the opponent's strong points or one's own weaknesses are better treated lightly or not at all. It will not help to engage in argument which is unconvincing. The only effect of such tactics is to emphasize the things that hurt.

In view of the tricks that memory is known to play, readier acceptance may be gained for a statement, in final argument, as to something which occurred during the hearing, if the statement is supported by a written memorandum. Notes made by the advocate during the course of the trial which record statements made by an opposing advocate or the testimony of witnesses may be used effectively. There is an obvious psychological advantage in being able to say, in substance, "I made a note of what the opposing advocate said in his opening statement on this subject and I shall read it to you."

Written exhibits should be read whenever they contain helpful material bearing directly upon the principal issues in the case. Such material may either affirmatively support counsel's own position or negate the position taken by the other side.

Many persons are visual-minded. There is truth as well as quaintness in the Chinese proverb that one picture is worth more than ten thousand words. The use of drawings, charts, photographs or other visual evidence is very effective in final argument. Demonstrating the function of a machine or the manner in which an accident happened, depicting the boundaries of a department or factory, and the like, by the use of exhibits will very often get the point across in a case in which mere words might fail.

14

Principles and Practices

The Moving Party

In all but discipline cases, the union is the moving party, the one asserting a claim, and it should make at least a preliminary or introductory presentation. In most cases, the union is expected to go ahead and present its whole case before the company does so. In an arbitration proceeding, the party with the substantive burden of proof, usually the union as the complaining party, has the task of presenting the initial evidence. The union must establish that a contract violation has occurred. If it establishes what is called a prima facie case (defined as support of the complainant's contentions by evidence that, if believed, would sustain those contentions), the employer must rebut that evidence.

The substantive burden of proof—whether in a court of law, in an arbitration proceeding, or in a grievance processing—rests with the complaining party. As we have said, in most cases the complaining party is the union. However, it seems a well-established tenet of labor relations that the burden of proof in disputes over discipline or discharge must be carried by the party who initiated the challenged action; the employer is, therefore, called on to establish the facts it asserts as the basis for having taken presumably positive corrective action. In such cases the employer must open the case and present its position first, and it will also be given the right to close the hearing with a position statement. This procedure may, of course, be altered or waived by agreement of the parties.

The Burden of Proof

One purpose of the labor agreement is to promote favorable relations between the company and its employees. This cannot be achieved if management acts under its contract without a fair and proper determination of the facts involved in any discipline or discharge action it takes. It must stand ready to support its allegations against employees charged with improper conduct.

Arbitrators differ on the quantity and quality of proof demanded from the employer. There are those who require that guilt be established "beyond a reasonable doubt," as do our criminal courts. Labor arbitrators are inclined to impose this measurement when the charges are by nature criminal, or involve substantial injury to the employee's work status, job security, or reputation. Others see the burden of proof as carried if a "preponderance of the evidence" establishes a prima facie case. In such an instance, the burden of proof may actually transfer from one party to the other during the arbitration proceedings. An example will illustrate this.

Let us imagine that a firm has discharged an employee for incompetence. To prove the necessity for the disciplinary action, it presents evidence of poor-quality materials, bad parts, and a low productivity record. It establishes that the particular employee charged with the misconduct is in fact the offender, and it shows that the corrective action was appropriate to his act of misconduct and his record. This evidence constitutes a prima facie case. However, the union alleges that the poor work was not the product of the discharged employee and that his low productivity was the result of some factors beyond his control. At this point, the burden of proof transfers to the union; it cannot establish its claim merely by stating it, any more than the employer can, but must present evidence in support of the employee's innocence. If it does so, then the burden of proof transfers again, back to the employer.

Evidence

Arbitral Treatment

Strict observance of legal rules of evidence is not a common practice in the arbitration process. If required by both parties, the arbitration hearing will be conducted in his manner, but it is done infrequently.[1] Furthermore, many labor agreements mention the American Arbitration Association (AAA), either as the agency to be consulted in selecting the arbitrator or the one under the rules of which the process is to be conducted, or both. Rule 28 of AA states that "the arbitrator shall be the judge of the relevance and materiality of the evidence offered and conformity to legal rules of evidence shall not be necessary."[2]

Arbitrator W. Willard Wirtz, secretary of labor under Presidents Kennedy and Johnson, has made the following observation on this rather flexible subject:

> Arbitrators have established the pattern of ordered informality; performing major surgery on the legal rules of evidence and procedure but retaining the good sense of these rules; greatly simplifying but not eliminating the hearsay and parole evidence rules; taking the rules for the admissibility of evidence and remolding them into rules for weighing it; striking the fat but saving the heart of the practices of cross-examination, presumptions, burden of proof, and the like.[3]

What this comes down to is that in the great majority of cases, "any evidence, information, or testimony is acceptable which is pertinent to the case and which helps the arbitrator to understand and decide the problem before him."[4]

The practice of most arbitrators of allowing a liberal introduction of evidence has its share of critics, most of whom are members of the legal community. Lawyers have an instinctive aversion to the words of the arbitrator: "Well, I am not sure myself about its relevance [i.e., that of the alleged evidence], but I will take it for what it is worth." However, Harry Shulman, late expert in arbitration, commented that "the more serious danger is not that the arbitrator will hear too much irrelevancy, but rather that he will not hear enough of the relevant."[5]

Arbitrator William E. Simkin, one-time national director of the Federal Mediation and Conciliation Service (FMCS), in commenting on the liberal acceptance of evidence, dwelt for a moment on the cathartic nature of such freedom:

> One of the fundamental purposes of an arbitration hearing is to let people get things off their chest, regardless of the decision. The arbitration proceeding is the opportunity for a third party, an outside party, to come in and act as a sort of father confessor to the parties, to let them get rid of their troubles, get them out in the open, and have a feeling of someone hearing their troubles. Because I believe so strongly that that is one of the fundamental purposes of arbitration, I don't think you ought to use any rules of evidence. You have to make up your own mind as to what is pertinent or not in the case. Lots of times I have let people talk for five minutes, when I knew all the time that they were talking it had absolutely nothing to do with the case—just completely foreign to it. But there was a fellow testifying, either as a worker or a company representative, who had something that was important for him to get rid of. It was a good time for him to get rid of it.[6]

The point is, of course, that, in the overwhelming majority of cases, arbitrators are receptive to almost any type of evidence the parties may wish to submit. What may not appear to be particularly germane at the outset may later be found intrinsic to the issue. Sometimes this can only be established as the case unfolds. It is a common practice for arbitrators to accept evidence "for what it is worth." This means that they are reserving their opinion of, and reactions to, the questionable evidence until they have had an opportunity to evaluate it against the record. Then, if in their judgment it is not sufficiently relevant to the issue at hand, they accord it no weight in their final determinations. While it is true that some arbitration statues require adherence to legal rules of evidence, the majority do not. If no such requirement is made, or if it is general rather than specific and explicit, the strict observance of legal rules of evidence is customarily not necessary.

It would take an entire volume to provide a comprehensive treatment of the subject of evidence, so the remainder of this discussion will be concerned only with examples of the ways arbitrators commonly apply certain rules of evidence.

Best Evidence—Real

The wisest rule is always to use the best evidence available. As an obvious example, eyewitness accounts will certainly provide more compelling testimony than will hearsay. If challenged, a supervisor's testimony that an employee was not at work will be considered more conclusive if it is supported by payroll and production records and other such evidence.

Arbitrators look askance at testimony or evidence introduced by the employer about events that occur after a discharge action. In determining whether the action taken by the company fits the accusation against the employee, arbitrators are concerned only with the employee's conduct preceding the discharge.

It is unwise to hold back records and information germane to the grievance issue. If time cards, production records, absenteeism reports, payroll records, prior grievance or arbitration settlements, and the like are available and related to the case, they should be introduced. To be of maximum effectiveness, such information should have been discussed and/or presented and made available to the other party preceding the arbitration hearing, preferably during the earlier stages of the grievance procedure.

Examples of real evidence include

Absenteeism records
Production records
Payroll records
Time cards
Discipline records
Tardiness records
Prior arbitration decisions
Prior grievance settlements
Photographs
Tangible or physical materials

Circumstantial Evidence

Circumstantial evidence is regarded with caution by arbitrators, just as it is by the courts. To be decisive, such evidence should preclude any reasonable theory or hypothesis other than that which it purports to establish. Such evidence, frequently given in arbitration proceedings, is generally resorted to in the absence of any direct proof of the fact at issue. It consists of a number of peripheral events or conditions that, taken together, reasonably point to the fact.

At the Stockham Pipe Fitting Company, circumstantial evidence was sufficiently persuasive to uphold a discharge action in a dispute over the discharge of employees for instigating an unauthorized work stoppage. Arbiter Whitley P. McCoy decided the matter and evaluated the web of circumstances surrounding it:

> Because of the secret nature of the offense of these men, proof is extremely difficult. It does not follow from this that proof may be dispensed with or that mere suspicious circumstances may take the place of proof, as I have indicated in sustaining the grievances of four men. But I think it does follow that something less than the most direct and most positive proof is sufficient; in other words, that, just as in cases of fraud and conspiracy, legitimate inferences may be drawn from such circumstances as a prior knowledge of the time set for the strike. Unusual actions in circulating among the employees just prior to 9:30, communication of the time set to employees, and signals however surreptitious, given at that hour. Mere prior guilty knowledge of the time set would not alone be sufficient since presumably many of the employees must have been told the time a half-hour, an hour, or several hours in advance. Nor would merely being the first in a department to quit at the stroke of 9:30, standing alone be sufficient. A wave of the hand, which might as reasonably be interpreted as a signal of goodbye as a signal to others to go out, as in the case of Hollingsworth, would of itself be insufficient. But these or other suspicious circumstances, in combination, and especially in case of known leaders in the Union's affairs, may be sufficient to convince the reasonable mind of guilt.[7]

The opinion of the majority of arbitrators is that circumstantial evidence is real evidence, providing every other possible explanation is eliminated. However, where too many imponderables remain, the doubt is resolved in the grievant's favor. Long experience has also taught that circumstantial evidence may in fact be more persuasive than the direct evidence in certain cases. However, arbitrators remain understandably cautious.

In deciding a dispute between the Illinois Bell Telephone Company and the International Brotherhood of Electrical Workers, Meyer S. Ryder discussed the standards of proof to be used when circumstantial evidence is involved.

> The Chairman holds that in discharge matters where the employee offense being treated with carries along with it connotations of corruption and illegality, were the employee to be held guilty of the offense, the standard of evidentiary proof to convict should be no real subjective question of guilt in the minds of him or those who have to decide. Acceptable to this proposition should be evidence of circumstances or combination of circumstances such as leave no doubt that what is indicated is actually present. Should it be considered that the application of standards of proof in a criminal proceeding under the law go beyond and are greater than these standards, then the criminal law standards should not be held to apply in an industrial relations arbitration proceeding. Accordingly, the Chairman has applied the standards he has enunciated above to the discharge matters.[8]

Arbitrator Paul M. Herbert has commented that the use of circumstantial evidence "does not eliminate in any sense the requirement that there must be a clear and convincing proof to establish that the offense charged was committed."[9] It has also been said that mere suspicion is not sufficient to establish a wrongdoing.

Putting it still another way, Clair V. Duff has stated that the arbitrator "must exercise extreme care so that by due deliberation and careful judgment he may avoid making hasty or false deductions. If the evidence producing the chain of circumstances pointing to guilt is weak and inconclusive, no probability of fact may be inferred from the combined circumstances."[10]

Hearsay

Briefly, hearsay is something heard from another. "Hearsay evidence" is testimony that consists in a narration by one person of matters told him by another. Hearsay evidence is usually barred in legal proceedings because it cannot be tested through cross-examination. A written communication may also be categorized as "hearsay" and be equally as inadmissible as oral testimony; the fact that a hearsay statement is reduced to writing does not render it admissible. Obviously, it is as impossible to cross-examine a written document as it is an absent third party.

Generally speaking, arbitrators also reject hearsay evidence when it is properly objected to. The reasons are self-evident—the contesting party has no chance to confront or cross-examine the alleged witness. Hearsay testimony may be motivated by self-interest, malice, or spite. It may be the misrepresentation of an irresponsible person or it may be partially or totally fabricated.

Inasmuch as arbitrators do not consider themselves bound by strict legal rules of evidence, they tend to admit hearsay evidence and weigh it in the light of the lack of opportunity to cross-examine. For example, Harold I. Elbert has ruled that doctors' certificates are admissible in an arbitration proceeding as proof of an employee's illness although they may be hearsay. An examination of reported arbitration decisions indicates that medical certificates are commonly admitted in evidence and given weight by arbitrators in determining whether an employee was sick.[11]

The observations of Benjamin Aaron on the weight to be accorded hearsay evidence are well worth consideration:

> A competent arbitrator may be depended upon substantially to discount some kinds of hearsay evidence that he has admitted over objection. He will do so selectively, however, and not on the assumption that hearsay evidence, as such, is not to be credited. If, for example, a newly appointed personnel manager, or a recently elected business agent, offers a letter to his predecessor from a third party, the arbitrator is likely to ignore the fact that the evidence is hearsay; if satisfied that the document is genuine, he will give it such weight as its relevancy dictates. On the other hand, hearsay testimony about statements allegedly made by "the boys in the shop" or by executives "in the front office," though perhaps not excluded from the record by the arbitrator, probably will have no effect on his decision.[12]

Another arbitrator, Arthur R. Lewis, has commented that "the reasons calling for the existence of a hearsay rule in common-law jury actions should at least guide the judgment of the arbitrator in the evaluation of the weight, if any, to be attributed to such evidence in an arbitration proceeding."[13] In any case, it is extremely unlikely that an arbitrator will decide an issue with a ruling based on and supported by hearsay evidence alone. It is worth noting that the rules of AAA allow the arbitrator to receive and give consideration to the evidence of witnesses by written document, but recommend that it should be given only the weight to which it is deemed to be entitled after consideration of any objection made regarding its admission.

There is no rule in arbitration which decrees that hearsay evidence is inadmissible. It is admissible in arbitration "for what it is worth." The "for what it is worth" rule is not a satisfactory yardstick, but it is a compromise between two extremes which are often more unsatisfactory.

The principal spokesman or witness, however, should not take it upon himself to relate alleged facts as told to him unless there is no other way of getting them into evidence. If the facts are worth putting in the record, let the foreman, personnel manager, complainant or grieving employee, the person with firsthand knowledge, tell his own story unless the facts are admitted by the adversary or unless they are such as can better be proved by authentic records or documents. *Prove your case by the best and most authentic evidence available to you.* A case resting on "scuttlebutt," hearsay, or other secondary evidence will in all probability be a weak one.

The basic objection to hearsay is that it is a secondhand, warmed-over version and gives the adversary absolutely no opportunity to cross-examine the person who is quoted and frequently misquoted, and thus amounts to the taking of an unfair advantage. In courts of law it is considered incompetent and is inadmissible, unless there are circumstances which are deemed sufficient to substitute for the oath and cross-examination, and unless it consequently falls under one of the many exceptions to the rule.

Parol Evidence Rule

It has long been a substantive rule of law in the English-speaking world that in the absence of fraud or mutual mistake, oral statements are not admissible to modify, vary, explain, or contradict the plain terms of a valid written contract.

The rule has ramifications and in arbitration is seldom referred to by its name—the Parol Evidence rule—but arbitrators and all parties should keep in mind that there is a very sound basis for the rule, and just as sound outside as inside the courtroom. To consider any or every oral statement made by one party or the other during contract negotiations so as to vary, modify, or contradict the plain language finally adopted could throw the best written contract into doubt and constant turmoil. Where a contract is plain and unambiguous, oral statements or reservations made by either party do not change it.

If the terms of the contract are ambiguous or clearly susceptible to more than one meaning, then parol evidence is admissible to show what the parties meant at the time of making the contract and how they intended it to apply. It is in the interpretation of ambiguous provisions or conflicting provisions that grievance arbitration serves a great need.

The rule seldom comes into arbitration under that heading, for it is more tactful for the objector to simply point out the unreliability of the claimed agreement based on no more than oral statements and faulty memories, especially when it conflicts with the written version.

Objections to Evidence

Each party is entitled to object when it believes the other party is seeking to introduce improper evidence or argument at the arbitration hearing. Such objections, when based upon some plausible grounds, can serve a useful function even if overruled, for the arbitrator will have been cautioned to examine the challenged evidence or argument more closely before giving it weight. A party is also entitled to object to evidence he considers irrelevant, for the record should not be burdened with a mass of material having little or no bearing on the issue.

However, objections which have no plausible basis, and those which are repetitious, should be avoided, as has been advised by Clarence M. Updegraff:

> Do not make captious, whimsical or unnecessary objections to testimony or arguments of the other party. Such interruptions are likely to waste time and confuse issues. The arbitrator, no doubt, will realize without having the matter expressly mentioned more than once, when he is hearing weak testimony such as hearsay and immaterial statements.[14]

Offers of Compromise—Inadmissible

The purpose of the contractual grievance machinery is to provide an instrument by which the parties may seek and, hopefully, find remedies to problems between them. To maintain its functional purpose, such machinery must be utilized by the parties in an open and uninhibited way. If their mutual interests and needs are to be served, each party must feel free to search for accommodation or negotiate compromises. Each must be free of fear that if its offers are refused they will not subsequently be interpreted as a sign of weakness by an arbitrator.

For this reason, arbitrators give very little weight, if any at all, to revelations of previous offers. The logic of this attitude is sound. One arbitrator put it succinctly: "It is clear that any offer made by either party during the course of conciliation cannot prejudice that party's case when the case comes to arbitration. It is the very essence of conciliation that compromise proposals will go further than a party may consider itself bound to go on a strict interpretation of its rights."[15]

The following is an example of this same concept in action: Upon returning to work after a back injury, an employee had refused, on the advice of the union, to consult yet another doctor, after having submitted to examinations by the employer's doctor and a clinic. Arbitrator John Sembower ruled that that evidence had to be disregarded. The arbitration was dealing with a dispute involving the employer's refusal to reinstate the employee. It appeared to Sembower that the final medical examination was part of an attempt to settle the grievance before arbitrating it. As such, he held that the parties' attempts to resolve their differences should not be allowed to prejudice their positions at arbitration.[16]

If proposals, counterproposals, and offers of compromise could be seized upon and used later in arbitration against a party, the result would be a throttling and stifling of the dispute-settling efficiency of the grievance machinery. Consequently, it is rarely allowed.

The De Minimis Rule

In denying grievance, arbitrators sometimes apply the rule of *de minimis non curat lex*, under which trifling or immaterial matters will not be taken into account. Often in applying this principle the arbitrator concludes that the action complained of is such a slight departure from what is generally required by the agreement that the action must be viewed either as a permissible exception or as not constituting an injury at all. The de minimis concept has sometimes been applied, for example, in denying grievances protesting the performance by management personnel of small amounts of bargaining unit work where a unit employee was not readily available.

Application of the de minimis rule has been rejected where "the amount has been small but the principle large." And in any event, Harold W. Davey has explained that no hard and fast mathematical line should be drawn between minimal on the one hand and substantial on the other, but that each case should be decided in terms of its own circumstances.[17]

Weight and Credibility of Evidence

It is within the province of the arbitrator to determine the weight, relevancy, and authenticity of evidence. The general approach of arbitrators in giving weight and credibility to evidence is effectively illustrated by a statement made by George Cheney in reviewing the discharge of an employee. He noted that the case was illustrative of the type of situation in which the facts are to a large extent determined by the weight and credibility accorded to the testimony of the witnesses and to the documentary evidence offered by the parties. He pointed out that, in arriving at the truth in such a case, an arbitrator must consider whether conflicting statements ring true or false; that he will note the witnesses' demeanor while on the stand; and that he will credit or discredit testimony according to his impressions of the witnesses' veracity. Arbitrator Cheney also pointed out that, in determining where the preponderance of the evidence lies with respect to any material point, the arbitrator will take into consideration whether the witness speaks from firsthand information or whether his testimony is largely based on hearsay or gossip. In summarizing, Cheney stated that the duty of the arbitrator is simply to determine the truth respecting material matters in controversy, as he believes it to be, based upon a full and fair consideration of the entire evidence and after he has accorded each witness and each piece of documentary evidence the weight, if any, to which he honestly believes it to be entitled.[19]

Arbitrator Clair V. Duff, in turn, has offered some considerations relevant in evaluating testimony:

> [A]ny attempt to sort credible testimony from that which is not worthy of belief is very difficult for at least four basic reasons. They may be briefly stated:

> *Interest.* While having an interest or stake in the outcome does not disqualify a witness, it renders his testimony subject to most careful scrutiny.... Few witnesses will deliberately falsify but there is a common tendency to "put your best foot forward." This tendency, either consciously or subconsciously, leads many witnesses to remember and express testimony in a way favorable to the result which they hope the Hearing will produce.
>
> *Perception.* Frequently the initial observation is faulty or incomplete because the observer has no prior knowledge that a dispute will develop concerning what he has seen or heard and his casual sensory impression is not sharp and keen.
>
> *Memory.* The remembrance of an event weeks or months after it occurred is frequently dim and inaccurate and a witness may be confused as to facts which initially he correctly perceived. By lapse of time precise details may elude his memory.
>
> *Communication.* The manner in which a witness expresses what he saw and heard may fail to communicate exactly his initial perception of the occurrence, so that after listening to the testimony and the cross-examination of the witnesses, the fact-finder may not have had transmitted to him a completely accurate impression of the facts, even though they were initially observed carefully and well remembered by the witness.[19]

Arbitrator Joseph Rosenfarb cautioned that while "both sides might be subject to the unconscious influences of self-interest, personal predilection or antipathy," it is the duty of the arbitrator "to examine the testimony of each witness on its own merits." [20] Rosenfarb considered that union members are not necessarily prejudiced witnesses any more than are supervisors. Arbitrator Samuel Krimsly has cautioned that if a grievant's testimony "is colored by bias," employees used as company witnesses also may have "a bias by reason of their employment."[21]

Widely differing versions of the facts are too frequently presented by the parties. Where the testimony is highly contradictory it ordinarily "becomes incumbent upon the Arbitrator to sift and evaluate the testimony to the best of his ability, and reach the best conclusion he can as to the actual fact situation." However, sometimes "it is unnecessary to resolve the substantial conflict in the evidence to obtain an unobstructed view of the scene. By piecing together the parts, the broad outlines of the whole picture emerges." Arbitrator Sidney L. Cahn has observed that, in discipline cases, the truth often "lies somewhere between" the widely conflicting versions of the facts. In any event, as arbitrator R.W. Fleming has aptly observed:

> Arbitrators are not equipped with any special divining rod which enables them to know who is telling the truth and who is not where a conflict in testimony develops. They can only do what the courts have done in similar circumstances for centuries. A judgment must finally be made, and there is a possibility that the judgment when made is wrong.[22]

Stipulations?

Before going to the hearing, how about trying to get an agreed stipulation of the issue the arbitrator is to decide?

It is a great idea if it can be obtained. It may save considerable time during the hearing and it would certainly (1) make it clear to the arbitrator what the parties agreed was the issue and the acceptable remedy and (2) narrow and confine the arbiter's freedom in resolving the dispute to that specified issue.

It is not unheard of that one side may present its entire case and still leave the issue obscure. It has not been unknown for the same condition of obscurity to persist after the whole case is in.

An advocate must strive to delineate for the arbitrator's comprehension what he contends the issue is, with the facts in crystal clear, unequivocal terms, and what he contends is the appropriate remedy for the disposition of the issue.

However, experience has shown that seeking to obtain stipulation in advance of the hearing is often frustrated by the other party's objections to particular words and phrases.

Therefore, if you make the attempt and fail, be neither surprised nor frustrated. Instead, merely prepare yourself for an assertively clear presentation to the arbiter of the issue and the remedy as you see it.

At the Hearing

Opening Statement

Always prepare an opening statement. This will be when you clearly define the issue and the appropriate remedy. It should lay out what the facts are and what you intend to prove. You will find that in drafting it, you will be greatly helping your own preparation for the hearing. You will realize what evidence must be assembled and proved, what witnesses, if any, must be prepared and used, and the order in which you will present each, using all of these as building blocks for an orderly, organized, and compelling persuasive presentation of your case.

Where Is the Hearing Held?

Arbitration hearings are not usually held in courtrooms. More often they occur in hotel or motel conference rooms, company offices, library or post office conference rooms, even the union's offices, though, for some unknown reason, seldom are they held there.

Ideally, the room will be large enough to accommodate a "T" or "U" shaped table arrangement with the arbitrator sitting at the head and the parties along either side. There will be a witness chair to the side of the arbiter and a functional chair and table arrangement for a verbatim reporter, if one is to be used.

You will want the advocate and the arbiter to have enough table space to spread out their papers and exhibits. You don't want them to be crowding each other. With too little space, papers and exhibits might get intermingled, or the privacy of notes and papers might be invaded.

Swearing to Tell the Truth

Do you ask the arbiter to swear in the witnesses, "to tell the truth, the whole truth, and nothing but the truth, so help you God"? If either party asks, he will. Some arbiters will even express their own wish to have all witnesses sworn, and will do the swearing in. Will it do any good? Will it ensure that all witnesses will tell only the truth? Who knows? My own individual opinion is that it may induce some who are religious, or who are strongly influenced by the need for a clear conscience, to be more truthful. I also believe that if a person comes to the hearing intending to tell only the truth, the oath is superfluous; and if a person comes intending to lie, he will refer to the oath as reason why he should be believed.

Nevertheless, I personally insist upon the swearing of witnesses. It seems to give more dignity to the proceeding, it impresses upon all the need for adherence to the truth, and it may tend to restrain improper volunteering of information and argument by onlookers.

I acknowledge that often witnesses are not sworn, although this is at the option of the parties.

A Court Reporter

Court reporters who record a verbatim transcript of the proceedings are sometimes used, more often by the employer. Without it, the arbiter must accept the onerous burden of taking copious and detailed longhand notes, while at the same time trying to evaluate witnesses and their testimony.

Without a court reporter, the advocate should pace himself in the presentation of evidence, in articulating argument, in direct and cross-examination of witnesses.

If you are presenting your case at fifty miles per hour and the arbiter is recording it at twenty miles per hour, he is missing thirty miles per hour of your stuff, and it could be the critical part of your stuff in that thirty mile per hour gap.

You should consider a verbatim transcript. Sound reasoning on this matter includes the following considerations: (1) You intend to file a post-hearing brief. It will assist you in that preparation. (2) The issue and facts are complex, or they involve jargon unique to the industry and perhaps foreign to the arbiter. (3) You want a verbatim record of witness testimony. (4) You are prepared to provide a copy to the other side if they request one and are willing to pay an appropriate per page price. (5) You are prepared to provide a copy to the arbiter, which you pay for. (6) You want to be better positioned if a post-hearing court test should occur.

Realize, however, that a court reporter's transcript takes time to type and thus delays the rendering of a decision. If time is of the essence, transcripts, though useful, may not be advisable.

Subpoena Power

Under state arbitration law, the arbitrator, and in some states the attorneys of record, may have subpoena power co-extensive with that available in a civil action. There is no precedent for it in a Section 301 suite directly. It can be inferred as being available through the court under Federal Rule 45.

Enforcement of subpoena must be through the court. Under either federal or state law, there is no contempt power.

15

Past Practice: The No Man's Land of Labor Arbitration

A collective bargaining agreement negotiated between an employer and a union represents the compromise reached by the parties during labor negotiations leading to its consummation. During the discussions which finally result in a contract sufficiently mutually acceptable for both parties to bind themselves to its provisions by signing, each has attempted to meet the needs and wishes of the party it represents. On the one hand, the employer has sought to satisfy the needs of its management and its stockholders, while the union, on the other hand, has tried to satisfy the needs and desires of its members and the International. Presumably, it contains what represents the sole and complete embodiment of the commitments each has made to the other for the duration of its term. But this is not to say that it always does—or that it clearly and precisely expresses what both parties understand it to contain—even if it presumably embraces all issues relevant to their relationship. Such can be the contract product for a variety of reasons. One is that even expert labor relations authorities who have participated in the bargaining of the document can unintentionally create articles of draftsmanship. Another reason which sometimes contributes is that often the final wording agreed upon is the product of the contributions of several people. Still another reason may be that because the parties have been unable to reach an agreement on a given subject, they have finally accepted wording which is ambiguous and susceptible to more than one interpretation (and since the wording does not clearly agree with the adamant position of either party, it represents a face-saving for both and a loss of face to neither). Another factor in the relationship which may produce an imperfect labor instrument is the fact that the typical industrial plant is a dynamic organization with changing conditions and operations rather than a static one. Thus, the parties may enter an agreement that fits the operation it serves, but as conditions change during the contract's term, they find themselves attempting to bend it to fit a new situation. Also, no contract, no matter how comprehensive, can explicitly and fully cover all situations. Inevitably, a management representative will be faced with the situation which does not appear to be embraced by his contract. And, finally, even when a contract phrase is clear-cut in its meaning, practices may be initiated or allowed to continue which run contrary to the intent of the contract.

Who does the creation or existence of a past practice benefit most: the company or the union? This is an age-old contest with the final score yet to be tabulated. Needless to say, there are arguable positions in support of either contention. Even the diehard who most strenuously argues that the union benefits must realize that occasionally management benefits also. Although grudgingly given, this admission must be made in view of the revealed truth of arbitration decisions. Many of these expose the fact that management sometimes defends its action on the basis of some supporting practice and occasionally does so in the presence of ambiguous language or in the absence of any wording whatsoever. More often, however, practices are used by the union as a means to obtain more from management than it could achieve by collective bargaining. This is the case since the union typically views the labor agreement quite differently than does management. Management considers the agreement as the final point in the concessions it intends to grant for the term of the agreement. To the union, the consummation of a labor agreement brings it only to a temporary resting place in its quest for more. During the term of the agreement, the union will regularly and consistently seek to obtain more than it achieved at the bargaining table through its use of the grievance and arbitration procedures. This is its role and it is an understandable one. One of the ways open to the union to achieve this objective is to search out and find where management has established some condition or benefit not generally or specifically provided by the contract. Using the grievance and arbitration provisions as the instrument by which they seek the established permanence of the contractually uncovered item, they obtain a grievance settlement or arbitration award which cements the condition or benefit as a now contractually covered item.

Management attempts to avoid this happenstance in several ways. First, it commonly adopts and practices a residual rights theory of management. Second, during negotiations it seeks the insertion of language into the agreement which limits the relationship of the parties to the expressed terms of the agreement and negates the influence of any unwritten understandings or practices which may exist. Third, it attempts to bargain into the contract a zipper clause which indicates by its phrasing that the union has had its opportunity during collective bargaining to present all issues and seek all concessions it has any interest in, and that failing to do so or failing to obtain what it had sought, it is now foreclosed for the term of the agreement from expecting to bargain with the company relative to any such covered or uncovered issue. This chapter will be concerned with these two exclusive agreement provisions.

The preponderance of arbitral opinion holds to the following view on an employer's residual rights: "it is now a well established generalization that every employer continues to have all powers previously had or exercised by employers unless such powers have been curtailed or eliminated by statute or by contract with a union...."[1]

While this is generally true and fairly typical of the concept endorsed by a majority of arbitrators, *there are some exceptions. A silent contract, that is, one which does not provide coverage to a given subject, does not necessarily dictate that any uncovered subjects are automatically left to management's sole discretion.* Therefore, it does not necessarily mean that any disputes which arise over matters not covered by pertinent contract language will be always resolved in the company's favor. Where this occurs, the customs and practices of the parties during the term of the agreement, and perhaps prevailing under prior agreements as well, may constitute a significant or even controlling factor in an arbitrator's final decision over the dispute.

Disputes between the parties may also arise over a subject dealt with in contractual language but by wording or phrasing which is not expressed clearly and specifically. In other words, the contract may give coverage to the subject, but the particular language adopted by the parties may be vague and ambiguous and susceptible to more than one interpretation. Employers argue that they operate properly when they exercise managerial discretion to fill in such gaps which are caused by this defective draftsmanship. Again, the residual rights concept is employed in this situation, positioned there by the argument that the ambiguity and vagueness of the language does not operate sufficiently to restrict, prohibit or limit managerial alternatives. *Failure to realize that practices and customs under an agreement can become as compelling a part of the agreement as the written word has sometimes led to unilateral actions of management which have led to findings that same were in violation of the governing contract.* There is no question that the presence of a written agreement imposes certain limitations on an employer's previously unfettered prerogatives. It should be recognized equally as readily that the existence of certain practices and customs under that written instrument may also provide additional limitations on management's rights not expressly indicated by the contract's wording.

This is not to say that management is obliged to admit to the compelling nature of any practice so alleged by the union. Of course, it should if its own investigation reveals that the practice as alleged by the union is a valid one which has become a controlling factor in the handling of that subject matter. To aid the parties in their determination of the weight and effect to be accorded to any practice is the objective here. But from management's point of view, *usually the wisest and safest course is to insist that the union find a base for its claim from some expressed provision of the agreement.* Most companies, in the construction of the grievance procedure of their agreement, attempt to obtain a definition for a grievance which requires that for a claim to be a valid grievance, it must allege violation of a specific provision of the agreement as expressly written and provided therein. Their attempt to obtain such a grievance definition is in accord with management's viewpoint that the labor agreement represents the extent of their total commitment to the union. To further protect itself against additional encroachments by the union, the employer also often seeks a provision in the arbitration article which limits the arbitrator's authority to interpreting the contract as written and expressed, and prohibits him from adding to, subtracting from or altering the document in any manner when formulating his award. But, as we will discover, despite the presence of such grievance and arbitration terminology, and despite vigorous argument of residual rights, practices and customs are often given compelling and controlling effect in arbitrator's opinions.

Before leaving this subject of the employer's concern for his management rights, it may be interesting to briefly examine how they declare such rights in their labor contracts. Management usually takes one of two approaches to protect its prerogatives during collective bargaining. The first is to avoid any statement of such rights in a contract on the grounds mentioned earlier—that certain prerogatives are inherent in management and need not be fully stated and enumerated. According to the advocates of this viewpoint, their concern is that a statement of such rights may be interpreted to not include other rights not fully enumerated, and thus actually operate to restrict. The much more common approach is to include a management's rights clause in the contract which spells out as many prerogatives as can generally and specifically be listed in order to clearly establish the scope of management action which is to remain free despite the limiting obligations of the contract. This approach is often the subject of differences of opinion between those believing in a broad and general statement of managerial prerogatives and those believing in the detailed statement. These two subgroups are divided by the same considerations as the two major groups. What this means is that those supporting the general statement theory fear that a full and descriptive statement of rights may turn out to be restrictive (in the sense that rights not specifically asserted may be denied). The result is that a good many labor contracts try to solve this question by incorporating both a general and a detailed statement—or by adding to the end of a full and detailed statement of rights a proviso which indicates that the list is not intended to enumerate all rights retained by management, and is therefore not all inclusive.

A review of trends and patterns relative to provisions contained in labor agreements shows an inclination over the past several years toward the insertion of saving clauses. The percentages have moved up steadily, though not dramatically, over the past 15 years. Also, labor agreements negotiated by large, major manufacturers show that a substantially higher percentage of these favor the detailed statement of management's rights, plus the inclusion of the savings clause.

Past Practice Clause

Management must realize that practices and customs are not established by the employees, nor are they established by the union. Such practices and customs first come into existence and then continue from one application of the practice to the next by the actions or inaction of management. This must be considered so since, under a labor agreement, management acts, the union reacts. The union operates principally as a defense organization. The union has no right of administrative initiative under the labor agreement. Practices commonly develop when management makes decisions and takes actions, in other words, exercises its right of administrative initiative. If there is contract language which is clear and explicit, it perhaps permits only one position. But as discussed earlier, not all contract language is clear and specific and without vagueness.

Where the contract is clear, it probably allows those members of management who administer it only one direction to take in their decision making. But where the contract is silent or is susceptible to more than one interpretation (any one of which may be persuasively argued), management commonly fills in such gaps by exercising unilateral managerial discretion. Compounding this potential problem is the fact that the terms of the labor agreement are an umbrella over many operations, perhaps many of them diverse. Therefore, such widespread application of a common provision to different operations and departments brings many different management members into the decision-making process. Under these circumstances, it is not uncommon for these management members not always to be singing out of the same hymnal. These are the circumstances which may produce different practices from one section of the plant to another, from one department of the plant to another, from one shift to another. *Realizing this and the potential dangers it can represent to the company, many employers attempt to insert a past practice clause into the contract during bargaining.*

One last point before turning to a discussion of such clauses. As mentioned, management can be responsible for the creation of practices, often undesirable, by its *in*action. This can result where management members responsible for administering the labor agreement acquiesce to conduct and behavior of employees and union representatives which is not in the best interests of the employer. This can occur irrespective of whether or not the particular practice allowed is given coverage by the contract, in whole, partially or not at all.

For example, the employer's representatives may permit union representatives a greater degree of freedom and latitude in carrying out their union functions than is allowed by the contract. Or, they may compensate or reimburse such union representatives for time spent during working hours on union activities related to the grievance and arbitration provisions where the agreement does not contemplate such payments, and perhaps fails to mention the subject whatsoever. Management's agents administering the contract may permit employees to have idle but paid time during working hours for rest periods, lunch periods, wash up time, lining up at time clocks and other various activities. Such allowances may or may not be provided by the contract or, if provided, not to the extent acquiesced to by the company. A listing of all the numerous and various problems such acquiescence can produce is almost endless. *It must be termed as inaction since management possess the power and authority to prevent it from happening in the first place, and has the authority to halt it once it has been allowed.* The major problem resulting from management inaction which continues for too long is that once management decides to no longer be inactive, it may discover that it has waited too long to assert its authority during the term of the agreement.

One of the things the parties commonly do in an effort to give coverage to such practices is to insert a clause into the labor agreement which limits their relationship to the expressed terms of the contract. Representative of such a past practice clause is the following phrasing:

> This Agreement supersedes all previous oral and written Agreements between the Company and the Union. The Parties herein agree that the relations between them shall be governed by the terms of this Agreement only; no prior agreements, amendments, modification, alterations, additions or changes, oral or written, shall be controlling or in any way affect the relations between the Parties, or the wages and working conditions, unless and until such Agreement shall be reduced to writing and duly executed by both Parties subsequent to the date of this Agreement.[2]

Such a provision is typically sought by the employer hopefully as a safeguard against the eventualities mentioned earlier. When the union submits a grievance which claims the continuation of a benefit or condition based on some alleged prior practice, management will often turn to such a past practice clause and cite it to support its denial of the grievance, and its rejection of the impact of the alleged practice. This contention has enabled some companies to escape the encumbrance of an undesirable practice *where they were fortunate enough to have selected an arbitrator who endorsed this theory.* However, other employers have found that such defense was to no avail before other arbitrators. Often, the difference between two opinions will be determined by the particular fact situation, the clarity or ambiguity of the pertinent contract language, the nature and extent and duration of the past practice, the bargaining history on the subject, and the ability of the contending party to establish that the practice in fact existed, and was known, acted upon and acquiesced to by the other party. To make this point, a few examples are provided. A dispute involving the weight to be accorded a past practice arose under a contract which contained the following provision:

> Article XXVII—Other Agreements
>
> Section 2. The parties do hereby terminate all prior agreements heretofore entered into between representatives of the Company and the Unions (including all past understandings, practices, and arbitration rulings) pertaining to rates of pay, hours of work, and conditions of employment other than those stipulated in this Agreement between the parties.[3]

You can see the close parallel of this language to that cited earlier. The problem in this case concerned the company's assignment of boilermakers rather than carpenters to install and erect aluminum. The union contended that management breached the agreement when it failed to assign certain aluminum work to carpenters. To support its position, the union provided clear evidence to the arbitrator that custom and practice plainly established formal recognition on the part of the company of the jurisdictional rights of the carpenters to all such aluminum work. However, the company argued that any customs and practices which predated the current agreement were negated by the Section 2 language cited above. A careful review of Section 2 clearly indicated an intention on the part of the parties to terminate all past understandings, practices and arbitration rulings. Under these circumstances, the question became, would the reference concerning the elimination of past understandings in Section 2 eliminate those understandings which served to clarify ambiguous contract language, which continued to exist in subsequent agreements? Obviously not, said the arbitrator, because to eliminate understandings which clarify an unclear contractual condition would revert the parties to their original point of uncertainty which necessitated the understandings in the first place. He further concluded that understandings and practices which arise by virtue of ambiguous contract language remain in force and effect until such time as contract language which necessitated the understanding is changed. Otherwise, he said, uncertainty would result from a constant attempt to reach understandings over the same unclear contract provision which results in insecurity regarding the sanctity of a promise. Therefore, he held that the terms of Section 2 did not terminate the prior understandings of the parties relative to the jurisdiction of the carpenters.[4]

Arbitrator Edgar A. Jones disposed of a dispute between the Fruehauf Trailer Company and the United Automobile Workers, where the contract contained both a past practice and a zipper clause.[5] The former provision stated: "138. This agreement supersedes and cancels all previous agreements, both written and oral and constitutes the entire agreement between the parties." The latter provision stated: "139. No agreement, understanding, alteration, variation, waiver or modification of this agreement, terms, provisions, covenants, or conditions contained herein shall bind the parties hereto unless made and executed in writing by the parties."

This dispute involved a union claim that the employer had violated the job bidding provisions of the agreement and that a prevailing practice should be considered compelling. The employer sought refuge behind the above cited contract provisions. In the substance of his opinion and award, the arbitrator theorized:

> The repeated execution of collective bargaining agreements which contain exclusive agreement provisions canceling "all previous agreements" *has no magical dissolving effect* upon practices or customs which are continued in fact unabated and which *span successive contract periods*. Although not verbalized in the current agreement, such practices may nonetheless comprise a part of it as *any of its written provisions*...[6] [emphasis added].

Thus ruling, he concluded that the company had violated the job bidding provisions of the agreement.

In fairness to arbitrators generally, one should always keep in mind how many factors enter the decision-making process. Examinations of arbitral opinion invariably produce a finding of remarks by arbiters that the particular opinion was based "on the facts of the case." Divergent opinions from arbitrators on what appear to be very similar issues should actually be understandable to the practitioner. Differing viewpoints from one case to another result even where the labor agreements in two different and unrelated institutions contain identical language. Despite these identical features, it is unwise to assume that arbitral examination of the language will yield identical interpretations. This is understandably true for a number of reasons—not the least of which reasons is that the history of bargaining on the particular contract phrasing may have been quite different. Also, the contract's interpretation may have been applied in a different way by different organizations. Still another compelling factor may be the differences in practices and customs in which the parties have engaged. Consequently, an arbiter may, on a particular occasion, assert an absolute doctrine that the practices and customs of the parties, in the language they choose to adopt, actually represents the true agreement between them. This same arbiter may turn around on another occasion and declare with no less conviction that his view of past practice is that it cannot alter the meaning of a clear contract provision. What all this says is that many factors operate, perhaps in combination, to make each decision of an arbitrator relatively unique. It is not intended to imply that arbitrators are considered by the author to be innovators. These professional labor problem solvers recognize the compelling need for stability of labor relations between the parties. *For this reason, an arbitrator, carefully researched by the parties before their selection and utilization of his services,* will usually exercise judgment in a very predictable way. The difficulty in examining arbitration cases dealing with past practice issues is that such cases invariably contain various of the aforementioned ingredients which can produce apparently different arbitral reasoning from one arbitrator to another, or from one case to another with the same arbitrator.

Now that this has been said, we will turn our attention to an examination of cases where arbitrators have given some weight and effect to a company argument based in part on a past practice clause.

A labor agreement between the National Can Corporation and the UAW contained a clause which read as follows:

> Section 2. Inclusion of Subsequent Agreements
> This agreement expresses all agreements and understandings between the parties. No subsequently negotiated agreements shall be of any force and effect unless in writing signed by the parties and made as Memoranda of Agreement supplementary to the Agreement. Such Memoranda shall terminate as of the expiration of this Agreement.[7]

This employer had an agreement with a customer requiring it, under threat of financial penalty, to provide sufficient cans at all times to meet the customer's needs. Because of the directly connected and closely integrated operations of the two companies, the hours of production shifts were arranged to coincide. Following the customer's alteration of its processing schedule, it became necessary for this employer to change his working schedule accordingly. This resulted in an elimination of "wash up time" which the union protested as violating a long-established company policy and company-union understanding.

The union alleged that the policy had been in effect for six years or more and had continued under two labor agreements. They demanded overtime pay for the time that was involved and a return to the long-standing arrangement. Their contention was that the company could only accomplish such a change in a long-standing agreement at the bargaining table and not in the midst of a contract term. The agreement also contained a management's rights article and a clause divesting the arbitrator of any authority to alter, modify, add to or subtract from any of the terms or provisions of the agreement. Standing in his path of awarding to the union was Section 2, the past practice clause. This arbiter concluded that he would be exceeding his authority if he were to give any weight to verbal agreements or understandings reached in negotiations leading up to the agreement or subsequent to the execution of the agreement sought to be modified. He went on to say that if the parties had intended to give effect to any agreements or understandings reached in negotiations, they could easily have incorporated them in the agreement. If fact, they were obligated to do so if they intended that they should have any force and effect. If the arbitrator should, as the union urged, give consideration to "verbal agreements and understandings reached during negotiations as part of the contract," he would render meaningless said Section 2.

One arbitrator was faced with the requirement to decide the weight and effect to be accorded to two different practices which gave rise to two separate grievances under one contract. This labor agreement embraced three plants of the employer, situated at three different physical locations. For a period of seven or eight years, the employer had voluntarily adopted the practice of giving an extra hour's pay for each day spent by employees on a certain type of work, even though no service actually was rendered for such pay. Upon the execution of a new labor agreement, the company discontinued this practice. The employer contended that the employees were not entitled to receive compensation over and beyond the regular hourly rate agreed upon by the parties in their new contract; that they were entitled only to pay for the actual hours worked and, further, that the additional compensation given to these employees discriminated against other employees performing the same tasks in the other plants operated by this same employer.

The union contended that such payment was now an established custom and practice in that plant and the employer had no right to change it, especially since there had been no discussion of such a change in the negotiations between the parties.

In view of the fact that such payment had never been made the subject of collective bargaining, and further that it discriminated against employees performing similar work in other plants who had never been granted such extra pay, and also because it was payment for services that were not in fact rendered and could not be justified, the arbitrator ruled that the company had the right to discontinue the practice it had unilaterally established.

The second question dealt with this same employer's practice of calling in an entire crew operating a large electrical shovel when it became necessary to make repairs on the shovel. Despite this practice of many years' standing, the employer began calling out fewer men on the premise that all were not required to perform the necessary work. The company contended that it had the sole right to determine how many men were needed on a particular job at a particular time. The company relied in large measure upon its management's rights article and an Article 22 as written below:

> All agreements heretofore made between the parties hereto are hereby cancelled and it is agreed that this instrument shall constitute the only agreement between the parties.[8]

At the arbitration hearing, the union testified that a prior oral agreement had been made between a responsible member of management and a union official to call out the entire crew when such work was necessary to be performed. The existence of this agreement was not denied or challenged by the employer.

On the basis of the management's rights article, as well as the inherent rights usually reserved to management, the arbitrator observed that the employer did usually have the right, regardless of past practice, to determine how many employees would be assigned to a repair job, unless in a particular instance it had agreed to limit that right.

In relying on the above cited Article 22, the employer contended that all prior agreements, written or oral, were abrogated. The union insisted that the employer did not have the right to change oral agreements previously made on this subject because the parties had never discussed or contemplated such a change. It contended that Article 22 merely cancelled all written agreements and written riders made between the parties and did not change the oral agreement pertaining to the point in issue.

On the basis of all the evidence, the arbitrator found that although management generally has the right to determine how many employees should be assigned to a particular job, it had limited that right by the agreement it made with the union which had remained in force for many years. Contracts can be changed by practice or custom where over a sufficient period of time the practice and custom amounts to a mutual acceptance. In situations such as this, oral agreements may be just as good as written agreements and supplement the written agreements. One last point of significance to this arbitrator was that when Article 22 was being discussed during the negotiations, the union representatives inquired what effect the clause would have. In those discussions, it was clear that the employer did not mention that it included oral agreements. *This, of course, did not prevent the employer from seeking a modification of such an agreement when the terms of a new collective bargaining agreement would be negotiated.*

Where labor agreements have contained some provision assuring to some degree the continuation of past practices, arbitrators have used the following general principles: *First*, practices under the agreement are sheltered and may not be changed or discontinued unilaterally by the company where the conditions surrounding the practice have not changed. *Second*, where the circumstances and conditions surrounding the practice have changed, the practice often may be discontinued or altered in some form by the company. *Third*, the practices under a labor agreement containing a clause guaranteeing continuation do not need to be the product of a direct authorization or management order. *Fourth*, where management can demonstrate honest efforts to prevent the development of some practice, it may be ruled by an arbitrator that they have effectively prevented it from achieving the status of a binding local working condition.

It is, therefore, safe to say in connection with labor agreements, either "silent" or containing "practice continuation clauses," that arbitrators have concluded that an established practice or custom is a condition of employment which continuation is implied by the terms of a contract. Usually, they arrive at this opinion where there is convincing and compelling evidence that the claimed practice or custom was well known to the management and the employees, that it was seated in a mutual knowledge, that it existed for a considerable period of time, and that it continued unchallenged up to and beyond collective bargaining.

This result is not inconsistent with holding by various courts that a contract includes not only the obligations expressly set forth therein, but in addition includes any implied obligations indispensable to effectuate the intentions of the parties.[9]

But one cannot apply the implied obligation theory blindly. In every case, the critical question must be whether the evidence warrants a finding of an inference that the parties tacitly agreed to the continuation of a specifically challenged practice.

Harry Shulman, one of the earliest outstanding spokesmen in the arbitration profession, in a case with Ford Motor Company and the UAW, under which he presided as permanent umpire, stated it in the following way:

> To imply an obligation is to find that both parties, not just one of them, in fact agreed upon it, even though they did not express their agreement in words, or that their conduct fairly leads to that result whether they thought of it or not. The propriety of the implication depends therefore on the circumstances of the case. Just as silence or certain other conduct may permit the implication, so also other conduct or expression may clearly negate it. If we assume that the execution of successive national agreements may imply, in general as well as by particular language, an obligation to continue local agreements or practices not mentioned in the national agreements, the question arises whether the claimed implication is proper in this case.[10]

Zipper Clauses

In a great many labor agreements today is located the provision popularly referred to by the parties as the "zipper clause." This clause is most often sought by the company rather than the union, although in some situations, the union has been as eager as management to obtain it. Management's interest in it comes out of the hope that such a provision will shut out the necessity for bargaining on issues uncovered by the expressed terms of the agreement. Its title is self-explanatory. It presumably zips the contract closed after the parties have consummated discussions leading to a finalized collective bargaining agreement. Saying that such a provision *hopefully* negates the obligation for bargaining during the contract's term is explained by the fact that the National Labor Relations Board accords it a varying amount of force and effect as a waiver specific enough to remove the obligation to bargain. Despite the presence of such a clause, Board decisions have turned on the particular fact situation, the individual and peculiar circumstances involved, the particular phrasing of the agreement, the practices and customs between the parties, the history of collective bargaining between the parties, and the company's good or bad faith.

The following clause is representative of a well-worded zipper clause provision—but, of course, there are numerous variations:

> The Parties acknowledge that during the negotiations which resulted in this Agreement each had the unlimited right and opportunity to make demands and proposals with respect to any subject or matter not removed by law from the area of collective bargaining, and that the understandings and agreements arrived at by the Parties after exercise of that right and opportunity are set forth and solely embodied in this Agreement.
>
> Therefore the Corporation and the Union, for the life of this Agreement, each voluntarily and unqualifiedly waives the right, and each agree that the other shall not be obligated, to bargain collectively with respect to any subject matter referred to, or covered in this Agreement, or with respect to any subject or matter not specifically referred to or covered in this Agreement, even though such subjects or matters may not have been within the knowledge or contemplation of either or both of the Parties at the time they negotiated or signed this Agreement.[11]

Another clause of this type which allows for bargaining on wages due to a wage reopener provision, and which results in bargaining during the contract's term, is stated below:

> This agreement expresses the complete understanding of the parties on the subject of working conditions, hours of labor and conditions of employment other than wages. This mutual understanding has been reached after many hours of collective bargaining and represents concessions which have been made by both parties in order to reach an understanding. It is, there-

fore, agreed that neither the Union nor the Company will present any demands or claims not included herein other than as to wages during the life of this agreement, unless it is agreed by both parties that changes or amendments of this agreement are desirable.

The opposite of such clauses is achieved under labor agreements where the parties have inserted clauses reading similar to the following statement:

> It is agreed and understood between the parties hereto that this agreement is limited to and embraces only such matters as are specifically set forth in this agreement and that all other matters shall be subject to further negotiations.

The latter two examples are provided only to show the type of language adopted by parties in the absence of a *true* zipper clause.

When defending against some union claim based on past practice or a demand by the union for bargaining on some subject supported by an alleged past practice during the term of the agreement, *employers often join the zipper clause with the past practice clause* and attempt to use the two of them as a shield against the union's claim. In some situations, the compelling force of customarily experienced practices may be diminished or eliminated *if* the contract language is sufficiently strong. And, where the past practice clause or zipper clause or both are clear and explicit, arbitrators have dismissed the binding effect of a prior practice.

> This contract represents complete collective bargaining and full agreement by the parties in respect to rates of pay, wages, hours of employment or other conditions of employment which shall prevail during the term hereof and any matters or subjects not herein covered have been satisfactorily adjusted, compromised or waived by the parties for the life of this agreement.[12]

Under the contract where this clause appeared, a bonus practice had been the result of negotiations between the parties and had been paid for several years. However, it had not been expressly written into the agreement and thus an arbitrator ruled that the employer could unilaterally discontinue it.

This, of course, is a representative example of a clearly and strongly worded zipper clause. It also represents the viewpoint of a particular arbitrator deciding a case in the light of its peculiar and individual fact situations. A different result would be derived under another collective bargaining agreement which contained a less strongly worded phrasing that "this contract expresses the entire agreement between the parties." Such wording was considered by this arbitrator to eliminate automatically *only* such practices as were in direct conflict with the contract's expressed terms. This arbiter said that practices were not necessarily matters for agreement.

With regard to the question of past practice and the requirement to engage in collective bargaining relative to it, perhaps a few remarks of explanation are in order. Nothing contained herein is intended to imply that practices must continue indefinitely. As a matter of fact, later herein the subject of collective bargaining relative to the preservation or discontinuance of practices will be discussed. It is certainly recognized that practices or customs which create benefits—and these may take an infinite variety of form, like other emoluments of value which accrue to employees out of their employment relationship—are a mandatory subject of bargaining which can be expanded or discontinued at the bargaining table. For this reason, employers are well advised not to unilaterally disturb that type of practice or custom.

Collective bargaining means the employer and union sitting down across the table from each other and engaging in a give-and-take relationship. It means affording to the union in advance of the employer's discontinuance of the practice an opportunity to discuss the matter with the company and exchange proposals relative to it. The typical ritual at the bargaining table is for the union to start with a position of having nothing and seeking to obtain something. However, in most instances of collective bargaining relative to past practices, the union and the employees have something and the company wishes to bargain it away. If an employer could abrogate its obligations and responsibilities by unilaterally discontinuing bona fide practices from which employees derive a real benefit, and which have become established and accepted by the parties over a considerable period of time, then the collective bargaining relationship between these parties would be seriously strained. Many are the number of such items which often are not specifically detailed in the labor agreement. Of course, it must also be recognized that the give and take of good faith bargaining cannot occur after the employer has unilaterally acted to short circuit or discontinue an existing practice. The grievance action provoked by the company's unilateral behavior, and the discussions which then surround it, obviously cannot be considered as constituting good faith bargaining to which the union is entitled.

16

Standards Determining a Fixed and Established Past Practice

Maybe it's futile to attempt to identify any standards by which arbitrators determine if a practice exists which should be given some weight and effect in their decision. The more one investigates the many published decisions where past practice has been involved, the easier it is to form the conclusion that there is no unanimity of opinion among arbiters as to *precise* standards. The easiest conclusion is that the decision reached in any particular case is greatly dependent upon the individual thinking of the particular arbitrator deciding the issue. Archibald Cox once made the following statement:

> Outside the areas controlled by statute, there is no more important treasury of experience than the record of grievance arbitration. Surely arbitrators have not labored at the administration of collective bargaining agreements for almost two decades without arriving at some generalization upon which the unbiased can agree, even though partisan interests preclude unanimity.[1]

It must be considered true that many practitioners representing labor and management have found some guiding generalizations in arbitral opinion which have provided some expectant and predictable outcomes on certain issues. But those practitioners engaged in such searches must certainly be somewhat disappointed when it comes to the question of past practice. *The best that can be said here is that there are only uncertain generalizations and no indisputable rules.*

Now that this has been said, an attempt will be made, which may prove to be merely a feeble one, to provide some idea of the type of standards generally utilized by the majority of arbitrators. Perhaps, in retrospect, it will be considered as an effort that went for naught—but it is better to have made the attempt and failed than not to have made the attempt at all.

I believe that in the majority of arbitration decisions involving past practice where such practice or custom was given some influential weight in the final outcome ... one or more of the following four characteristics was present. Conversely, where the party pressing for compelling consideration of past practice failed to establish that one or more of these same characteristics existed, the award went to the other party.

The four characteristics are as follows:

- *The practice is unequivocal.* That is to say, the practice has been granted or applied consistently, uniformly, regularly and without break.
- *The practice is clearly enunciated.* This means that the practice has been acquiesced in by the parties and has operated without protest or objection from one party or the other.
- *The practice is of long duration.* That is to say that it has existed and been followed over a reasonably long period of time. In this regard, as will be shown, a bridge effect may be of significance to some arbitrators. The bridge effect results from a practice commencing under one agreement and continuing unchanged and unprotected into a renewed agreement. Thus, it bridges the collective bargaining negotiations between the parties without having been changed or discontinued. It should also be noted that the *frequency* of the practice may not be as consequential as the *consistency* of its application. In other words, a practice which occurs only three times a year, but which on each occasion is consistently executed, may conceivably have more weight and effect than another practice which occurs fifteen times a year, but is inconsistently administered from one time to another.
- *The practice is jointly accepted and acted upon.* This means to say that both parties, through their line representatives, have operated as though the practice in fact existed and was a guiding rule. This may signify to some arbitrators a mutuality aspect which then conceivably makes the practice one resulting from bilateral action as opposed to unilateral action.

Turning now to case examples where these factors were influential, we first consider the case in which Arbitrator Whitley P. McCoy, serving as chairman of a tripartite board for Kaiser Aluminum and Chemical Corporation and the Aluminum Workers International Union, ruled in favor of a binding past practice in a call-in pay dispute. In view of the practice, employees who completed their regular 8:00 A.M. to 4:00 P.M. shift on one day, and were then called and told to report early on the following day, were not entitled for four hours' pay for time worked prior to 8:00 A.M. on the second day, even though the contract provided (1) that the work day was from 8:00 A.M. to 8:00 A.M., and (2) that employees called in to work on the second shift within the same work day should be paid for not less than four hours' work.

Three features—(1) uniformity; (2) acquiescence by the parties; and (3) long-continued existence—were all present and influenced by the decision.

The company proved that a uniform practice had existed, where the man called out has continued to work on into his regular shift, to count the time on had regular shift in computing the minimum of four hours paid for. An employee of the company's payroll department testified that so far as he knew payment had always been made as it was made in this case, when a man called out continued working into his regular shift. He testified that he had made a random check and had been unable to find any instance of paying allowed time under the circumstances. Other supervisors testified as to instances that they recalled where payment had been made in the same manner as in this case. They testified as to these instances, giving names and circumstances. The union offered no evidence of an instance where payment had been made in accordance with its interpretation of this contract section.

Uniform and long-continued practice, known to and concurred in by both parties, is of course good evidence as to the intent placed upon contract language by the parties.[2]

As mentioned earlier, a practice may be deemed as possessing compelling weight even though it may occur relatively infrequently, if it is regularly and consistently applied in a given fashion. Such was the case in a dispute resolved by arbitrator Hubert C. Callaghan for the North American Cement Corporation and the United Cement, Lime and Gypsum Workers union. The arbiter ruled that evidence of four instances over a period of eight and one-half years was sufficient to establish a practice of filling job vacancies by lottery when two of four applicants for the vacancy had equal seniority and the minimum ability required for the job. Since the situation was necessarily one of infrequent occurrences and, therefore, one in which a relatively small number of instances would be required to establish a practice, consistency of administration was easily and clearly established. Another element—that of acquiescence—was evident since the union heretofore had not protested. On the matter of relative infrequency of the occurrence here, the arbiter posed a question which he then endeavored to answer for the parties: In labor relations, how many instances are necessary to establish a practice? Naturally, the answer will vary with the nature of the situation. If the problem is one which normally occurs fairly frequently, and is not dealt with in the contract, a relatively large number of instances might be required to establish a practice. But, if the problem is one which does not occur very frequently, such as in the instant case, a relatively small number of instances might be sufficient to establish a practice.[3]

The bridge effect of a practice continuing from one agreement into the next was one of the principal ingredients in a dispute resolved by Harold M. Gilden. Despite the fact that a retirement plan was unilaterally established, compulsory retirement of employees when they reached retirement age fixed by the retirement plan was ruled as proper, since the retirement plan had been in effect for a long period of time and the union had never protested against the compulsory retirement feature. In addition to the bridge effect referred to in the arbitrator's decision, the case had two features: (1) existence over a reasonably long period of time; and (2) acquiescence by the parties.

> (7) In this issue, the union is attempting to do by means of arbitration what it could not accomplish during negotiations. It bargained with full knowledge of the company's retirement policy and accepted the language which appears in the local agreements. The union, by its silence, either has abandoned its objections to the retirement program, or at least has yielded to an established management prerogative.
>
> (8) This is not a situation where the company is attempting to inaugurate a retirement policy. The arbitrator is here presented with a tenuous claim based on an unrealistic and startling definition of the word "discharge." He is being asked to rewrite a contract agreed to by the parties in the light of years of past practice and interpretation, and to throw open to dispute the resulting multitude of thorny problems.[4]

Arbitrator Edgar A. Jones also endorsed this bridge concept when he made the following remarks in a case decided by him:

> It is well accepted that a course of conduct engaged in by one party and acquiesced in by the other party to a collective bargaining agreement, spanning two or more contract terms—without any interim contractual reaction to it—becomes a part of the agreement between the parties and cannot be substantially altered or discontinued except by bilateral negotiations....[5]

Arbitrator Whitley P. McCoy revealed his agreement with the bridge doctrine when he stated the following in one of his many published decisions:

> The contract does not contain any provision concerning this matter. However, it could hardly be denied that plant practices and customs have existed at *the time the contract was executed*, bearing on working conditions and which *the parties did not contemplate changing*, are by implication a part of the contract....[6]

Past practice was clearly controlling in the next subject case. The factors of the bridge effect, acquiescence by the union without protest, and long and consistent administration were all compelling features of this controlling practice. The involved contract granted vacation pay at the employee's regular rate and defined it as the employee's regular straight time rate on the job to which he was regularly assigned at the time of becoming eligible for vacation. The employer computed the vacation pay of the aggrieved employee who was transferred to a lower rated job one week before vacation on the basis of the wage rate for the lower rated job, since the employee would have been assigned to the lower rated job had he not taken vacation at that time. The company's practice under this agreement for many years, without protest from the union, had been to pay for vacations at the same rate the employee would have received if he had actually been at work. There was no evidence that this disputed method of computation had been deliberately used to give an employee less vacation pay than he was entitled to receive. The pertinent remarks of arbiter Joseph M. Klamon were as follows:

> It is a universally recognized rule that in interpreting a contract clause capable of more than one meaning the intention of the parties as evidence in long-established past practice is an important and often a controlling factor.... When a method of computing vacation pay is not challenged either in grievance procedure or during contract negotiations for many years of collective bargaining history, it is reasonable to find and to hold as we do that the past practice of the company in computing such vacation pay on the basis that it has used for many years has met with at least the implied assent of the union.... If the parties wish to effect a drastic change, or spell out more specifically a different interpretation than the one clearly established and accepted by the union without protest over many years of past practice, they can only do so during the next contract negotiations or by supplemental agreement to the present contract....[7]

This case is interesting for more reasons than its revealed accord with the standards which were outlined earlier. It also discloses one of the avenues open to the parties who have become encumbered by a practice undesirable to them. Obviously, either party may find itself in this position; in this particular case, it was the union.

The specific avenue of escape suggested by the arbitrator here was for the union to bargain it out. This probably meant that the union would be waiting until the expiration of this agreement to accomplish this objective, since the company was probably satisfied with the outcome of this arbitration case. However, it is conceivable that the union might be able to persuade the employer to engage in negotiations on this subject during the term of the agreement, provided it was willing to enter those discussions ready to grant a concession to the employer of greater consequence to the employer than was this vacation decision.

Arbitrator Paul Prasow found the duration of a practice and the union's acquiescence to it to be controlling in a Procter and Gamble Manufacturing Company case with the Procter and Gamble Employees Association. The job of jar unpacker was ruled properly considered by the company as a job within the general classification of packer. The classification of packer was one which under the contract was confined to female employees, and in its performance, jar unpacking was inherently related to, and an integral part of, the packing line. This ruling resulted despite the union's contentions that unpacking, as contrasted to packing, was unsuitable for women and that jar unpackers were not included in the contract listing of women's jobs. The governing factor was that of past practice.

> ... in every instance, whenever the company indicated, by practice, that it considered and understood jar unpacker to be a woman's job and part of the packer title, the union apparently went along with this interpretation. For over two years, there was an acceptance by the union of the company's interpretation inferred by the union's conduct. It is clear that there is an acceptance where the relations of the parties, through their previous dealings or through other circumstances, are such as to impose a duty to speak, but where silence is maintained. Silence on the part of the union to a company interpretation of a clause, as practiced over the two-year period, could conceivably, in management's mind, constitute acceptance of this interpretation.[8]

In the above cited case, the company also pointed out that the union did not raise the issue in negotiations on the new contract, which would have been the proper time for it. This they failed to do even during specific bargaining discussions regarding packing lines in the factory.

Another employer did not have the right, without the consent of the union, to discontinue its practice of granting leaves of absence to pregnant employees and to adopt instead a policy regarding the discharge of such parties when their work deteriorated or risk of injury became evident. Accordingly, an employee who was discharged under this new policy, rather than be given a leave of absence, was reinstated with back pay from the time of her discharge, except for a five-week period during which she would have been absent on leave. On the evidence presented to the arbitrator, it was clearly apparent that the granting of maternity leaves was a long-established, important and known practice, not referred to in any specific contract clause. As such, the long-standing practice ripened into an integral part of the bargaining relationship and became a condition of employment which the employees and the union understandably had a reasonable expectation would continue.[9]

The scheduling of lunch periods and the impact of past practice upon management's right to change them was the question presented to arbitrator Clarence M. Updegraf by the Bake-Lite Company and the United Glass and Ceramic Workers union. On the shift of work which ran from 8:00 A.M. to 4:00 P.M., the practice had been to schedule lunch periods in four thirty-minute periods between 11:00 A.M. and 1:00 P.M. The employer unilaterally changed the schedule of lunch periods to five thirty-minute periods between 10:45 A.M. and 1:15 P.M. The text of the agreement contained nothing restrictive as to the time for lunch periods of shift workers. However, the union's concern was that the change in schedule placed the earliest and latest lunch periods unreasonably near the beginning and end of the shift. The changes actually caused some men to work two hours and 45 minutes before lunch and then four hours and 45 minutes after lunch. Others would work four hours and 45 minutes prior to the half-hour lunch period and then work two hours and 45 minutes thereafter. In the view of the union, if the employer could extend the lunch periods by 15 minutes each way, why not thirty minutes or more at its convenience, bringing them even more unreasonably remote from the mid-time of the shift. Although the agreement was silent with regard to when particular lunch periods should be scheduled, the arbiter felt that this was a case where the usage of past practice had been virtually *uniform* and *so relied on in the past* that the time for luncheon periods had to be regarded as restricted to the two-hour period from 11:00 A.M. to 1:00 P.M. theretofore scheduled, and *apparently concurred in by the parties.*[10] Again, we see a situation here where ingredients from the above-mentioned four were instrumental in the final results.

Arbitrator Paul M. Hebert clearly stated his complete agreement with the various principles under discussion here.

> Past practice to be binding must be unequivocal, clearly enunciated and acted upon and readily ascertainable over a reasonable period of time as a fixed practice accepted by both parties. The past practice under a disputed contract provision is not controlling where the interpretation of the clause has long been the subject of dispute between the parties....[11]

Applying these principles, he decided that past practice seemed inconclusive in deciding a case that involved questions of seniority, job classifications and the filling of vacancies by the posting of jobs for bid. While the employer in this case had maintained its position that jobs in its warehouse were not subject to the bidding procedure, the union had disputed this interpretation. Furthermore, the company had permitted bidding on some jobs so that its practice of denying bids had been contaminated by its own actions.

Confusing evidence of past practice was presented to arbitrator Charles A. Reynard in a case where both parties invoked arguments of past practice to resolve an ambiguity in their contract terms. Arbiter Reynard acknowledged that where contract language is capable of yielding different interpretations, resort may be made to past practice in order to resolve the ambiguity. The difficulty here, however, was that there was no agreement upon what that past practice had been. The evidence on the point was in substantial conflict, so much so that the arbiter was not persuaded by either version. The union's evidence appeared to show that on two occasions it had protested the assignment of the challenged work and the work was stopped. The company's evidence relating to these same two incidents indicated that the work was stopped, not because of the union's protest, but because its use of the particular equipment involved was concluded in both instances. The company further presented evidence that it had performed the challenged work with the challenged equipment on several other occasions, that some of these assignments were protested by the union, but in all instances, the company rejected the protests, and the union acquiesced in the assignment. Because of his inability to determine the validity of either practice, one cancelled the other, and he viewed it as his unavoidable duty to resolve the issue in terms of the burden of proof. The union, being the complaining party here, was held to have failed to sustain the burden of establishing a clear pattern of past practice to support its claim.[12]

An employer may handicap its ability to act unilaterally in imposing discipline for breach of plant rules based on some prior conduct in its administration of discipline. This happened to the Coca-Cola Bottling Company in its agreement with the Teamsters union. Over a period of ten years of contractual relations between the parties, the employer had established a custom that no discharge for dishonesty was made without *first* giving the union the opportunity to investigate and act on its own. Finally, a dispute developed when the employer broke this custom. It failed to formally notify the union of the company's belief that an employee was guilty of theft until the very day of his discharge. In so doing, the union was accorded no opportunity to make an investigation on its own and to discuss the problem in advance with the company. By violating the established contractual custom for handling such cases, the company breached the labor agreement. Here again is a past practice, which had been unequivocal, of long duration, and one that had been accepted and acted upon by representatives of both the company and the union. As time went on, it evolved into a binding commitment by the company to proceed in strict accordance with it, or be found in violation of the contract of which it had become an integral part.[13]

Another past practice was considered as cemented into the relationship between the parties where a successor union incorporated into its first agreement with the company language which had existed in the former agreement with the predecessor union for 10 years. By bridging the negotiations and failing to raise any question about the prior interpretation of the clause, the officers and members of the new local were presumed to have been satisfied with the interpretation and operation of the particular clause. In so ruling, arbitrator Leo C. Brown charged this succeeding union with knowledge of the prior practice under the same contract language as it permitted it to appear in its first contract.[14]

Arbitrator Russell A. Smith found himself deciding a reporting pay dispute in which the union contended that on one occasion reporting pay, under the same contract provision and like circumstances, had voluntarily been paid by the employer thus establishing, by practice, the intent and meaning of the contract. Arbiter Smith could not agree that a single incident established a practice of the parties in the interpretation and application of their contract. The fact that the company had paid reporting pay under like circumstances did not, standing alone, afford an independent basis for upholding the union's grievance. As he observed, if the situation were reversed, and payment had been refused on this prior occasion, the union certainly would have been justified in contending here that, just because it failed to make a case of the one incident, it should not be precluded from making one in this instance.[15]

In order for a past practice to be important in determining the meaning of language, "the practice must be of sufficient generality and duration to imply acceptance of it as an authentic construction of the contract." So holding, arbitrator Robert E. Mathews, appointed to resolve a call-in dispute, ruled that an interpretation of the contract contrary to its apparent intent was not justified by the bare showing of the practice of a few payments over an 18-month period.[16]

Ordinarily, an arbitrator might uphold a union's contention that a contract provision requires payment for 56 hours to an employee who works six consecutive eight-hour days beginning on Sunday, where the governing provision states that the overtime rate will be paid for Sunday work and work in excess of 40 hours per week, but that the premium will not be granted twice for the same hours. However, in one case a long-standing practice complicated matters.

The company argued that Sunday premium was paid as daily overtime and should not be counted as a day of work for the purpose of computing weekly overtime over forty (40) hours. If the overtime was figured on both a weekly and a daily basis, the company would be required to pay a premium on both a daily and a weekly basis which was greater than that required by the contract. In order to pay overtime for the sixth day of work, the company asserted it would be necessary to count the Sunday hours worked which were paid for at a premium rate, in order to pay the overtime rate on the sixth day of work. This would amount to paying overtime on the same hours worked.

Looking at the contract language alone and *without* regard to the bargaining history, the arbitrator might have been inclined to agree with the union's interpretation, which was that an employee who worked six 8-hour days commencing on a Sunday would be entitled to a payment of fifty-six hours' pay. However, an ambiguity existed as to the proper interpretation of the contract language. The existence of the ambiguity was underscored by a twelve-year bargaining history where the union involved had repeatedly sought a change in the contract wording which would have agreed with the interpretation placed upon the disputed clauses by the union. Throughout the parties' bargaining history, the company refused to make this language concession sought by the union. Also, throughout their bargaining relationship of the prior twelve years, the union had lived with the company's interpretation and the past practice which developed and grew as a result of it. For these reasons, the arbitrator recognized this practice and interpreted the ambiguous provision in its light, deciding finally in accord with it and ruling that the company had not violated the overtime premium pay clauses.[17]

This is another supporting example of the established concept that practices growing up under one agreement are strengthened and entrenched when they survive contract negotiations between the parties and are continued unchanged and unabated into another contract term, particularly where any relevant contract provision in unclear, vague, or ambiguous. Such a continuation of like practice with readoption of identical contract language usually gives rise to the presumption that the parties intended to continue the prior practices established hereunder.

What this can mean to the respective parties under the agreement is illustrated again where a dispute centered about a contractual phrase that vacation pay should be computed on the basis of "the regularly scheduled work week," as that phrase appeared in the vacation article of the contract between the parties. The problem in this situation was between the A.O. Smith Corp. and the United Electrical, Radio and Machine Workers union. The union contended that this phrase meant the regularly scheduled work week of the *individual employee*, or at least, of the *department*. The company claimed that this phrase could mean only the regularly scheduled work week of the entire *plant*. Depending upon which method was used for computation, the earnings of employees could be materially affected. Naturally, the interpretation sought by the union provided a more liberal vacation pay allowance. The section in question was not as clear or well written as might have been wished, and, on its face, was ambiguous in that it might be susceptible to more than one interpretation.

Faced with this type of problem, the arbitrator did that which is commonplace to all arbitrators faced with similar controversies. Since the parties had failed to express their intent with clarity in the labor agreement, the ambiguity had to be resolved by making reference to the collective bargaining of the parties on this subject, and to any past practice which surrounded this contract clause's administration. The evidence on the record was clear and undisputed that the interpretation of the language was as the company contended, plant-wide, rather than according to the scheduled work week of the individual employee or department. Since the practice favored the company's plant-wide interpretation, and since the union was knowledgeable of this fact prior to and during the negotiations, it was the union's responsibility to alter the vacation wording to make the union's intent clear. The arbitrator made the following remarks:

> ... for in accepting the identical language, without expressing a clear change in intent, the union ran the risk of having any ambiguity in the language resolved on the basis of the contract established by the practice.... Any party desiring a change in application or meaning must assume the responsibility of seeing to it that the wording of the provision involved is qualified or modified to make explicit the change intended.
>
> It is a well-settled principle of industrial arbitration that where past practice has established a meaning for language that is subsequently used by the parties in a new agreement, the language will be presumed to have the meaning given it by past practice.[18]

The precise question placed before arbitrator Peter M. Kelliher had been placed before another arbitrator in a previous arbitration hearing, involving the same parties, and precisely the same contract language. The only difference in the case before arbitrator Kelliher was that the aggrieved was different than the aggrieved employee in the prior arbitration hearing. Subsequent to the prior arbitral decision, the parties negotiated and entered a new agreement in which the same language was repeated. The allegations of the past practice put forth by the union were not denied by the company, nor was their evidence of the prior arbitration award. The arbiter had no choice but to find that on the basis of the prior award and the settled past practice, the same construction and interpretation of the labor agreement had been carried over into the new agreement.[19]

Again, we find the importance of the bridge effect to the arbitral conclusions, but in this instance supported by the additional weight of a prior arbitration award of precedential value.

Arbitrator Whitley P. McCoy was another who stated this principle in the case of Dwight Manufacturing Company and the Textile Workers of America. In this opinion, he stated the following:

> Such practice, on familiar principles of law, constituted a construction of the contract by the parties themselves, and became a part of that contract by virtue of such construction. Therefore, when the identical language, thus

construed by the parties, was incorporated into the latest contract, the construction was also reincorporated.[20]

One of the essential ingredients to make a practice compelling and binding is that it be acquiesced in by the parties. Even where it may meet the test of having continued for a long period of time with consistent and uniform administration, it often falls before an arbiter where either party can demonstrate its long-standing *objections* to the practice. Such was the case at the Hotpoint Company in its agreement with the UAW. Despite a company claim that its practice in vacation administration was a long-standing one, it could hardly speak of its actions as reflecting an *accepted* practice. The union in its early negotiations with the company, in its presentation of several grievances before an arbitrator, and in the instant case it was presenting to arbitrator Otto J. Babb, had certainly and definitely objected to this so-called past practice. Therefore, although it had endured for a considerable period of time, it was rejected in the final analysis.[21]

My intention in reviewing these cases has been to provide the reader with some general standards which may provide insights into the role of past practice in arbitral decision-making. Such an objective, at best, is very difficult to achieve. Although past practice is not the sole problem that has perplexed those in the labor-management arena, it certainly ranks high on the list of difficult issues. Arbitrators' decision-making is actually not the mystical process that it might appear to be at first glance, and the weight and effect arbiters accord to past practice is not I hope that in some small way I have dismissed the notion of this possibility from the minds of some practioners.

Conclusion

No one possesses all of the characteristics which make for the perfect arbitral advocate. Gifts of memory, ready wit, clarity of thought, facility of expression, grasp of figures, experience in business, technical knowledge, ability to simplify the complex, an understanding of human psychology, a fine appearance, physical stamina—these and other qualities are meted out to all of us in different measure. One thing, however, that we can do is to review objectively our efforts and profit from our own mistakes and from the experience of others. Seldom has anyone ever tried a case so well that in retrospect he does not see some aspect of it which might have been better presented.

Hindsight will not avail in a case tried and lost, but retrospection is a useful exercise as a guide to the manner in which the next case should be tried. The advocate who reviews every case he has tried (regardless of its outcome), testing what was done against established principles so that his presentations will be improved in subsequent cases; the advocate who is not too readily discouraged by early failures nor too satisfied with early success; that advocate can, whether his gifts be great or small, achieve reasonable competence in the presentation of a case.

I have dealt here with the various considerations and methods of procedure which are available to every practitioner. Less has been said of the arts of putting these into practice. That depends to so great an extent upon the early education and the physical and mental attributes of the individual advocate that general rules cannot readily be formulated.

Training and education are helpful, but should be so complete that no suspicion of acting can arise. Training and practice in debating are also helpful, since ability to think quickly and to express one's extemporaneous thoughts clearly is prerequisite to success in the hearing room.

An imposing presence, a winning personality, and a pleasing and powerful voice are also valuable assets. More important than any of these is a retentive memory that enables one to carry a witness's story in mind and a mental alertness in grasping the significance of every phrase.

The *sine qua non* for success in the field is unflagging industry, in advance and throughout the trial, to obtain mastery of every feature and development of the case. Without this, even a person with outstanding faculties and most thorough training will fail.

Citations

Chapter 1

1. See Archibald Cox, "Reflections Upon Labor Arbitration," *72 Harvard Law Review* 1482–1489.
2. See BNA, *Labor Arbitration Reports*, 43 LA 1262.
3. See 29 LA 372.
4. See 43 LA 322.
5. See 41 LA 18.
6. See 39 LA 607.

Chapter 2

1. See Owen Fairweather, "Employer Actions and Options in Response to Strikes in Breach of Contract," in *Proceedings of NYU 18th Annual Conference on Labor* (Washington DC: BNA, 1966).
2. *Proceedings of National Academy of Arbitrators*, Jan. 27, 1956.
3. See 43 LA 1262.
4. Local 174, *Teamster v. Lucas Flour Co.*, 369 U.S.95 (1962).
5. *Ibid.*
6. Section 301(a) LMRA, 29U.S.C.—185(a).

Chapter 3

1. See *NLRB vs. Jones & Laughlin Steel Corp.*, 301U.S.1, 45, 1 LRRM 703–713 (1937).
2. See *H.J. Heinz Co. vs. NLRB*, 311 U.S.514, 7 LRRM 291.
3. See Donald Crawford, "Challenges to Arbitration," *Proceedings of the Thirteenth Annual Meeting of National Academy of Arbitrators* (Washington DC: BNA, 1960), pp. 52–53.
4. See Sidney Wolff 14 LA 31.
5. See 25 LA 151; 24 LA 883.
6. See 37 LA 442.
7. See 26 LA 723. Also see 30 LA 851; 22 LA 251; 13 LA 991; 24 LA 158; 35 LA 397.
8. For arbitrators who have supported this concept, see 19 LA 503; 20 LA 432; 24 LA 158.
9. See 8 LA 720.
10. See 28 LA 491.
11. See 21 LA 713.
12. See 29 LA 67.
13. See 12 LA 707.
14. See 19 LA 219; 27 LA 174; 28 LA 270; 29 LA 594; 28 LA 491.
15. See 22 LA 608; 25 LA 118; 26 LA 870; 24 LA 33.
16. See 30 LA 678; 27 LA 57; 29 LA 609; 27 LA 233; 28 LA 461.
17. See 27 LA 174; 19 LA 815; 23 LA 171.
18. See 27 LA 233.
19. See 26 LA 438; 27 LA 281; 21 LA 330.

Chapter 4

1. See 20 LA 749; also 2 LA 295.
2. See 34 LA 262; also 34 LA 332; 23 LA 311; 23 LA 785.
3. See 33 LA 112; also 9 LA 269.
4. See 10 LA 265; also 28 LA 543; 15 LA 842; 1 LA 447; 9 LA 765; 43 LA 46; 33 LA 701.

5. See 16 LA 307. Also 39 LA 298; 30 LA 143.
6. See 6 LA 965.
7. See 30 LA 41.
8. See 34 LA 464; also 10 LA 372.
9. See LA 146.
10. See 33 LA 174.
11. See 33 LA 879.
12. See 10 LA 75.
13. See 8 LA 75.
14. See 21 LA 10; also 31 LA 144; 14 LA 925.
15. See 10 LA 355; also 9 LA 861.
16. See 33 LA 103.
17. See 3 LA 779. Also, 6 LA 988; 9 LA 447; 19 LA 43.
18. See 42 LA 923; 30 LA 250 21 LA 421; 4 LA 744; 16 LA 99; 21 LA 843; 21 LA 239; 9 LA 447; 42 LA 131; 42 LA 142; 42 LA 328; 13 LA 304; 30 LA 181.
19. See 28 LA 369. Also 35 LA 699; 20 LA 875; 33 LA 488.
20. See 28 LA 782. Also 16 LA 99; 29 LA 622; 43 LA 608; 8 LA 758; 13 LA 143; 6 LA 617; 13 LA 295; 14 LA 475.
21. See 33 LA 807.
22. See 9 LA 563.
23. See 37 LA 1076.
24. See 64–1 AARB—8376 (CCH).
25. See 32 LA 719.
26. See 8 LA 765.
27. See 14 LA 986.

Chapter 5

1. See 37 LA 794; 24 LA 141; 20 LA 416; 26 LA 501.
2. See 5 LA 175.
3. See 31 LA 917. Also 26 LA 505; 12 LA 311; 35 LA 412.
4. See 10 LA 664.
5. See BNA Collective Bargaining Negotiations and Contracts, Basic Patterns in Union Contracts" (Washington DC: BNA 1996 [pamphlet]).
6. See 30 LA 301. Also 30 LA 519.
7. See 34 LA 429.
8. See 3 LA 840; 24 LA 294; 26 LA 393.
9. See 33 LA 553; 25 LA 534.
10. See 4 LA 170; 9 LA 595; 31 LA 959; 19 LA 186.
11. See 11 LA 98; 12 LA 786; 13 LA 387; 13 LA 874; 13 LA 949; 15 LA 318; 15 LA 640; 26 LA 550; 27 LA 157.
12. See CCH-64–1 AR3–8400.
13. See 48 LA 496.
14. See 45 LA 275.
15. See 17 LA 187.
16. See 28 LA 659.
17. See 13 LA 468.
18. See 7 LA 387.
19. See 7 LA 785.
20. See 7 LA 621; 7 LA 192; 10 LA 244; 6 LA 1025; 6 LA 107; 14 LA 970.
21. See 36 LA 781.
22. See 36 LA 1463.
23. See 26 LA 395.
24. See 20 LA 34.
25. See 13 LA 266.
26. See 5 LA 742.
27. See 2 LA 481.
28. See 44 LRRM 0064 and 45 LRRM 2379.
29. See 31 LA.
30. See 34 LA 189.
31. See 7 LA 954.
32. See 25 LA 243.

Chapter 6

1. Bureau of National Affairs, CBNC, No. 397, BNA, 1969.
2. Labor Agreement between National Dress Manufacturers Association and International Ladies Garment Workers Union, 1966.
3. Labor Agreement between Gulf Oil Corp. Port Arthur Refinery and OCAW, 1970.
4. Labor Agreement between Coleman Company, Inc., and Tool Craftsman Independent Union, 1966.
5. See 60 LRRM 2222, 59 LRRM 2745, 57 LRRM 2528, 58 LRRM 2344.
6. *John Wiley & Sons v. Livingston*, 376 U.S. 543, 555 (1964).
7. *United Steelworkers v. Enterprise Wheel and Car Corp.* 363 U.S. 593, 597 (1960).
8. For these criteria and a full coverage of the subject, see Herbert Schmerty, *When and Where Issue of Arbitrability Can Be Raised* (Englewood Cliffs NJ: Prentice-Hall, 1966).
9. For this and other coverage, see "Procedural Arbitrability—A Question for Court or Arbitrators," *Labor Law Journal*, Dec. 1963, p. 1010.
10. *Ibid.*
11. See 24 LA 761.
12. See 34 LA 617, 33 LA 777, 28 LA 659.
13. See 28 LA 321.
14. See 46 LA 473.
15. See 46 LA 369.
16. See 33 LA 130.
17. See 33 LA 390.
18. *John Wiley & Sons v. Livingston*, 376 U.S. 543, 555 (1964).

19. See 25 LA 39.
20. See 1 LA 78.
21. See 1 LA 215.
22. See 25 LA 50.
23. See 21 LA 502.
24. See 22 LA 456.
25. Labor Agreement between International Harvester Co. and UAW, 1964.
26. See 22 LA 456.
27. See 19 LA 737 and also 15 LA 474. Also, Jules Justin. *Arbitrability and the Arbitrators Jurisdiction: Management Rights and the Arbitration Process*, (Washington DC: BNA, 1956).

Chapter 7

1. For complete coverage of this subject see Walt Baer, *Discipline and Discharge under the Labor Agreement*, (New York: American Management Assoc., 1972).
2. See 45 LA 515 and 42 LA 555.
3. See 16 LA 616 and 32 LA 586.
4. See 45 LA 1128 and 24 LA 132, and 42 LA 947.
5. See 28 LA 330.
6. See 23 LA 252.
7. See 25 LA 736.

Chapter 8

1. "A Profile of Labor Arbitration," BNA, 166A970 by Edgar L. Warren and Irving Bernstein (238 responding arbitrator).
2. See Von Moschzisker, "Res Adjudicata," 38 *Yale Law Journal* 299 (1929); "Symposium on Res Adjudicata," 39 *Iowa Law Review* 213 (1954).
3. See 25 LA 426, Carroll Daugherty.
4. For examples, see 24 LA 193, 32 LA 247, 25 LA 146, 22 LA 181, 16 LA 74, 22 LA 336. (Many other such cases are found by an examination of any volume of published awards.)
5. Erick Heller, *Oswald Spengler and the Predicament of the Historical Inauguration in the Disinherited Mind* (New York: Farrar, Straus and Cudahy, 1957).
6. See 25 LA 149.
7. See 63-1 ARB 8063.
8. See 62-2 ARB 8611, 62-2 ARB 8584, 63-2 ARB 8695; see also 11 LA 945, 25 LA 896, 37 LA 830.
9. See 62-3 ARB 8882.
10. See 62-3 ARB 8946; see also 39 LA 567, 28 LA 476.
11. See 62-3 ARB 8964. For another case between different local unions in different plants of the same firm, see 33 LA 25.
12. See 24 LA 379, 9 LA 761.
13. See, for example, 16 LA 111, 16 LA 844, 32 LA 126, 32 LA 156, 26 LA 84, 26 LA 258, 24 LA 193, 24 LA 181, 23 LA 39.
14. See 15 LA 934, Douglas B. Maggs.
15. See 16 LA 217, Whitley McCoy.
16. See 32 LA 360. For similar rulings, see 16 LA 816; 22 LA 721; 33 LA 826; 35 LA 826; 37 LA 119.
17. David A. Wolff, Louis A. Crane and Howard A. Cole, *BNA Proceedings of the Eleventh Annual Meeting—National Academy of Arbitrators, The Chrysler-UAW Umpire System*. Washington DC: BNA, 1966.

Chapter 9

1. See 43 LA 1262.
2. See 43 LA 1262.
3. See 43 LA 1256 at 1262.
4. H.D. Fuller, "The Adversary System" (New York Vantage, 1961), pg. 42.
5. See 33 LA 667, Arbiter R. McIntosh.
6. See 3 LA 846.
7. See 34 LA 288, Arbiter Charles W. Anrod. Also see 12 LA 230, 10 LA 487, 5 LA 410 and 7 LA 767.
8. See Arbitrator Paul M. Hebert in 29 LA 469. For similar rulings see A. Langley Coffee in 12 LA 1117, H. Platt in 9 LA 91, P. Killiher in 27 LA 798.
9. See Arbitrator Marlin Volz in 48 LA 409.
10. See 47 LA 726, p. 732.
11. See 47 LA 26, Arbitrator James P. Whyte.
12. See 28 LA 879. See also 28 LA 198.
13. See 29 LA 415, Arbiter Carl Warus, Jr.
14. See 1 LA 215. For a similar decision see 13 LA 949.
15. See 5 LA 684. For other cases dealing with a demand for a foreman's discipline see 1 LA 75, 15 LA 528, 19 LA 8, 1 LA 68.
16. *Ostrofsky v. USW* (36 LC ¶65,329), 171 F. Supp. 782 (D. Md. 1959), aff'd per curiam (39 LC ¶66,117), 273 F.2d 614 (4th Cir.); and Gregory, "Fiduciary Standards

and the Bargaining Grievance Process," *8 Lab. L.J.* 843 (1957).

17. *Humphrey v. Moore* (48 LC ¶18,670), 375 U.S. 335 (1963); *Hostetler v. Brotherhood of Railroad Trainmen* (42 LC ¶16,806), 287 F.2d 457 (4th Cir. 1961).

18. *Thompson v. Brotherhood of Sleeping Car Porters* (47 LC ¶18,200), 316 F.2d 191 (4th Cir. 1963); *Falsetti v. Local 2026, UMW* (40 LC ¶66,590), 400 Pa. 145, 161 A.2d 882, 895, 87 A.L.R.2d 1082, 1098 (1960) (dictum).

19. 45 Cornell L. Q. 25, 46 (1959).

20. *Aluminum Ore Co. v. NLRB*, 131 F.2d 485, 6 LC ¶61,332 (CA 7, 1942).

21. *NLRB v. Southland Cork Co.*, 342 F.2d 702, 51 LC ¶19,567 (CA 4, 1965); Weinacker Bros. Inc., 153 NLRB No. 40, 1965 CCH, NLRB ¶9478.

22. Fafnir Bearing Co., 146 NLRB 1582 (1964).

23. Metropolitan Life Insurance Company, 150 NLRB 135 (1965).

24. Fafnir Bearing Co., (UAW) 146 NLRB 1582 (1964).

25. See 136 NLRB 1648 (1962).

26. Celotex Corp., 146 NLRB 48 (1964); Ingalls Shipbuilding Corp., 143 NLRB 712 (1963); Administrative Decision of General Counsel, 1963 CCH NLRB ¶12,657, Case No. SR-2595.

27. See cases cited below. For summary, see LRX (Labor Relations Expediter), Collective Bargaining, Sec. 19. Compare *NLRB v. Truitt Mfg. Co.*, 351 U.S. 149, 38 LRRM 2042 (1956).

28. Otis Elevator Co., 102 NLRB 770, 31 LRRM 1334, 33 LRRM 2129.

29. Otis Elevator Co., *supra*, arose from a grievance. See also General Controls Co., 88 NLRB 1341, 25 LRRM 1475 and *NLRB v. New Britain Machine Co.*, 33 LRRM 2461.

30. 36 LRRM 2220; 35 LRRM 2215; 35 LRRM 2730; 27 LRRM 2524, 25, 26.

31. 10 LRRM 49; 11 LRRM 693; 36 LRRM 2220.

32. See 6 LA 426.

33. *Aluminum Ore Co. v. NLRB*, 131 F.2d 485, 6 LC ¶61,332 (CA 7, 1942).

34. *NLRB v. Southland Cork Co.*, 342 F.2d 702, 51 LC ¶19,567 (CA 4, 1965); Weinacker Bros. Inc., 153 NLRB No. 40, 1965 CCH NLRB ¶9478.

35. See 17 LA 121, Arbitrator Michael I. Komaroff.

36. See 19 LA 385.

37. See 43 LA 1256.

38. See 24 LA 541. For a similar case see 25 LA 437.

39. See 39 LA 652, Arbitrator Leonard Oppenheim. For similar cases see 24 LA 145, 43 LA 864, 44 LA 20, 44 LA 711, 22 LA 819.

40. See 38 LA 313.

Chapter 10

1. Labor Agreement between Englehard Minerals and Chemicals Corporation and Local 238, United Cement, Lime and Gypsum Workers, International Union, Gardner, Ga., 1972.

2. Labor Agreement between the Boeing Company and International Association of Machinists, effective 12–12–71.

3. Labor Agreement between McDonnell Douglas Corporation and IAM, 1972.

4. Sherwood Medical Industries, Inc., and Dist. 50, UMW, 1969.

5. Labor Agreement between American Enka Corporation and United Textile Workers of America, 1969.

Chapter 11

1. See 26 LA 122.

2. Emanuel Stein. "Problem Areas in Labor Arbitration," *New York University Third Annual Conference on Labor* (Albany NY): Mathew Bender, 1950), pp. 267–86.

3. Labor Agreement between Brunswick Corporation and UBCJA, Local 824, 1972.

Chapter 14

1. See 10 LA 955.

2. See 30 LA 1086.

3. Willard W. Wirtz, "Due Process of Arbitrations," *The Arbitrator and the Parties* 1, 13 (Washington DC: BNA, 1958).

4. Williams, Simkin and William Kennedy. *Arbitration of Grievances*, Bulletin No. 82, (Washington DC: U.S. Dept. of Labor, Div. of Stds., 1946), p.25.

5. Shulman, "Reason, Contract and Law in Labor Relations," *Harvard Law Review* 68 (1955), pp. 999, 1917.

6. *Conference on Training of Law Students in Labor Relations*, Vol. 3, Transcript of Proceeding, *Harvard Law Review* (1947), pp. 636–37.

7. See 4 LA 744; 7 LA 239.

8. See 39 LA 470; 45 LA 490; 40 LA 598.

9. See 29 LA 604.

10. See 19 LA 413.

11. See 29 LA 718.
12. Benjamin, Aaron. "Some Procedural Problems in Arbitration," *Vanderbilt Law Review* 10 (1957), pp. 733–44.
13. See 29 LA 291; 20 LA 451; 19 LA 417.
14. See 16 LA 727.
15. See 48 LA 496.
16. *Ibid.*
17. See 23 LA 146.
18. See 24 LA 430.
19. See 23 LA 171.
20. See 43 LA 46.
21. See 43 LA 1262.
22. See 29 LA 718.
23. See 43 LA 46.

Chapter 15

1. See 43 LA 1262.
2. See Labor Agreement between I.A.M. Local 1813 and Brunswick Corp. Technical Products Division.
3. See 37 LA 297.
4. See 37 LA 297.
5. See 29 LA 372.
6. See 29 LA 372.
7. See 45 LA 470.
8. See 19 LA 421.
9. See *E.G. Sacramento Navigation Co. vs. Salz*, 273 U.3.326.
10. See 10 LA 272.
11. Labor Agreement between Rubber Workers and Samsonite Corp., Murfreesboro TN.
12. See 26 LA 627.

Chapter 16

1. See Institute of Industrial Relations, University of California, *Law and National Policy*, vol. 12 (1960), p. 143.
2. See 28 LA 439.
3. See 28 LA 14.
4. See 17 LA 81.
5. See 29 LA 372.
6. See 31 LA 137, also 3 LA 760.
7. See 29 LA 256.
8. See 1 LA 313.
9. See 23 LA 277.
10. See 29 LA 555.
11. See 27 LA 762.
12. See 27 LA 793.
13. See 9 LA 197.
14. See 21 LA 524.
15. See 22 LA 835.
16. See 10 LA 617.
17. See 29 LA 45.
18. See 23 LA 27.
19. See 15 LA 87.
20. See 10 LA 786.
21. See 23 LA 562.

Bibliography

Association of the Bar of the City of New York. *An Outline of Arbitration Procedure.* New York: Author, 1996.

Baer, Walt. *Collective Bargaining: Custom and Practice.* Jefferson, NC: McFarland, 1989.

_______. *Discipline and Discharge under the Labor Agreement.* New York: American Management Association, 1972

_____. *Grievance Handling: 101 Guides for Supervisors.* 3d ed. New York: American Management Association, 1970.

_____. *The Labor Arbitration Guide.* Hornewood, IL: Dow Jones–Irwin, 1974.

_____. *Labor Relations for the Practitioner.* Jefferson, NC: McFarland, 1989.

_____. *Labor Relations Guidebook.* Dubuque, IA: Kendall-Hunt, 1978.

_____. *Labor Union Representatives: Allowed and Prohibited Practices.* Jefferson, NC: McFarland, 1989.

_____. *The Operating Manager's Labor Relations Guidebook.* Dubuque, IA: Kendall-Hunt, 1978.

_____. *Practice and Precedent in Labor Relations.* Lexington MA: D. C. Heath, 1972.

_____. *Strikes.* New York: American Management Association, 1975.

_____. *Winning in Labor Relations.* Chicago: Crain, 1982.

Bureau of National Affairs, Editorial Staff. *Grievance Guide.* 5th ed. Washington, DC: Bureau of National Affairs, 1996.

Davey, Harold W. *Improving Grievance Arbitrations: The Practitioner's Spear.* Ames: Iowa State University, Industrial Relations Center, 1970.

Elkouri, Frank, and Elkouri, Edna Asper. *How Arbitration Works.* 7th ed. Washington, DC: Bureau of National Affairs, 1981.

Justin, Jules. *How to Manage with a Union.* IRWS, 1969.

Landis, Brook. *Value Judgments in Arbitration: A Case Study of Saul Wallen.* Ithaca, NY: Cornell University, New York State School of Industrial and Labor Relations, 1960.

Levin, Noel A., and Gerald Aksen. *Arbitrating Labor Cases.* New York: Practising Law Institute, 1974.

National Academy of Arbitrators. *Proceedings of the Annual Conferences on Labor Arbitration.* 58 vols. Washington, DC: Bureau of National Affairs, annually 1948–.

Reich, Robert. *The Future of Success.* New York: Alfred A. Knopf, 2001.

Sinicropi, Anthony. *Management Rights.* Washington, DC: Bureau of National Affairs, 1986.

US Department of Labor, Bureau of Labor Statistics. *Grievance and Arbitration Procedures in State and Local Agreements.* Washington, DC: US Government Printing Office, 2000.

Zack, Arnold M. *A Handbook for Grievance Arbitration: Procedural and Ethical Issues.* Lexington MA: Lexington, 1992.

Zack, Arnold M. and Bloch, Richard I. *The Arbitration of Discipline Cases: Concepts and Questions.* New York: American Arbitration Association, 1959.

Index